KU-053-152

DEAR MUMMY,
WELCOME

by
Bethany Hallett

HONNO

Published by Honno

'Ailsa Craig', Heol y Cawl, Dinas Powys,

South Glamorgan, Wales, CF64 4AH

© Bethany Hallett, 2011

The right of Bethany Hallett to be identified as the author of this work
has been asserted in accordance with the Copyright, Designs
and Patents Act 1988.

ISBN: 978-1-906784-30-0

All rights reserved. No part of this book may be reproduced, stored in a
retrieval system, or transmitted, in any form or by any means, electronic,
mechanical, photocopying, recording or otherwise, without
clearance from the publishers.

Published with the financial support of the Welsh Books Council.

Cover design: G Preston

Cover photograph: Maxim Bolotnikov/Getty Images

Printed in Wales by Gomer

For my daughter,

who has brought such joy into my life

and into the lives of many others

OLDHAM METRO LIBRARY SERVICE	
A33478396	
Bertrams	14/12/2011
A362.73409	£8.99
LIM	

Acknowledgements

I owe much to Michael, for encouraging me to write this book, for his assistance with the editing and for his, as always, unswerving support.

Part One

My Story

It was January – no different to any other January except that it was the first month of the new millennium and on this particular evening in January, the train was on time. I was in good spirits as I mumbled 'Good Night' to the ticket collector, walked up the steep hill, passed the darkened windows of the estate agent's and looked in at the garish-coloured kilims in the fluorescent-lit Turkish takeaway, before quickening my step in anticipation of dinner and a warming glass of red wine.

What *was* different was that my knock at the door elicited no response. I stood, impatiently, outside in the cold, and then rummaged through my bag for the keys to unlock the door.

It was quiet as I walked into the hallway – only the sound of my hungry cat's cry pierced the silence. I descended the stairs to the basement to discover that his cases had gone. 'He's buggered off!' I exclaimed out loud, with a mixture of regret and relief. But only a few seconds later, the realisation hit me. With no one around I wanted to share a bottle of wine with, let alone to father my child, at 42 – to all intents and purposes – my time had finally run out.

Sitting alone, the silence punctuated only by the slow tick of the sitting room clock, a myriad of thoughts rushed through my mind. Just as a drowning man is said to see his past flash before him, in an instant I saw my childless future. I was swept away by images of a lonely auntie tossed scraps of comfort by visiting nephews and nieces, by images of perhaps teaching some ill-disciplined class of other people's offspring – or even a spell in the Voluntary Service Overseas. 'So this is where I've finally landed up,' I said, incredulously. I looked around at a room that looked no different. But *something* had changed. For years, I always assumed I would give birth to a little 'me'. For years, I had pictured that child in my mind's eye. I thought it my God-given right to become a mother. Apparently not. The slow ticking of the clock sounded in the otherwise silent room.

'Let's talk it over this weekend,' he suggested by telephone, the next day. 'I'll book you a flight.'

I clung to the receiver, my mind racing, drawn in two directions. I finally heard myself speak, head winning over heart. 'But I've got tickets for Covent Garden this weekend.'

Only much later would I know that this January *was* different to all other Januaries. In the first month of the new millennium, the little girl I was to adopt was conceived.

'I have an Italian clock that some Italian friends many years ago literally put in their bin as their child had damaged its face. It's one of these rather lovely, ornate brass ones and has a loud tick. One Christmas many years ago, my parents secretly had it repaired for me and it has worked perfectly ever since. In fact, I can hear it ticking now. I like to hear clocks ticking ....'

As far back as I can remember, I always wanted a child. I cannot say, though, that I have always hankered after actually being pregnant. I did not like the thought of sagging breasts, stretch marks and a big bump. It was only in my early forties that the idea of being pregnant started to appeal and I began to enjoy looking in shop windows, at booties and wicker cots. No doubt, it had something to do with time running out.

My mother had six children, three girls and three boys. I came second, four years after my brother, Nick. The youngest – my sister Caryl – was unexpected, a late baby, born when I was 14. I was delighted to have a little sister and was effectively a second mum. But I never liked my mother's bump. I remember the look on my eldest brother's face one day as he glanced over at her belly. I could see he wasn't happy

2

with the fact that Mum was pregnant. She was wearing a burnt-orange dress with a flower pattern; I imagine I only remember that dress because of the look on my brother's face.

Years ago, my sister Molly, who was living in Hong Kong at the time, was home on holiday and we had gone to Wales together for a few days. We stayed with my uncle and auntie, and I have a clear memory of Molly crying, at the foot of Cardiff Castle, as we ate our sandwiches on that hot, sunny day. After years of no success having their own natural child, Molly and her husband, Tom, aware of the number of Chinese orphans awaiting parents in Hong Kong, had decided to adopt. Now, in the midst of the adoption process Molly was upset because they had just heard from Hong Kong social services that there was a surplus of boys available for adoption, but she desperately wanted a girl. I had never realised until then that she wanted a baby so badly. Then, just before her return, Tom rang from Hong Kong to say that a little six-month-old girl had just become available.

Molly later related how simply things were done. 'The baby was like a rag doll,' she said. 'The lady from the orphanage just handed her over to me and that was it… After we left the orphanage, we realised we had no nappies. It was late so we had to drive around Hong Kong, the baby in my arms, looking for a chemist's that was open.'

My adopted niece, Poppy, must have been two years old when they first brought her back home to see the family. I remember how Poppy had burst into tears standing on my doorstep. She was wearing the little red-and-white striped dress that I had sent for her birthday. I still have the photo I took of her that day; she's wearing a very solemn expression. The photo is on the bookshelf in my study.

Unlike Molly, my friend Diane never wanted a child. 'My *caree*r is my baby,' she once told me in her soft, diluted

Geordie accent. Paradoxically, I envied her: she never seemed to suffer that niggle that had so plagued me.

'*How* you've survived so long as a contractor at Robert Flemings, I'll never know,' Diane scolded me one evening, as we sat down for a drink in the Oxo Tower to celebrate the new millennium.

'The people are nice,' I replied, 'and on the whole it's been interesting work – and you *can* learn a lot from how things are done wrong! I have to admit, though, that these last few months have just driven me nuts. I was forced to go on this Y2K project called the MOR – the Millennium Operating Regime,' I laughed, as I nibbled hungrily at the olives. Diane began to giggle, too.

She and I had got on since the first day we met, on a structured business analysis and design course. We agreed that it must have been six years since we had taken that course together.

'You sometimes see the rich and famous in here,' Diane now said excitedly, as she tossed her head nosily at the stream of people entering the bar. 'How about a glass of champagne to wish you luck in your *interview* at Credit Suisse?'

'Let's not get ahead of ourselves now,' I smiled.

Later, ensconced on the train clanking its way through the station tunnel, I wondered whether Diane would one day look back with regret… Probably not, I decided, as the guard came along to check my ticket. Her career really was her baby.

One morning, early in the new century, my boss – a tiny man with a disproportionately large nose – had enquired of me unexpectedly: 'Didn't you say you have experience of the 'Wall Street' system?' He carried the unenviable title of project manager of MOR, and lost no time in surfing job websites once the millennium clock had made its benign strike.

'Yes, I do,' I called out disinterestedly, whilst concentrating on the lunch menu pinned to the notice board behind me.

'Credit Suisse First Boston,' he went on, 'are looking for a contractor business analyst in Emerging Markets IT. It might be worth looking into…'

'You'd lose nothing by attending a Credit Suisse interview,' my friend, Ruth, later encouraged me on the telephone. 'It'll be far more dynamic; you could do with a change.'

I still hesitated, however.

'Isn't the money better than where you are now?' she persisted. Upon hearing earlier how much contractors' daily rates had risen since her days in the City, she had joked, 'You'd clean toilets for that sort of money wouldn't you?'

'I already *am* the City's highest paid cleaner,' I laughed. 'The "permies" got irritated with me swanning around with little or nothing to do, so last week they made me clear out the desks of the Y2K testers they'd just sacked!'

Seated on the Docklands Light Railway, I surveyed the extraterrestrial-seeming landscape stretching out before me. Punctuated by odd-looking shapes, parts of the East End looked like another planet with the Millennium Dome spaceship in the foreground and, further in the distance, the pointed-hat towers. I felt like an alien as the train trundled through unfamiliar-sounding stations like Shadwell, Limehouse and West India Quay, eventually to find myself in the squeaky-clean shopping mall under the Canary Wharf tower.

Outside the mall, the unexpected tranquility was broken only by the footfalls of the joggers, and by a few gardeners tending the perfectly manicured flowerbeds and lawns. It was hard to believe I was in the midst of one of the world's largest financial centres.

Like a shrinking violet, I stood in the investment bank's foyer feeling apprehensive and conspicuously old-fashioned in my newly pressed jacket and skirt, as confident and composed women in trousers strode by. I shrank even more when I was greeted by the female IT director, obviously into no-nonsense power dressing. Her sober outfit was matched by a 'don't mess with me' expression, and as she escorted me to her office, she simultaneously barked New Jersey-accented orders to rows of software developers.

'What do you think makes a good business analyst?' her male colleague, brought in to ascertain my analyst's credentials, asked during my interview.

'Getting the detail correct,' I responded, assertively.

'We don't waste time on detail here,' he announced disdainfully, 'so long as we get it broadly right...'

Oops, I had forgotten: I was now with the big guns, the big American investment banks that favoured quick and dirty solutions – detail is for wimps. But whenever I didn't get the detail correct, it *always* came back to haunt me; I whimpered inside.

I was then asked about my last assignment, which I briefly described.

'Embarrassing wasn't it?' the IT director said, dismissively. 'Better not advertise the fact you worked on Y2K!'

It was only towards the end of the interview, when she uttered the words, 'We're about to go "e",' that I knew I wanted the job – 'e-commerce' was the buzzword in front office IT at the time; I was ambitious, it was new and hot and I wanted to be part of it.

Funny to think, I was made to have a child and yet never did. All those premenstrual problems I needlessly suffered over the years. I looked out of the train window to see that we had just passed the row of Edwardian cottages where I used to live, and that we were now running parallel to the river. And all those wasted eggs – these days you would be advised to freeze them. I caught sight of the little Norman church in the near distance. I had only been there once; it was my first Christmas in Sussex and I attended a service there with my mother and two sisters. We had walked along the river in the snow and arrived late. Squeezed together on the last empty pew, I remember how our faces glowed in the candlelight.

Sometimes, in summer, I would get off the train a stop early and walk home along the river. What a contrast to the City: one moment I was applying a change to a plan or a presentation, an hour later I was thrilled to see a heron, or simply to note that the honeysuckle in the hedgerows was already in blossom.

I thought of how rarely I looked out of the train window nowadays – although I *still* enjoyed my first sight of the Downs in the morning, and my first sight of the river signifying that I was almost home… This area was flooded not long ago. I remember looking out of the window of my newly renovated house to see the large, silvery lake where once there had been a green meadow.

I bumped into an ex-neighbour in town shortly after the flood. I felt embarrassed, guilty even, that I had got out in time. 'Is that why you moved,' he asked me, 'because you knew about the flood?' I was taken aback, for how could I have known?

When I told my friend James that I had put the cottage on the market, he had exclaimed, 'But you always said you'd be happy there for ever!' I think the realisation that my current relationship was going nowhere was a major factor in my decision.

'I want a house with a garden and a view,' I told the estate agent who responded with a smirk. I knew he was thinking, 'Doesn't everyone in this town?' And twice, I ignored the details of the house sent to me by post until, by chance, James invited me to lunch at the pub opposite.

'What do you think of that house over there?' I asked James.

7

'It looks nice,' he said, 'and there's probably a garden at the back, and I bet there's a view, too…'

The house, though a significant renovation project, turned out to be exactly what I wanted.

My first thought before boarding a flight to New York (at short notice and without clarification of my objective from Credit Suisse – I got the job!) was, 'What about my cats?'

The tall, bearded Russian, whose office I entered straight from the airport, droned on for hours. A ball of tangled wool came to my mind as I looked at the diagram he was now drawing on the flipchart in front of me, a diagram which revealed that despite this new age of e-commerce, all the old software development errors prevailed. The bottom line: the bank's new electronic trading system was under-performing.

Soon after, when the Russian asked the London IT director – who was his boss, too – if I could join the New York team permanently, she vetoed his request.

'It's because of me you've got to where you are,' she later told me, owl-like and accusingly, down her gold-rimmed pair of specs. (How did that reconcile with the, 'I want to help women get ahead,' she had uttered at my interview?) 'Besides, they're having problems with that 'e' project,' she went on. 'It won't be long before the whole thing will be canned…and I need you here – there are a number of firm-wide projects to co-ordinate for Fixed Income IT.'

She did not know that for the past year I had been trying to come to terms with the fact that I might never have a child. She did not know that I recently had decided that a potential role in senior management might solve my dilemma. Now, rebuffed, I gazed out of her office window at the 'other side', where the timeless church spires and the dome of the old Poplar town hall were set like a cardboard cut-out against a blue, sunny sky. *It's OK for you,* I silently protested. *You have it all. Your son, your nanny, your doting husband – and you have your career, too. I'm 43, childless, with not even a partner in sight.*

It was time, I knew, to acknowledge the truth I could no longer ignore. There was a gap in my life that a career never could fill.

Applying to become adoptive parents for a child can seem a move into the unknown and the process itself can seem very daunting for any individual or family…

Preparation Course notes

In August 2001, on my 44th birthday, I finally decided to ring social services. I tried to look on it as a present to myself. Yet instead of making the call like an excited child might open a gift – not wasting a second – I was constantly darting glances at the telephone but not daring to make a move. I was excited and yet frightened – frightened that once I had made that first phone call and stepped into the unknown, the life I had built for myself and to which I had become accustomed, might begin gradually to collapse.

Sometimes one has to think of the overall picture, disregard the dangers and go for it, I encouraged myself as I sat alone in the sunlight in my sitting room… *Perfect weather for a housewarming party*, I thought distractedly.

Suddenly the telephone rang, making me jump. 'Do you have a large bowl for the cocktail?' my caterer asked.

'Yes, I think I do,' I replied, 'I'll go and check. I'll call back.' The party was another reason I was on edge.

Instead of ringing her back, I dialled another number.

'Hello, I wonder if you could tell me whether, as a single person, I would be allowed to adopt?' I asked.

9

The cheery warble on the other end sounded surprisingly pleased. 'Yes, indeed you can,' she said, before enquiring as to whether I was interested in foreign or domestic.

I wanted to ask her, 'So what do you think about it – would you adopt or do you have your own children?' But I said nothing.

'I'll put a leaflet in the post,' she said. 'If you decide to go ahead, call us back and we'll put your name down for the next information evening. They can get quite booked up though, so it's best not to delay.'

'Can't you book me on it now?' I said. 'I know I want to proceed.'

'I'm sorry but you do need to read the leaflet through first, to be certain it's something you really want.'

Later, that night, for a few moments I stood alone on the patio. My new Moby CD was playing in the background and it suited my now buoyant mood – the house was finished, the party was a success *and* I felt relief, tinged with a sense of excitement, at having made that phone call. But I had told no one.

A Czech friend came out and joined me. She commented on how much sky you could see from the patio and, as we looked up at the stars, added, 'You have a beautiful home, and a good job, too… Now all you need is your Prince Charming.'

Her words brought me back to earth. How I wished I could pursue my dream, my dream of having a child with someone by my side.

'I hope he *will* come along, one day,' I said, wistfully.

'Don't worry, he will,' she said.

On a balmy September evening, I found myself surrounded by a dozen or so uncomfortable-looking couples, all seeking information on adopting. For a moment, I regretted not having taken up my mother's suggestion that she accompany me. To my relief, another woman on her own entered the room. She was in her thirties, short and plump, with long, dark hair. She did not, however, look like a 'me', I decided, feeling more and more a square peg in a round hole.

A fifty-something female social worker now thanked us for making the effort to attend and gave us our first glimpse of the obstacle course that lay ahead.

Step 1:   Information evening (where I was now)
Step 2:   Initial home assessment of applicant by social services
Step 3:   Preparation course
Step 4:   Home Evaluation (study) by allocated social worker/subsequent written report
Step 5:   Approval Panel evaluation of report and approval of applicant
Step 6:   Matching between a child and adopter
Step 7:   Introductions and placement of the child
Step 8:   Legal process.

It was whilst I was still trying to get my head around this labyrinthine process that I heard the few words that gave me my first shiver. Once we had adopted, the smiling woman assured us, the child's birth certificate would be re-issued to hold our own name. I knew I was not buying a puppy but for some reason I found this unsettling. Whilst I was still trying to take that information in, the social worker and her colleagues then began to bandy about unfamiliar terms like 'stickability'. 'Stickability' meant – literally – sticking it out: enduring a child's behavioural difficulties; accepting the bad as well as the good; above all, seeing it through. Familiar words like 'abandonment', 'grieving' and 'loss' were mentioned, too, but they were set in unfamiliar – and scarier – contexts and communicated via a flipchart, which back at the office would have been used to show the predictable flows of settlement and trade data. Here it spoke of the unpredictable difficulties with which we, as adoptive parents, would most likely be challenged.

There was now a silence in the room as we were introduced to the faceless third party in the scenario: the mother, whose child would one day be calling *us* Mummy, or Daddy. 'No matter how neglected the child has been,' the social worker said, 'the mother still loves them.'

The mother! I hadn't even thought of the mother before. I had, up to now, thought only of myself, and my desire for a child. For the first time, the real sadness of it all hit me.

I was tired and hungry by now, and there was still a video to be shown. Its purpose was an attempt to clarify further the process. I stayed – partly out of interest, of course, but partly out of fear that my premature departure might be noticed and that, as a single applicant, I might be penalised in some way.

Some of the children portrayed in the short film were lovely, but some disappointingly un-endearing, and for just a moment, I was struck by the guilty thought that I might have been enjoying a glass of Sauvignon Blanc at a Canary Wharf riverside bar instead.

At the end of the evening, I was mentally exhausted, no longer even sure that adoption was something I wanted to pursue. Until the social worker beamed at us and spoke eight final words: 'The joys of adoption far outweigh the pain.'

I rose from my seat, tired, but with a darling cherub of a child in my mind's eye. I filled in a form that would take me to the next step.

As yet, I had told only my parents, my sisters and my friend, James, of my intentions. For just as a woman usually keeps her pregnancy under wraps until she is certain, so I, too, wanted to wait until I was approved by social services before publicising *my* equally personal decision. *And*, to tell the truth, at times I was still blowing hot and cold about it all. Anxious to hear another's view, I confided my plan to an acquaintance on the edge of my social circle.

'Isn't it rather selfish of you, to consider adopting as a single person?' he replied, to my utter amazement. His response touched a nerve: I had been brought up with an ever present Mum and Dad so had had my own occasional feelings of doubt as to whether it was right to bring up a child without a father.

I spent days afterwards analysing myself as to whether I *was* being self-indulgent in some way.

I looked out of the window at the net curtains opposite. I could have sworn I saw them move – had my neighbours guessed what I was up to?

I had reached Step 2 of the adoptive process – the initial home assessment – or what I would have called the feasibility study. In the context of my work, a feasibility study ascertains upfront a project's cost-effectiveness, technical viability and resource availability. I opened my front door to June, the social worker who was to carry out an upfront assessment of my own viability: my financial resources, my mothering capability, and whether or not I had the available emotional resources – family and friends – to form a 'support network'. June would be the first to pass judgement on my worthiness to become a mother.

In contrast to the aggressive type I had expected, I was pleasantly surprised: June was a charming and pretty, middle-aged woman whose grilling of me over the next hour – firm yet gentle, probing yet non-intrusive – I could almost say I enjoyed. Most of her questions – how did I envisage making the enormous transition from career woman to mother; did I intend to go back to work afterwards – were, of course, expected. One or two, however, were not.

'Have you ever married or cohabited with anyone?' An

obvious one. But not her revelation that social services were now interviewing ex-husbands and ex-cohabitees as part of their investigations. She informed me that this change in policy followed a recent case in Brighton, where a father was convicted of killing his new adoptive son; later investigations revealed he had beaten an ex-wife whom the case worker had failed to interview.

I was somewhat relieved that I could reply in the negative to both marriage and co-habitation – could one really be sure there would be no sour grapes? However, I felt rather sensitive about my status, living as I did in a town where there were very few single women in their forties, and was therefore afraid she might judge me as somehow having failed in my relationships or, perhaps, as gay.

'Good for you,' she replied, to my relief, before changing tack.

'Do you have sufficient funds to adopt?' she asked. I was told I would need funds enough to enable me to take six months off work. 'And once a social worker is assigned to you,' she warned, 'they'll be asking you for proof... You can always, somehow, have a natural child on a wish and a prayer,' she went on to explain in mellifluous tones, 'but *not* when you adopt.'

When I made that first phone call to social services in August, this question would not have bothered me. For I already had made a financial plan and was determined to pay off my mortgage as quickly as possible. But September 11th hadn't happened then, and now there were rumours of redundancies. Only that week a former boss had said, 'Contractors are likely to go first,' before telling me that she was now the sole breadwinner in her family: her husband, a management consultant, had become one of the City's first post-September 11th casualties. The contract market had thinned considerably and if I lost my job, I would almost certainly end up a permanent employee somewhere else on a much-reduced income. Sometimes, when I saw a plane flying close to the Canary Wharf tower, I would wonder how long before the terrorists struck here. Was it possible that my adoption plans might be in jeopardy because of September 11th?

There was nothing for it but to *forget* my real job uncertainties and to assure June of my financial viability; and I did so.

'Are you totally committed to adoption?' came June's final question that day.

It should have been an obvious one, too, but it was unexpected. Had June guessed that throughout her gentle interrogation, I had, in fact, been questioning all this myself? Had she seen me gaze round my designer kitchen without a thing out of place? Had she caught me looking into my minimalist sitting room, wondering whether a child would fit in? But June was nodding her head *for* me – I swear – and I heard my voice squeak in the affirmative.

'Then the next step will be the preparation course,' she said, with a smile, as she put her notepad away. 'It's quite a tough course,' she warned, as I showed her out. 'Some people find it emotionally difficult.'

I looked both ways down the street before closing the door behind her. The possibility of my motherhood now lay in social services' hands.

The last thing on my mind that evening, as I drove over the Downs towards Gillian and Donald's for supper was to reveal my adoption plans to anyone else.

As soon as I arrived, I checked the table setting, recalling that the last time I had sat there I was dining with a newly engaged couple. Then, I had sat, alone, at the top of the table, feeling single and singular, with only my knife and fork for company. This time, however, it seemed we were to dine *à trois*.

Gillian and I went back a long time – ever since my early thirties, when I first moved to Sussex. I was at the end of a relationship, and Gillian at the end of her first marriage. We met at the local tennis club, where I asked her for a game – what gall I had, I remember thinking, she's far better than me! Gillian later said she thought it was the other way round.

'Beth's one of *the* success stories,' Gillian once said with a laugh to a group of friends. I had just come back from a business trip to New York with Deutsche Bank, my first job in the City. To me, however, Gillian was the success: she had recently left a senior post in the civil service to pursue her ambition to become an MP.

'Do try the broad bean paté – it's one of Nigella's,' Gillian urged. 'Donald's not keen on it.'

Gillian always loved cooking: the 'Babette of all feasts' I used to call her. 'Donald loves cooking, too,' she had told me, some other time.

'It must be difficult, then, deciding on who does what?'

'No, I generally do the starter and main course, and Donald does the pudding,' she'd smiled. 'You can make *anything* work,' she often said when I first met her.

'Do you think you'll get married one day?' Donald had asked me earlier in the evening as he was pouring me a gin and tonic.

'No, I don't think I will now,' I had replied. 'I always assumed I would marry one day but it hasn't happened yet, so I doubt it ever will… But it doesn't bother me. I think I'll just have a series of affairs for the rest of my life,' I told him, rather flippantly. I could see from the look on his face that, as a devout Christian, he was not over-impressed with my last statement. So later, to justify my existence on God's earth, and for Donald's sake, I told them my news.

'Surely, you can't think of adopting at your age,' Donald scolded me. 'These should be some of your best years, not a time when you're financially burdened with bringing up a child.'

I helped myself to some endives coated in Gillian's delicious vinaigrette.

'I don't want to have a lot of money in my fifties, yet feel unfulfilled,' I replied firmly. 'I don't want to look back on my life with regret.'

Donald was silent for a long moment. 'Well, that's fair enough, I suppose.'

After Donald had removed the empty dishes and left the room, Gillian said, 'I think what you're doing is marvellous! It's the sort of thing *I* might have done.' She then wickedly added, 'But I adopted Donald instead.'

Donald was right: the stork would eventually drop not just a child but the whole financial burden of adoption into my lap. But what I did not know was that in the end the Twin Towers tragedy, which I feared might threaten my financial future, in reality ensured my continuing employment at Credit Suisse.

Due to the demands of the external regulators for more stringent money laundering controls, a new project arose out of the ashes of September 11th and my contract was renewed. Not long after, I was assigned to a new electronic trading project in equity derivatives, and whilst the new Chief Executive sacked thousands of employees my contract was renewed once again. As one of just a *handful* of contractors still employed by the bank in 2002, I was reasonably happy and enjoying my role in the small, friendly team.

Seven months had passed since my initial phone call to social services the previous year and I now received notification from them that I had a place on the adoption preparation (or prep) course in May. But the whole thing now felt like a dream.

It is hard to imagine, but one of the scruffiest houses in the street where I live belongs to a painter and decorator by trade. And although *I* am someone well trained and fully experienced in project planning, I naively failed to recall that an unexpected event can set a project wildly off course...*even* put it on hold.

Back in January 2000, when I realised that my chances of having a birth child had just about fizzled out, so, too, I was released from the urgency to find Mr Right. Never did I think that Prince Charming would turn up – that seemed the stuff of fairytales – but when I said 'hello' to the new handsome, young employee at the water-machine (according to the *Evening Standard* a good way to meet your new mate) I thought, why not?

I soon embarked on a spring affair – clubbing, fine dining, theatre and opera, travel to exotic places – but rather than landing on terra firma after a sensible time, I began to wonder, fancifully, if *he* might be *the one*.

'I'm thinking of postponing my preparation course,' I told my sister Molly who had popped in to see me one Saturday morning. 'There doesn't seem to be any real point,' I explained. 'We're happy, and despite my age, there's still a chance we might be able to have a baby together.'

Molly paused for a moment, and then said, 'Make sure you give social services a good reason as to why you're delaying, so they don't become suspicious...just in case.'

I called them the next day and told them that something unavoidable had cropped up at work, making it impossible for me to attend the prep course. 'Give us a call back when you're able to make it,' the receptionist said, pleasantly.

Well before a long-planned trekking trip to the Galapagos Islands, the relationship had begun to unravel. I realised that I no longer desired a holiday in which every waking moment was packed with non-stop activity. Instead, I hankered after the sort of holiday I had not had in years: I wanted my *only* decisions over that fortnight to concern where I should place my sun-lounger and whether I should have my main meal at lunchtime or at dinner; I wanted to walk no further than from the hotel to the beach, and drink cocktails whilst the sun set.

Years earlier, I remember reading, astonished, that an American woman filed for divorce on the grounds that her spouse kept failing to replace the cap on the toothpaste tube. Things came to a head for me on the evening before our departure, when he was on the phone for hours droning on about the impact of the government's recent changes to the tax status of contractors. Instead of clutching at the receiver and holding on to his every word, this time I let the receiver dangle. What about *my* need to finish my Christmas cards, wrap presents, arrange for the cats to be fed while I was away, *pack!* After replacing the receiver, I had to face the unthinkable: this relationship was to all intents and purposes nearing an end.

After the holiday, I was momentarily depressed on learning, via a Christmas card, that an ex was now the proud father of two. That could have been me, I realised. And in the same way as one might look back nostalgically on a snowy, childhood Christmas, so I began to think back to those days when I had been contemplating adoption.

I made my second phone call to social services from the office.

I was stunned to hear the response on the other end of the phone. A dismissive voice expressed doubt as to my commitment. It was the last thing I had expected. I clung to the receiver in desperation, terrified that I had tossed my chances overboard – and for what? I looked round the office as I silently drowned. Had my colleagues guessed at the subject of my conversation? I could see the team manager pacifying a trader; otherwise, everyone had their eyes glued to their computer screens. I stared at my own screen as I listened in horror. Social services had assumed that I would call back within a few weeks, but I had left it almost a year. So this is it, I thought, my chance to become a mother will end the moment the social services manager puts down the receiver.

'I needed more time to pay off my mortgage,' I explained. 'Things haven't been very secure in the City since September 11th.' I was surprised at how calm I sounded. Inside, I was churning.

The voice eventually said, 'Then I'll need to schedule another home assessment. It's been too long since the last.' I breathed a huge sigh of relief.

After I put the phone down, I sat at my desk, quite still. Why had I built this relationship into something that it was not? Had I used it as a distraction, a means of escape from the prep course and the daunting intrusion of home visits? Or was I, in reality, more fearful of adoption, and the prospect of doing it all alone, than I had thought? I decided it was a bit of both. Even so, I was incredulous at the situation I had put myself in.

But I had been given a reprieve. For the moment, at least.

June, who had carried out my previous home assessment more than a year ago, again appeared at my door. After settling down with her cup of tea, she asked, 'Why the postponement?'

I knew it was essential to stick to the story I had told the social services manager, so I mentioned the effects of September 11th and my desire to pay off my mortgage, to strengthen my finances.

Then, the other dreaded question was raised: 'Have you had any significant relationships since we last met?'

I wanted to be honest, but the last thing I could admit was that a man had been responsible for the delay. 'She'll do the same again,' I could hear them say. If I wanted to become a mother, it was essential to keep mum.

Many people who pursue adoption do so after a prolonged period of fertility investigations; others already have children and a happy family life, but are prompted by hearing of children who have themselves been deprived of a normal family life. And some families may have made a decision not to have children themselves, perhaps because of medical or genetic advice…

Preparation Course notes

In May 2002, a place finally became available on the prep course. The week before it was to begin, I had diligently read through the wad of material sent to me, on the train. In particular, I was struck by a statement that, 'In adoption all parties have experienced a major loss.' And no one completely gets over that loss, it went on, for throughout one's life there are times when one re-experiences the pain of the original grief – 'rubberbanding', as it is sometimes called. 'These feelings may last a few minutes, hours or days but do not usually continue for long if the person has been able to go through the tasks of grieving…' Whether parents come to adoption through having lost a child, or have been unable to create one together, all, apparently, have suffered loss.

But there was no mention of women like *me* included in the category of those coming to adoption, women who had simply waited too long…and no mention of someone doing this alone.

If someone had asked *me* whether I had suffered a loss, I would have said a categoric 'no', that first morning. It was not a sense of loss *I* felt as I sat there, feeling like a spare part, waiting for the preparation course to begin – just surprise; surprise at where I found myself.

'The *other* single woman has failed to turn up,' a social

worker whispered in my ear. 'One of us will sit by you if it'll make you feel better.'

With my best, bravest face I said that I was feeling just fine. But after her well-meant offer, I felt more ill at ease. As the only single participant, I was sticking out a mile. I glanced at the empty chair by my side. Did the other single woman know something that I did not, I wondered. I looked at my watch; it was 9.15am. I visualised my colleagues in the office, getting on with their daily tasks, faces fixed to screens, ears to phones. Suddenly, I, too, wanted to be doing safe, familiar things. I wanted to be complaining about the train or tube journey in; I wanted to be checking my e-mail or fetching a coffee from Starbucks—

'It's time for a coffee,' the course leader announced, interrupting my thoughts.

'Hi,' said a buoyant, sporty-looking couple in their mid-forties. 'We've already two of our own,' they volunteered in unison. 'We always wanted another so we thought we would adopt.'

I was taken by surprise. *Why want more?* I thought. *Haven't you already got what the rest of us haven't?*

Next, I met a plump lady in a kaftan who appeared to be in her early fifties. 'I always wanted to adopt a baby,' she confided, 'but I could never have afforded it on my own. Besides, I didn't have a good enough support network... Only recently, I met someone and got married.' She then introduced me to her diminutive Mr Right who approached with a plate of chocolate biscuits. He looked lost, I thought, as he clutched at his cup and saucer. She hoped, she said, for a baby. 'Isn't a baby too much work?' I heard him mumble.

A young couple then approached me for a chat. They, too, already had a birth child. 'Our daughter was born a dwarf,' the mother explained. 'We want to adopt another child like her so she'll feel less isolated growing up.'

'There's an agency that specialises specifically in the adoption of dwarf children,' her husband added, and I felt a lump in my throat: if there was a competition for the saddest story then surely they would get the prize? On the other hand, it was obvious they were happy and committed, and evidently adored their tiny child.

All the while during the coffee break, I wanted someone to ask me why I was there. I wanted them to know I wasn't a man hater, I just hadn't met my Mr Right. Then, I caught sight of a couple standing apart from the rest of us, a straight-faced, tight-lipped couple, here, I judged, after years of trying for a baby; his face in particular said it all. And it struck me that if *I* found it difficult being here, then how must *they* be feeling?

Back in the meeting room, I glanced down at some of the topics on the agenda:

- Who we are and how we live
- Bringing adoption into our lives
- The developing child
- The abused child

The course leader told us to close our eyes, take a temporary leave of the present and flutter back into our own childhoods.

'Think back on the good times,' he told us, and I whizzed back to South Wales. I remembered the wet and windy times spent on the beach (hoping the sun might come out), the long walks to the Gaumont cinema on Saturday mornings, and playing cowboys and indians. I recalled the gang fights with the children on the nearby council estate, the delight at seeing icicles in the snowy fields at the back of the house, and playing in garden sheds. And I thought of the pale-faced and freckled twins who lived over the road – but who never played with the rest of us and were never part of the gang. 'They're adopted,' I remembered my mother once saying.

And I thought of my childless Great Aunt Peggy who would take Molly and me to the funfair each year; how all three of us would squeal with delight on the ghost train as we roared through the tunnels, saw the flashing lights and heard the mummy groan. And how disappointed we always were when the ride finally came to an end.

'Now think of, and tell us about, some bad memories,' a social worker requested.

I spoke of wetting my knickers on my first day at school. 'They only had a big pair of boy's khaki shorts for me to wear,' I related. The whole room burst into laughter and again, I felt like that little girl standing in the playground, sensing the other children's stares.

At this point, the leader stressed, 'Empathy is the key. As adoptive parents, you will need to be able to empathise with your child's feelings of abandonment and loss… Now try to remember some of your own losses.'

I was only nine, I recalled, when we moved from Wales to the Midlands; it was just before the Aberfan disaster. How I had missed our little school, the Welsh lessons, sitting on the teacher's knee. And how shy and introverted I became at the new school – 'like a crab in a shell' my school report stated, though academically I excelled. Only now did I realise *that* experience was a loss. And only now did I wonder how my mother must have felt about taking five children (my sister Caryl had not been born at the time) all that way.

'I didn't want to,' Mum later told me. 'But I didn't think of saying no – though looking back, it would have been far more sensible for Dad to have stayed up there on his own and come back at weekends… I missed my mother,' she added.

I recalled the little flat where Nana made us Welsh rarebit, the sound of the gas kettle whistling and the faint smell of cigarette smoke. But it was to our *paternal* grandmother's house that we returned so often at weekends. I remembered the smell at breakfast of hot buttered toast that Nana cut from a large crusty loaf whilst the tea brewed, and the smell of fried bacon, eggs and tomatoes she made for Papa. I remembered her playing 'patience' in the front room and hearing her gossip. I remembered the shopping arcades and the little Italian café where our father treated us to sarsaparilla, and the indoor Cardiff market where we looked forward to paper cartons of cockles doused in vinegar and sprinkled with pepper. And I recalled hearing the night train thunder through St Fagan's woods whilst we lay under thick, crocheted blankets and winceyette sheets. And Sundays, when 'the men' returned from the pub to my grandmother's roast, always followed afterwards by a piping hot fruit tart with a sugar-crusted top; and later, for tea, how we would eat thinly sliced bread spread with Welsh butter, and homemade egg custard tarts.

'Think of the types of children that come from a care background,' the leader urged, and I thought back to Nana's neighbours, in particular our friend, Gaynor, who would take us to the corner shop to buy sweets, or the swimming pool or the park.

My reverie was interrupted when the leader asked us to come back to the present and examine a case study of an adoptive child, one in which Gaynor herself, I now realised, could have appeared. There was just time for me to recall us all piling into my father's car, waving out of the back window, seeing Nana with a hankie at her eyes…and our arriving safely, hours later, in the Midlands, where I never really felt I belonged…

By the afternoon, I began to feel part of the group, actually enjoying the company of the other participants, all of whom seemed to be genuinely nice people.

We now had reached that part in the agenda where we were to consider what made a good adoptive parent; 'parenting plus' they called it. In addition to providing love, acceptance, attention and all the usual needs of the child, as 'parents plus' we also had to be open-minded and flexible; optimistic and tolerant; resilient and accepting of the children as they were – and accepting also of the other people who are important to them. Lastly, a sense of humour was essential to being a good adoptive parent.

Finally, on that first day, we studied the stages – disbelief, searching, anger, guilt, depression, adjustment, rehabilitation and acceptance – of loss and grief that the adopted child would experience. The same stages of loss and grief that some of the participants sitting there would themselves have experienced; some might even still be stuck in the middle somewhere, re-experiencing those emotions due to their participation in the course. Again, empathy was the key; if we were able to understand our *own* grief, it would benefit our adopted children and help them to mourn their own losses.

Driving home later that afternoon, my mind fluttered back again, this time to 1997. I distinctly remembered the year because a friend of mine had died in a sailing accident, leaving me quite devastated.

I also had been in a relationship which I thought might be lasting, one that might lead to children. But at the end of the day, it turned out, my partner didn't want to make the ultimate commitment to marriage and children, so the relationship ended. I had moved out of my Edwardian cottage that year into a house that needed extensive renovation. At the time, I couldn't understand why I often felt low. It was due, no doubt, to the stress associated with months of having builders and decorators, but also to starting all over again, this time *alone*.

I remembered the year, too, because I had switched from permanent work to contracting, having joined Robert Fleming merchant bank…and New Labour had just come into power. I also went to a concert at the Royal Albert Hall to hear the country singer, Nanci Griffith. I remembered her saying how different it felt to be in England this time; that there was a feeling of hope in the air and people were talking again about politics; it was as though we had come out of a period of stagnation. And I remembered her haunting song about the Texas bluebonnets.

I felt at the time that I, too, had come out of a period of stagnation. My sister, Molly, and I had taken her dogs out for a walk on the Downs one day and I burst into tears – how often I did that then! We stood in the long, wet grass among the dandelions, and Molly encouraged me to get into all the things I had once enjoyed. So I joined the local athletics club and a yoga class, and rang Covent Garden – I hadn't been to an opera for ages. And with time, I felt happier than I had done in years. It was as though I had emerged from a tunnel and shed a layer of skin en route…

On the morning of the second and final day of the preparation course, I was late. I entered the silent room and experienced once more the same intense atmosphere and the serious expressions on the participants' faces.

The first item on the agenda was attachment. We were told a child's secure attachment to the adoptive parent was paramount in a successful adoption. We learned that some of the common causes of attachment difficulties were: abuse, neglect, sudden separation from the primary caretaker and the child's inability to accept nurturing due to neurological problems caused by a number of things including crack cocaine exposure. If any, or all, of these occurred in the first two years of the child's life, there was a high risk of problematic attachment. Problematic attachment could result in a superficially charming child, or a child who might avoid eye contact, be indiscriminately affectionate with strangers, refuse cuddles or be inappropriately clingy. The effect might also be incessant chattering, poor peer relationships due to telling tales, low self-esteem, the need to be in control, and impulsive behaviour.

An amiable, softly spoken woman introduced herself to the group and then addressed the subject of child development.

My sister, Molly, who worked as a health visitor, later told me she had once met the woman at a social services meeting to discuss the welfare of one of her caseload. 'She adopted a child who's now a teenager and apparently a nightmare,' Molly revealed.

But that day the woman gave no indication of having endured any adoptive nightmares as she informed us of the impact of neglect and abuse on an adopted child's development. We were shown a chart of how 'normal' children developed: that at two years, the child was toilet-trained, could initiate their own play activities, liked praise and could show sympathy and shame; and at age three, a characteristic was their readiness to conform to the spoken word. We should not expect our adopted child, however, to necessarily follow this timeline. They would almost certainly regress, to a greater or lesser degree, in an attempt to catch up on missed years.

Later, we reached that item on the agenda to which none of us were looking forward, abuse. We learned that abuse might be physical, emotional and/or sexual, as detailed in some harrowing case studies they presented us. We were encouraged to fully consider the risks in adopting a child who had suffered severe abuse or one born to alcoholics or drug addicts, or even one with *no* available medical history.

I began to worry now that perhaps *all* children in care came from such brutal backgrounds – until the course leader explained that the children in these case studies would have probably been too highly traumatised to be considered eligible for adoption.

We then were shown a diagram depicting the labyrinth of

lengthy investigative and legal processes we must undergo in order to successfully become an adoptive parent. It looked like a game of snakes and ladders.

As the course drew on, an adoptive mother cradling her newly adopted baby addressed us. I envied her at first her blond-haired baby boy; envied her until I learned that not only did the child have two half-siblings by different fathers, but that all three babies had been placed separately, with only two sets of adoptive parents agreeing to sibling contact. What's more, the birth mother – in the need to replace the lost children – was again pregnant by yet another father. I wondered what her baby boy would one day make of it all.

We were then shown a book containing details of available children: the babies and toddlers awaiting new mummies and daddies. The lady in the kaftan got there first. I looked on as she and her anxious-looking partner flicked over the pages. Immediately, I felt concern at how few children there appeared to be on social services' books, and that the faces of those that stared up at me seemed strangely unreal. I tried, in vain, to imagine any of them running around my garden or clambering up the stairs. I recalled the Grattan's catalogue my grandmother used to run – those dress rings that her neighbours ordered, or the elegant shoes, totally unsuitable but they could always be sent back. Would any of these children get sent back, I wondered, as I studied their eager smiles.

'How do you know if a child is the right one for you when you first meet them?' someone asked. I had a sudden flashback to my sister telling me about the moment little Mei had been placed in her arms: 'I knew as soon as I held her that I would never give her up.'

The social worker advised the questioner that 'chemistry' often played a role, but that we should not necessarily worry if we *didn't* start to bond immediately. 'However,' she warned, 'if there's a *niggle* when you first meet the child, it's more than likely that that niggle will still be there in a year's time.' It was *crucial* to be as sure as possible about a child *before* they moved in.

'Disruption' was the term for sending a child back. I wondered how many adoptions actually ended up in a disruption. For that matter, how many people adopted at all? What proportion of those who did the prep course? And how many of them were single? I looked at the statistics in the course handbook but they were dated 1990!

Lastly, we were told never to expect an adopted child to be grateful: 'They didn't ask to be adopted.'

I was relieved, but a little sad, too, at the end of the course – sad that I would never know the others' outcomes after having connected with them in very singular and special circumstances. Was I ready now for all this, I wondered, as I collected my notes. I glanced over at the social worker with the adopted teenage daughter. She was handing out the forms that we were to complete, should we wish to proceed. Would she say it was all worth it in the end? Did the joys really outweigh the pain?

Outside, everything appeared normal as I drove home and then made a mad dash for the station, fearful of missing the train to London. I had arranged to meet a friend at Covent Garden later that evening. I climbed on board and was soon glad to be miles away from the prep course. Would I or wouldn't I? I deliberated, gazing out of the grimy window. My mind was in turmoil.

'How did it go?' my friend asked, as I arrived at the opera house.

'Really well,' I replied, and we rushed to our seats on hearing an announcement that *Der Rosenkavalier* was to begin in five minutes. I felt for the adoption form in my handbag, during the last-minute round of coughing and shuffling of programmes. Then, the exit doors were closed. Would I go ahead and fill it in? I asked myself, as the lights dimmed and a sudden hush fell over the auditorium. *It's not something I have to do,* I reasoned. I saw Pappano make his way to the rostrum, whilst the audience clapped and cheered. Suddenly, I was clapping and cheering, too. My answer became clear. I would!

Standards of housekeeping should not be on trial and no one should feel the need to tidy up before the social worker arrives...

Preparation Course notes

My adoptive journey was like the slow shuttle of the daily commute I had endured for fourteen years. For it was not until five months *after* completion of the preparation course that my home visits commenced.

That summer, I was content in the knowledge that the adoptive process was now well under way, so I planned a fortnight's holiday with my youngest sister, Caryl, in Cornwall.

'It was like a boot camp,' Caryl later recalled, laughing.

We stayed in a friend's converted boathouse and each morning, would put on our swimsuits and make our way across the field to the cliff edge where we descended a hundred or so steep steps to take our early morning swim. Afterwards, we would rush back for a hot shower, eat breakfast in the company of a ginger cat called 'Rommel', and plan the day – sometimes just lying in the grass and eating Cornish pasties bought from a local shop.

'Do you make crumble with self-raising or plain flour,' I had asked the shop owner.

'I'm not sure,' he replied. 'Does anyone know whether you use self-raising or plain flour in a crumble?' he called out to the customers in the shop.

'Plain,' someone shouted back.

'Self-raising,' said another.

Later, using blackberries we had picked from the bushes outside the boathouse, and windfall apples from a nearby tree, Caryl and I made the most delicious fruit crumble, the likes of which, it was agreed, we would never be able to duplicate.

As we celebrated the last evening of our holiday in a local pub with a bottle of wine, and reminisced over our blissful week, I suggested to Caryl that the two of us might come again.

'But Beth,' she exclaimed, 'the next time you come, it might be with your new son or daughter!'

What would Sylvia, my new social worker, be like, I wondered, one early morning in October, as I nervously awaited her arrival.

I recalled again the preparation course leader's reply in the affirmative, when I had asked if any social workers were against single adopters: 'You can make a formal complaint if you ever think you're being unfairly treated,' he said. His comments had unnerved me and as I opened my front door, I half-expected to find a battleaxe waging a personal crusade against me and all single adopters.

A woman with a cheerful demeanour and a reassuringly maternal air entered my hallway, however; someone instantly likeable and certainly unlikely to arouse any neighbourly gossip.

Our relationship would be vital: Sylvia would gather all the evidence, dig into my past, evaluate my financial viability, search for any deep-seated anxieties, or misplaced intentions. *She* would be the one to make a recommendation to the adoption Approval Panel on my behalf. Sylvia's approval was essential.

'How did you find the prep course?' she enquired, as I brought her a cup of tea. 'Did you find that adoption started to become more real?'

'Yes, I did,' I fibbed, assuming this was what she wanted to hear.

'I hope to write up your report for the Approval Panel early in the New Year,' she said, as she leaned back on the sofa. 'That should give us enough time to conduct around ten fortnightly sessions.'

I sat on the edge of my chair, nervously bracing myself for the forthcoming interrogation. 'I'd like to learn about your career first,' she began. 'It'll help me to learn about what sort of person you are, your work ethic, your motivation...'

It was quiet when I began to talk, the traffic outside just a faint drone after its early morning rush as I transported myself back sixteen years to the start of my City career. 'My banking career started in the mid-eighties, at Deutsche Bank,' I told Sylvia, 'following several years in the diplomatic service...'

I later looked over at her on the sofa; she appeared to enjoy hearing me rattle on about my past.

'As my career took off with increasing responsibility and frequent trips to Frankfurt to improve my business and IT skills,' I continued, 'in my personal life, my relationship suffered. I was sad that my boyfriend at the time was resentful of my success.'

'So you *have* been in love then,' Sylvia interrupted.

'Oh yes, more than once,' I responded and we giggled together in the dim, autumn light. 'In fact, he asked me to live with him. I remember it gave me such a nice, warm feeling on the one hand, but on the other, I knew I would have felt stifled if I couldn't have pursued my career to the degree I wished. We had talked about moving out of London, and when the relationship failed, I decided to do it anyway, on my own. I sold my flat in south London and bought a little Edwardian cottage here in Sussex, which I adored. I still enjoyed the buzz of the City, however, so I ended up splitting my life between the two places. Commuting wasn't so bad in those days; the trains were nearly always on time.'

For the balance of the session I talked about the other banks I had worked for and, in passing, mentioned that one of them had been particularly aggressive. Sylvia then questioned me at length about my remark, and explained that children from care could also be aggressive.

At the end, Sylvia gave me an extract as background reading, and said that we would be discussing my *significant relationships* in a fortnight's time. I was taken aback, having assumed from the home assessment carried out by June that they were only interested in past husbands or cohabitees.

On the whole, I felt I had come out of the session well, and had even enjoyed it.

After seeing Sylvia out, I rushed down the high street, past the empty Turkish take-away and the estate agent's, where an arm-in-arm couple were looking at some over-priced house advertisements, and calculated that I had just enough time to buy a sandwich and a coffee for the train.

It struck me, a little while later, as I settled back into my seat to read the extract I'd been given – taken from a book with a strange-sounding title, *The Primal Wound* – how paradoxical it was that this time I looked forward to the safe and familiar routine of my daily commute.

Several minutes later, I stared in disbelief at the words I was reading. I already felt rejected by a child I had never even seen.

The connection between a child and his biological mother appears to be primal, mystical, mysterious, and everlasting. It can no longer be presumed that one can replace the biological mother with another 'primary caregiver' without the child's being both aware of the substitution and traumatised by it. The mother/infant bond takes many forms and the communication between them is unconscious, instinctual and intuitive. To those researchers who want to believe only what they can observe, this may not seem very scientific. It is understood by mothers, however, to whom it does not seem to be all that mysterious. The significance of that bond is confirmed by the increasing numbers of adoptees and birth mothers who are out there searching for each other...

I felt tense before the next session and I wasn't looking forward to it at all – the poking and prying into what, after all, was my business, not theirs. As far as I could see, my significant relationships really had nothing to do with my fitness to adopt a child – and what, in any case, did 'significant' mean?

I had already decided I would tell Sylvia about a three-year relationship that *was* significant as far as I understood the meaning of the term; it certainly had been significant in its effect on *me*. So I regaled Sylvia with the hopes I had felt back then; how low I had felt at the relationship's end and at the thought of starting over again on my own; of standing in the long, wet grass and the dandelions with Molly; and coming out of my period of stagnation.

'I'm not sure that relationship qualifies,' Sylvia told me afterwards. 'Significant, to me, means living together for a long period or being married.'

'But it was still *significant*,' I replied.

'But you weren't paying bills together,' Sylvia explained.

I wanted to ask her, *What if, instead, I had had a three-year marriage that had been a disaster from start to finish? Would that have made it more significant?* But I said nothing.

At the end of our session, Sylvia said, 'By the way, I've

already initiated your police checks; I should have the results back soon…and I'll need the addresses of your referees soon.'

I had already provided her with the name of my sister, Molly, back from the Far East and the mother of two adopted children herself; my friend, Ruth, and another friend, Nigel, whom I had known for some years.

'I'll be writing to them,' Sylvia informed me, putting on her coat. 'I'll need to meet them all.'

Eager to get to the train station, I grabbed my coat and accompanied Sylvia to the door. I hoped she would not interpret my haste as any lack of commitment to adoption on my part.

It was just after noon, on a blue-skied, crisp winter's day and I had met Ruth, one of my referees, for lunch. The Royal China was buzzing with the high-pitched chatter of traders, secretaries and accountants temporarily released from the stresses and travails of the office.

'It's good to see you again,' Ruth said. She had been working from home these last few years, bringing up her two girls, and since their move from Sussex, we rarely had been in touch.

'I'm really pleased to see you, too,' I replied, as I took a sip of green tea and opened the lunch menu. 'How are Greg and the girls?'

'They're all doing well. Why don't you come up for another visit?'

Ruth had always been a supportive friend, and not only in regards to my career. 'You *will* be a mother,' she would often tell me whenever I expressed some concern, always managing somehow to reassure me. When I had told her about my plans to adopt, she was delighted. And when I learned that I would be unable to adopt an infant, she laughed. 'I can see you with an older child – someone who can travel around with you, like Dervla Murphy and her daughter.'

'The social worker didn't seem to want to know much,' Ruth now told me, recounting their recent meeting. 'I thought she'd be bombarding me with questions, but I had the impression she was just pleased to have a day up in London; I gave her some ideas as to what to do with her spare time. She told me her main concern was whether you'd be able to make the transition from career woman to mother – does she know what you do for a job? She didn't appear to have a proper understanding of it.'

'We discussed my career a lot,' I said, a little disconcerted. 'Perhaps I wasn't very clear.'

'Anyway,' Ruth went on, 'I explained to her that you spend most of your time getting other people to do what they don't want to do – perfect training, in my view, for bringing up a child!'

We were still laughing when lunch arrived.

I pulled at the cord that night to lower the bedroom blind but first, as was my custom, I peered into the house over the road to see Cynthia sitting there in the lamplight. Cynthia always knew when I was up late or when I was away, she said, by my blinds. She too, had once commuted for many years – far longer even than me – and had never married. Well into her nineties now, she had lived on her own for a great many years.

'Do you think it's a good idea, my adopting?' I had asked my father earlier that week.

'Yes, I do,' he told me, 'otherwise you might be lonely having no one around when you're older.' He mentioned his childless sister, the auntie with whom Molly and I had stayed in Wales just before Molly heard the news about the availability of little Poppy. And I thought of my neighbour, Cynthia, sitting alone, at her window.

'Did you mention Nana's neighbours to the social worker?' my sister asked. What a strange question, I thought, glancing at her, bemused.

Molly had rung earlier to ask if I would like some supper with her and Tom. It was quiet when I arrived, the two girls already up in bed. 'I've made a chicken coconut curry,' she said, 'is that OK?'

'It smells delicious…Yes, I did mention Nana's – why?'

'Sylvia came yesterday. It went well – you've no need to worry,' she added quickly. 'But I was surprised when she said she was concerned that you were very middle class and therefore had little experience of the types of children in care.'

'But I told her all about Nana's! I even mentioned Gaynor…and I said you often talked to me about the children on your caseload.'

'It should be OK, then,' Molly said, offering me a glass of wine. 'I told her about Nana's neighbours, too, and the fact that there wasn't a lot of money going around when we were little.'

I was feeling so positive about my sessions by then that it did not occur to me to bring it up with Sylvia later; in fact, it had already gone from my mind when Molly enquired as to the likely timing of the adoption.

'Apparently, matching can happen as soon as I've been approved.'

'Are you sure?' Molly said. 'Some friends of ours were approved months ago and they haven't heard a word. Their social worker told them there just aren't enough children available.'

'How strange,' I replied, though I was not overly worried. 'Perhaps there just aren't as many children available in Hampshire.'

'Or it could just be that their situation is a bit complicated,' Molly said. 'But again, you might just check with Sylvia.'

By the time of the next fortnightly meeting, however, my sister's advice had slipped from my mind.

'What sort of mother do you think you'll be?' Sylvia enquired of me.

What sort of mother does any woman think she will be, I wondered. We all surely expect to be wonderful. I thought how I had often been surprised to see that friends who were dominant forces at work, were at home dominated and undermined by their own children. So, who really knows? But I gave what I hoped were acceptable responses. 'I expect to be a warm and affectionate parent,' I told her, 'and when necessary, firm.'

Sylvia asked if I had had any experience of looking after children and I replied that I often babysat for my nieces.

My brother-in-law, Tom, would bring Mei's cot over and she would sleep in the study next to my bedroom, whilst Poppy slept with me (Poppy refused to spend a night away with anyone else). Tom would close the curtains and give Mei her bottle, assuring me that she would sleep solidly until the morning. Mei always did so. Sometimes, in the morning, I would go in and watch her lying there, staring up at the ceiling, making baby noises. And once or twice I would awake to the sound of her 'singing'. I could hardly believe it the first time I heard Mei singing. I would lie in bed, listening to her.

During our conversation, Sylvia stated two specific things about the mothering of an adoptive child that she felt were important – the need to reinforce boundaries by gently but firmly reiterating them; and never to forget that because of their insecurity, it might take longer to build trust with a child taken from care – therefore one needed to make their life as reassuring and predictable as possible, for example by establishing routines.

'Do you still think you'll be able to maintain your current friendships?' Sylvia enquired.

'I'm sure I will,' I replied. (Why not, I wondered.)

We went on to discuss those friends. Who were the closest

among them? In whom did I confide? What was my attitude to any gay friends I might have? This led on to a discussion of support networks.

'A good support network is critical to the success of an adoption,' Sylvia said.

We discussed the various family members, friends and neighbours who would form my post-adoption support. Obviously, my family would form the main source of emotional and practical support for me. My sister Molly was not only a health visitor, but had adopted two children herself and lived just 20 minutes' walk away. My parents, too, and other family members were not too far. 'I'll be the one you can ring up to scream and shout at,' my eldest brother, Nick, a GP, had offered. I was touched, though privately discounted ever needing such help.

'Do you know any single mothers in the area?' Sylvia asked.

'I have a friend, Cindy, who lives close by,' I told her. 'She's a single mum.' I saw Sylvia nod her head enthusiastically, inserting Cindy's name in a little box on a diagram.

'Have you told her about your plans yet?'

'No, I haven't, but then I've hardly told any of my friends. I thought I'd get my approval first.'

And then there was Kay, I told Sylvia, who lived up the road with three children and was effectively a single mum – though I refrained from mentioning that Kay had been brought to the attention of social services because she was home-schooling her children.

'And I have a cycling friend, Maureen, who lives in Brighton,' I added. It had actually been on the tip of my tongue to tell Maureen of my adoption plans the previous weekend but, out of the blue, she had suddenly started bemoaning the lot of a single parent. I listened in dismay as she told me what hard work it was trying to bring up a child, do a day's work, and have a social life, too. And living in

Brighton made it practically impossible to meet a man, she moaned: 'Everyone is either a student or gay.' All this detail, of course, I did not reveal to Sylvia.

'It's important to include some male role models in your support network, too,' Sylvia urged me, and so my friend James was inserted into another box on the diagram.

'He's the only friend locally I've actually told so far,' I said.

When, at the next session, I saw Sylvia's now completed diagram showing me in the centre of my support group with a series of nice, comforting, straight lines emanating outwards to the neatly boxed names, I felt secure. I never considered that some of those boxed names might not know how to deal with my changed situation. I never dreamed that for some friends it might even raise personal issues about childlessness. It never occurred to me that some of the names I had given Sylvia were, in reality, little more than acquaintances in my social network, people who would flutter off the instant I was no longer one of them...

During a time at work when I was growing increasingly disenchanted and, at times, weighed down by the slowness of the adoptive process, it was a support network I discovered on my Docklands doorstep that proved to be a godsend – and no neatly drawn diagrams were involved. To find it, one only had to cross over the road from Canary Wharf, walk up Poplar High Street and turn the corner at the Victorian-built town hall that housed the local adoption support services. There, tucked away opposite the attractive group of mews houses once owned by a lady of ill repute called Lucy Love, lay the little church of St Matthias.

It was at the end of my lunch-hour and I was walking back from a nearby school, where I had participated in a reading scheme for disadvantaged children, when a cheery-faced, well-built, blonde-haired woman approached me as I stood

41

admiring a gravestone depicting a jaunty ship with billowing sails.

Her name was Kath, and she told me the church was the oldest building in Docklands, built in the 1600s with money from the East India Company. It was now a community centre, run primarily by her. 'The Canary Wharf developers never cared about the community on "our side", Kath said, 'so we formed a committee called SPLASH to help protect the rights of all of us whose lives were being changed.' She said she was surprised to see me for hardly anyone visited from 'the other side'.

'Are the banks contributing enough?' I asked her guiltily, thinking of the plush apartment blocks and hotels, and the increasing number of office blocks mushrooming all over the 'other side'.

'They've done a lot,' she said, 'but they could do more.' Kath went on to tell me that she was recovering from breast cancer. 'I've just been given the all clear at my latest three-monthly check,' she said, in the same tone she might have used to tell me she had had a boil lanced. It was her work in the centre that had helped keep her going. And her writing, too.

'I'm writing a story for my grandchildren,' she told me excitedly. 'I've read them the first few pages but I haven't had time to finish it.'

From then on, in my free time, I would often walk over to the 'other side'. There, I saw the crèche facilities; the lunches laid on for the elderly; the meetings of local Bangladeshi women, many of whom were unable to speak English; and the gatherings for stroke victims, some of whom could not speak at all.

I told Kath about my adoption plans. 'A lot of people round here used to adopt during the war years,' she said. 'There was no formal process then. If a child lost their parents, someone in the neighbourhood would always take them in and make sure they were clothed and fed.'

Whenever someone entered her office, she always said, excitedly, 'This is Beth – she's going to adopt!'

Sometimes, over a cuppa, Kath would entertain me with tales of her grandfather who had sired fifteen children and worked in the docks. 'Would you help me write it up one day?' she asked. 'I'm afraid it'll all get forgotten.' I assured her that I would and I still have the map she drew, showing all the pubs she remembered as a girl. Only a fraction still exist; they carry names associated with the sea: famous admirals, naval battles and seaside places that evoke romance and the exotic. My favourite is The African Queen.

At one of our meetings, Kath passed me the first pages of the story she had been writing for her grandchildren. It was about a child who had been dropped into a loving home by a stork.

December 2003 and the stork was still a long way from my home…

'How do you expect to make the transition from career woman to mother?' was Sylvia's latest topic for discussion. Social services were obviously concerned as to whether I could leave my career and play a new and different role in the world of motherhood. Would I be able to manage the lifestyle changes and the loss of social events and activities – and, most importantly, adapt to a child living with me?

I knew what Sylvia wanted to hear, and I parroted it dutifully, but it felt like being at work and giving someone else's presentation.

Sylvia persisted that I might find the transition difficult because, as she put it, I hadn't ever lived with anyone before.

I reminded her that I came from a large family of six children. And I told her that after I left college, I had shared a flat with a friend for a couple of years – and that I would have been happy to share a flat during my Foreign Office tours but that each of us had been allocated our own accommodation. 'That took some getting used to,' I told Sylvia. 'It was my first experience of living alone…And when I later came back to London and bought a flat my sister, Molly, shared it with me for the first two years. And I've had lodgers from time to time…So I do have some experience of living with others.' Even so, I privately acknowledged that having a child round me all day would take some getting used to, at first, but I didn't dare admit it to her.

'It won't be so easy to go out for a meal,' Sylvia pointed out.

'I'll invite my friends round for dinner, instead,' I replied, naively imagining the little one in bed sound asleep whilst I served my friends a series of *cordon bleu* dishes. I did admit to Sylvia that it might not be so easy to go up to London to see an opera or ballet – 'but as they get older,' I said, 'I can take them with me.'

'You'll find your child will introduce you to *their* interests, too,' Sylvia smiled.

Sylvia often used the word 'family' when talking about a child living with me. I had previously assumed that 'family' meant mother, father and children, so I liked the way she used it in reference to my prospective situation. It caused me to think back to a weekend I had once spent with my eldest brother and his wife and children: we all of us sat round the breakfast table on Sunday morning, to the constant sound of cereal boxes being opened and chatter, when it suddenly struck me that for all that I had – my City career and non-stop social whirl – there was something fundamental missing in my life: *family* life.

I thought the session was going well enough until, out of the blue, Sylvia stated that the Approval Panel might need some convincing as to my commitment. 'One way of assuring them,' she said, 'would be to give up your job. Perhaps you could get one locally, or go part-time.'

44

'But changing jobs could take months!' I blurted out.

'Yes, that's so,' Sylvia agreed.

'Just so I'm clear,' I said, incredulously now, 'how long will it actually take for me to be matched with a child?'

'It could take a considerable time,' she replied, gravely. 'That's the one thing I think might put you off in the end: the time you have to wait.'

Since timescales were so woolly, there was no way I was going to leave my job immediately. Why forfeit the high daily rate I was on when I would get nothing from social services in the way of financial help – and perhaps not even be approved? Everything I earned was going towards paying off my mortgage and accumulating some savings for the adoption. Why give up my career if, at the end of the day, they took forever to match me with a child?

Looking back, I have no doubt Sylvia's gut instinct was that I would make a good parent – and she told me so as well. But as a single adopter and, moreover, one who had delayed the process, I was obviously not on the A list, reserved for the perfect couples. More likely, I was on a D for dodgy list: candidates who could not be failed on paper but who, hopefully, might have given up on adoption by the time social services finally got in touch with a match.

Christmas was approaching and Sylvia arrived for our last session of 2003 to discuss the types of child in care.

'Because of their background, it's not likely that your adopted child will be bright,' Sylvia mentioned casually, as though she were telling me it was unlikely he or she would have blonde hair. 'Genetically, the odds are not in their favour. And many of them will come from families with learning difficulties.'

All the time I had been wondering whether I might have a boy or a girl, whether he or she might be tall or short, boisterous or shy – it never occurred to me to wonder whether they might be bright or dim. More was to follow.

'And some of them won't have an imagination, because they've never received any stimulation. An imagination has to be nurtured.'

So not only would my future child be thick, they would have no imagination either! I somehow managed to keep a fixed smile on my face right up to the end of the session.

I walked to the train station in a state of horror. It had been too good to be true, this whole adoption thing. I waited in the queue at the station café only to find out that even my favourite bacon and egg sandwich was sold out.

It was Benny who convinced me that I would be able to adopt the type of child that Sylvia had described. Earlier in our home visits, I had told Sylvia how, whilst at Credit Suisse, I had become involved in a reading scheme for disadvantaged children. The idea was for volunteers to give up a lunchtime each fortnight and use that time working to improve the children's reading and conversational skills. 'When the bank's Human Resources department decided they were too busy to manage the scheme,' I told Sylvia, 'I myself set up and maintained it.'

'Benny was the first special needs child to participate,' I explained to her. 'He went to a school in All Saints, a part of the East End I'd never heard of – although it was less than a mile from my office. The school rang to warn me in advance that Benny was shy and under-confident. He needed to be treated sensitively, so I chose him as my own reading partner.

'I felt terribly nervous when I went along to meet him for the first time. What would he think of me? Would he accept me? What would we talk about?'

The school looked much like a prison, surrounded by high fencing and iron entrance gates. It couldn't have been more different to the school I went to. After passing the eleven-plus, I attended a red-brick, ivy-clad girls' school which sported grass tennis courts, hockey and cricket pitches and a sunken rose garden. I thought of my own school uniform – velour hats and gym slips in winter, and straw boaters and blazers in summer – when I first saw Benny's ill-fitting grey trousers and grey-white, curled-up shirt collar missing a button.

'Though I tried in vain to engage Benny in some general conversation,' I told Sylvia, 'he hardly opened his mouth. I remember how he gawped as though I were an alien and I suppose that's what I was: an alien from the 'other side' who worked in one of the tower blocks that dominated the horizon for miles. I'd landed in an area suffering from generational unemployment.

'At the end of the first session – by which time Benny had hardly said a word – I decided it was a hopeless case trying to engage him so instead, I chattered on about myself. Then, just as I was about to go, I could hardly believe my ears: 'My mum's just had a baby,' he announced.

'Oh really?' I said. 'Is it a boy or a girl?'

'The school coordinator later told me she'd never seen him chat before, and from then on, he seemed to look forward to my visit, always giving me such a nice smile when I walked into the classroom. I deliberated whether it was fair to tell him about my trip to the Galapagos Islands, but Benny loved looking at the postcards, and when he saw the one with the blue-footed boobies, he began to tell me about the gulls at Southend…'

There was a real benefit for me, too. After a dreary day in the office, seeing Benny's face light up made me feel like I was on cloud nine. Looking down at him affectionately one day, as he stumbled over some vocabulary and then told me about the panto at Shoreditch, it occurred to me that I *could* love a child irrespective of their background, or their ability to achieve A

47

grades in their GCSEs. And when the school gave a small party for us at Christmas, there I was like the proud parent, sitting on the front row…

When Benny took his Christmas school break, I likewise took a break from the office, the commute and Sylvia's home visits and began to anticipate a forthcoming trip to Mexico. I planned to spend the New Year with an old friend, Jim, whom I had met in Berlin, almost thirty years previously.

Jim's e-mail had arrived out of the blue, on a cold and dismal November afternoon. 'We've just finished renovating our new villa in Mexico – how about coming to visit?'

I immediately saw the invitation as an opportunity to avoid the usual New Year celebrations at home and, moreover, as a breather from the intensity of the adoptive process.

On Christmas Eve I drove my two nieces to my parents' house, to meet my younger brother's children down from London for the day. It was the first time the latest addition to the family – little Mei, whom Molly and Tom had recently adopted from mainland China – met her new cousins.

'She's worse than our new puppy Buster,' my brother, David, laughed as she tore around the house. I could not help noticing how, despite his being only 15 months younger than me, my brother seemed to have aged; I put it down to marital stress – things had not always been easy.

'She's a handful but she's lovely,' I said, as Mei rushed into the dining room where we were about to eat lunch and started to poke her little podgy finger up on the table for anything edible within reach. The 'magpie' tendency, social services called it – common amongst adoptees.

'She was well fed at the orphanage, I think,' Molly said, 'but probably never had *quite* enough to eat.' And never given any opportunity to stretch her little legs either, I was told. Despite which, within days of being handed over to Molly, Mei could stand up and waddle around; in fact, since then, she had been unable to keep still. But how would any child behave after being left in a cot or a chair with no stimulation for over a year? I first saw Mei through the window of my sister's home. It was the day Molly, Tom and Poppy arrived home from China with her. There she was, lying on the floor on her tummy, totally unfazed, her big dark eyes staring curiously up at me.

On 28th December, with the sound of Jingle Bells being sung by four generations of family resonating in my ears, I flew out of the family nest, headed for Mexico. The villa was in Puerto Vallarta, a place famous as the location for John Huston's film, *Night of the Iguana*, which starred Richard Burton and Ava Gardner. There's a pretty pink house there that Burton bought as a love nest for Liz Taylor.

What would Jim and his partner's reaction be to my adoption plans, I wondered, as we sat drinking margaritas on their hill-top patio, where pea-green parrotlets and yellow and black-striped caciques flew in and out of the tulip trees, and banana trees swayed against the backdrop of the sea below.

After revealing my news, I half-expected them to say I was taking too much on. To my relief, they both expressed delight.

'We, too, wanted to adopt some years ago,' Jim told me. 'But, in those days, it would have been difficult for a gay couple...so our Corgis are our family instead!' he laughed, as one came yapping up.

I had always thought, from our correspondence over the years, that in some ways their life sounded idyllic: retiring early, splitting their time between several homes, travelling and pursuing hobbies... But, privately, I could not help but get a whiff of 'what can I spend my money on next?' syndrome. Then, I recalled how offended I had been when an acquaintance once said the same about me.

As I lay back in my sun-lounger, I looked forward to the

pleasant two weeks that lay ahead…I had no idea that a major change in my life was about to occur, a change that would often cause me to think of the turns life can present just when you least expect them…

e-mail, 2004

Dear Beth,

I know you don't believe in hocus pocus but this whole thing between us and how it came about and its overall timing smacks of something out of the ordinary to me. We met through A, who was introduced to me by T, who I can barely tolerate and usually try to avoid, at a dinner I almost didn't attend. Later, you and I ran into one another at the sidewalk coffee shop and I cannot imagine why I gave you my e-mail address in the first place. Then there was our chance meeting at Puerto Vallarta airport on the leaving day. And later I learned that the first e-mail you sent was returned and then re-sent but might have been missed altogether. This whole thing came very close to not happening at all on many, many occasions. But it did happen. And for some reason, I believe…

Mike was from Texas, a long way from England. When I asked him, later, what *he* had been doing at the turn of the millennium, he said he had been in San Francisco with his daughters. One of them lived there and had hosted a New Year's Eve party. So at the same time that I was working on the Y2K project, anxious as to what might happen once the millennium clock struck twelve, he was concerned as to how the banking systems would cope because funds from his business were tied up in them.

'Whenever I spoke to some banking official,' he told me, 'they said there was no need to worry, the dangers were being vastly exaggerated.'

At his daughter's party that night, aware that everyone had become apprehensive about the dire things predicted for midnight, he and a friend decided that when twelve o'clock came they would switch off the electricity in the house.

'All hell broke loose,' he laughed, 'until someone noticed that all the other lights in the neighborhood were still on and then everyone began to laugh.'

I was told by an acquaintance, whom I met in Puerto Vallarta, that Mike was intelligent, and an avid reader. 'You'll like him,' he said. An erudite Texan – I liked the sound of that combination.

We were introduced at a club on the beach where a band played Cuban music, and a number of couples interpreted the salsa. Everyone was drinking.

Was it love at first sight? I *do* know that I was immediately attracted to Mike, and that I was disappointed that there was no space at his table; throughout the evening, I kept looking round for a glimpse of him.

When he came over to my table at the end of the evening, I felt like a shy schoolgirl and hardly said a word.

A few days later, I saw Mike *again*, this time walking past the pavement café where I was having a coffee. Unable to resist, I called out to him. In the brief time we had that morning, he told me about Oaxaca. It was his favourite place in Mexico, he said, and he tried to visit there each summer. Immediately, I knew I wanted to be there, too, that summer. Equally, I knew that by then, the adoption might have happened.

I once more felt that familiar feeling of disquiet at the thought of the ongoing process back home.

When I landed at a cold and wet Gatwick Airport a couple of days later, my mind had already turned to work, the commute and my social worker's visit the next day.

'I've received the results of your medical and they're fine,' Sylvia informed me that morning. She had first complimented me on my suntan and enquired at length about my trip.

She sounds suspicious, I thought, paranoia rising; perhaps she's looking for evidence of something that might divert me from the adoption. I remembered her once saying, 'You'd be surprised how people's lives can change by the time they're approved.'

So I mentioned that the friends I had been staying with were gay.

'Oh really?' Sylvia smiled. But then, her expression changed. 'I'm sorry,' she announced, 'but I'll be moving from your case soon. I'm moving to another department...I really should be leaving immediately but my boss and I agreed it wouldn't be fair on you if I left at this stage. They haven't found my replacement yet. I'm very sorry.'

I felt a moment of shock upon hearing her words. But this is my life, my future, my child's future, I felt like shouting. It was Sylvia who knew me, Sylvia who had been party to all the information I had revealed, Sylvia who knew the sort of child I wanted – the one that would best suit me. With another social worker, I would have to start from scratch. I sat there, feeling abandoned and alone.

'I'll be staying on until I've written up the report,' she continued, '*and* it might even work to your advantage, because *now* I'll be working with the families whose children are coming up for adoption, rather than with prospective adopters. I'll be able to keep a look out for you,' she promised.

I began to feel a little better. Who knows, I thought, encouraging myself, perhaps Sylvia's departure was even fated and because of it I would end up with the perfect match.

'I feel strongly,' I quickly said, 'that I want a child of two, and at most three. I'm seeing a lot of my little niece, Mei. She's starting to walk and talk and I'm worried I'll miss out on these stages with an older child.'

'It would still be better if we put "up to fifth birthday",' Sylvia insisted. 'Then, you'll have more choice.'

'But I don't want a child of five,' I objected.

'Up to fifth birthday actually means four, not yet five,' she replied, calmly.

'But I thought there were lots of children needing homes. Is it because I'm single that I'm not being allowed a younger child?'

'Not at all. But I can see you with an older child,' she said reassuringly. 'I believe it would work well.'

I had to admit that there were pros to having an older child. For one, I would still be able to enjoy some freedom whilst they were at nursery, or school. But it seemed difficult, impossible even, for me to make up my mind. I thought back to the first day of my business analysis course, years earlier. 'I want you to list all your positive attributes,' the course leader said, and I wrote a long list, at the top of which was the word 'decisiveness'. If true, then why did I always find it so difficult to decide what to order when eating out? *The chicken sounded nice but then so did the sole.* Decisiveness, I later realised, belonged to my working life; indecisiveness belonged outside of it. But – in my defence – I wasn't choosing a meal now. I was taking on a child, one who would become my son or daughter.

To reassure me, I imagine, Sylvia cited the example of a single woman who had adopted two lovely older boys. The youngest sounded ideal, I thought, and my spirits rose – but then sank when I was told he suffered from foetal alcohol symptoms and consequently had a small head. I don't want a child with a small head, I felt like crying out. Why are you telling me this? My adopted child might have blonde hair whereas mine is dark; they might even not be very bright...but why should I have one with a small head?

'His sibling is also a delight,' Sylvia carried on, oblivious to my distress. 'He's very well-behaved and well-mannered but due to his experience of abandonment, I imagine he'll always be a little detached. It wouldn't surprise me if he never had a girlfriend or if he did, he might not be able to form an attachment.'

This is getting worse, I shrieked inwardly. I now had visions of a son with a charming but disengaged smile, a son who found it difficult to have girlfriends, or would chuck them at the drop of a hat; I imagined a layabout refusing to move out, a spotty youth with bum fluff who spent all of his time in his room playing music.

But with the maiden aunt image once again entering my mind, an age range with which I did not completely concur, was entered into Sylvia's report.

e-mail, 22 February 2004

Dear Beth,

...The weather here in North Texas has been very odd lately. I'm sure Bush is somehow responsible. Two weeks ago Friday we had 3 or 4 inches of snow, the most in more than 30 years or so, but most all had melted by the afternoon, leaving some disappointed children and the remnants of some pretty disreputable-looking snowmen...

I was now more than two years into the adoption process, with the end seemingly far from sight. My father was becoming impatient for me and had recently suggested, 'Can't you ask for a little coloured child? That way, you might get one quicker.'

I laughed at his remark, thinking it very sweet. And I *was* drawn to the Bangladeshi community I passed through on my walks to see Benny and Kath. I liked to see their costumes flow in the wind as they crowded round the grocery van that pulled up at the tall blocks of flats, hear the Bangla music at the corner shop where I bought the occasional tin of cat food, and see the men in their embroidered caps hovering outside the mosque tucked next to the grocer's on Poplar High Street...

At the next – our penultimate – session, I was surprised to discover that my religious beliefs were of interest to social services. Did being a Protestant, Catholic or atheist affect one's ability to be a good mother? I could only assume that Sylvia's questions were to find out if I belonged to some fundamentalist religious cult.

'Up to the age of nine,' I told her, 'before we left Wales, my brothers and sisters and I went to a High Anglican Church – but only because it was the nearest church to the house. For the most part, I found it boring and spent my time giggling in the back pew.

'I later switched churches when I couldn't get into Brownies, which was over-subscribed, and started attending a little Methodist church. I remember feeling guilty when I later received a card with a picture of Jesus on the front from my former Sunday school teacher, saying how they missed me.'

I went on to tell Sylvia that, although I had not been to church in years, a colleague had recently persuaded me to attend a lunchtime session on the church barge of St Peter's at Canary Wharf. I had often seen the little boat bobbing up and down on the water in front of Beluga's Champagne and

Oyster Bar. My main concern on walking over the gangplank was being spotted by someone I knew. When the smartly dressed preacher opened his sermon with the words 'Work is *unimportant*!' you could have heard a pin drop.

'So how would you feel about having a child whose birth parents wanted them to be brought up as a Muslim?' Sylvia asked me.

'It would feel too alien to me,' I told her, puzzled – for what were the chances, anyway, in this predominantly white county to be offered a child of a different race, let alone one whose parents wanted them brought up in their faith?

Almost six months after our first meeting, Sylvia came into my home for our final session. The gap analysis, I called it. In the office, the gap analysis helped prioritise what was required to ensure a successful implementation: the critical 'must-haves'.

In adoption, the gap analysis meant the dreaded tick-boxes that the social worker would read out, and then check; responses that would delineate the 'must-haves' in my future child: what could I live with, and what was unacceptable? Would I accept a child with Asperger's, or one who had a limited life expectancy? What about a child born as a result of incest, or born blind, or deaf? The list is long and sad.

Molly revealed to me that *she* had agreed to a child without a limb when she and Tom filled in the tick-boxes for their second child and, during the long wait, she became increasingly concerned that she and her husband might indeed be presented with a one-legged baby when they arrived in Guangzhou.

I felt heartless saying a categorical 'no' to most of the conditions, my mind on the innocent children I was rejecting, crossing them out of my life before we had even met.

There was also a tick-box concerning 'contact'. 'Would you

take on a child requiring face-to-face contact (i.e., regular meetings) with their birth parents?' Sylvia asked.

'No, I wouldn't,' I replied immediately.

'Most people say that,' she said, as she entered her tick. 'You do have a lot of 'no's',' she said, finally, after having gone through the long list.

I told her that I was, after all, doing this on my own, and I *knew* my limitations. How could I take on a child who had severe behavioural issues, or who needed regular hospital treatment, or who was terminally ill? My mind went back to my medical examination when my doctor mentioned that there were children with cerebral palsy who needed adopting. At the same time, however, I knew I was walking a tightrope: by ticking too many 'No' boxes I risked being accused of wanting one of those 'normal' children that apparently just did not exist in care.

At the end of this final home visit, Sylvia informed me that her boss had given her the following week off to prepare her report to the Approval Panel before she moved on to her new job. 'As soon as it's ready I'll send a copy for you to comment on.'

I could hardly believe that my home visits were over. It was with a feeling of great relief that I watched Sylvia walk towards her car.

But later, as I sat on the train, I became apprehensive and felt as though I had been taught to drive using a flipchart but was expected, when the time came, to put my key into the ignition and drive away.

A week later, Sylvia's report arrived via e-mail and I printed it off eagerly. Immediately, I felt concerned. It did not read well, it was confusing, and I experienced a feeling of disquiet at a comment or two that sounded rather negative. Was Sylvia on my side? I worried for a moment, before discounting the thought. She had, after all, recommended me for adoption –

the report made that perfectly clear. *And* I remembered her saying that, as a senior social worker, the Approval Panel would almost certainly abide by her recommendation.

What I had forgotten, however, was one of the concepts I learned as a business analyst: *never assume.* I assumed the forthcoming Approval Panel would simply be a rubber stamp exercise and therefore eschewed Sylvia's suggestion that we go over the report together. I just sent back a list of changes by e-mail, which again – I assumed – would be incorporated.

e-mail, 27 March 2004

Dear Beth,

…I was so distressed to hear the news about your brother. I'm afraid most all of us wander around engrossed in things of slight importance and then occasionally we are brought back to reality. We are not as impervious to life as we'd like to believe…

Early one morning in March, I received a call from my father saying that my brother, David, had collapsed from a possible stroke, and was lying in a coma.

For the next four days, David lay in a semi-comatose state, on a general medical ward because the stroke unit was full. And only after much haranguing from the family was an MRI scan scheduled.

As the family sat around his bed in those desperate early days, I recalled the stressed face I had seen last Christmas Eve. *Let him live,* I pleaded to God, *if you're up there.*

His doctor told us not to lose hope: he had seen similar cases where a patient had woken up, spoken a few words and walked away as though nothing had happened.

But something *had* happened

At work, I went around in a daze, my thoughts on my brother and whether or not he would survive – and if he did, what his life would be like. I focused on the hour hand of the large overhead clocks that hung above the rows of identical desks; clocks set to reflect the time zones of London, Tokyo and New York, worlds away from the misery my family endured. For weeks, I watched the hour hand creeping its way slowly around the clock-face until it reached an acceptable hour, when I would dash away to the hospital.

It was a world of crowded lifts filled with patients on trolleys, hospital wards with grimy windows, the nauseating scent of hyacinths and a stream of 'Get Well' cards, as though David were simply suffering from a bad bout of flu.

My brother survived, but when he did come out of the coma, it was determined that he had suffered a severe stroke; he had lost his speech and the whole of his right side was permanently paralysed. The only way he would walk away would be with the help of a stick.

My brother's tragedy affected my life in ways that I would not have imagined, including my relationship with Mike.

Since that first e-mail I sent, we had been corresponding regularly. I would arrive home from work and log in with a feeling of excited anticipation, wondering whether he had sent a reply to my latest.

Mike later told me that, thousands of miles away, he was feeling and doing exactly the same. He said he had been concerned in mid-March when I had not responded, and wondered whether he would ever hear from me again.

When I finally got in touch and shared the news of my brother's illness, the tables were turned: *I* was the one wondering whether I would ever hear again. For I had taken our correspondence – hitherto long in length and deep in content, but rarely touching on the personal – onto a different level. Why should he want to be tainted by the misery my family and I were undergoing?

I burst into tears when I read Mike's response. I later told him, it gave me great comfort at a time when the rug had been taken out from my feet and my family's lives had been turned upside down.

Mike said he was pleased to hear that because he had been greatly saddened by the news and found it difficult to come up with the right words.

After my brother's stroke, I no longer experienced any push and pull about giving up my City career. For what was the point of getting up each morning and groaning at the thought of the commute and an unsatisfactory job?

As the smartly dressed preacher said, work *is* unimportant.

e-mail, 9 April 2005

Dear Mike,

It's Good Friday and I am sitting in my study, the window is open as it is really quite warm today; the birds are singing and the bulbs are out in the garden…and there's a lovely view of the Downs from the window. The cats just chased a tom from the garden – the two usually don't get on at all and are always trying to outwit each other, so it was nice to see them attacking in unison…

e-mail, 11 April 2004

Dear Beth,

...I had you figured as a cat person. I'm not much on pets, since I was 11, more trouble than human kids. But I believe that cats are much preferable to dogs. The problem I have with dogs is that they are way too stupid, and way too sycophantic. I know my own shortcomings and any creature that is soooo crazy about me must be short of intellect. I really prefer the independent nature of a cat. Who needs all the flattery dogs provide, anyhow?...

I'm pleased to hear your brother has improved some. I know you have much pulling on you right now, and if these e-mails are more of a responsibility than a distraction, please let me know and I will save my banal bullshit for another day.

Don't let life pull you down...

There were only two weeks remaining until my Approval Panel in May, and although Sylvia had not been in touch since she had come with her manager to sign off my report, I assumed no news was good news.

The phone rang one evening just as I arrived home from work. 'I'm sorry I don't recognise your name,' I said to an unfamiliar voice after dashing to pick up the receiver.

'I'm not surprised,' she laughed. 'It's been a few weeks since we met. It's Elaine, Sylvia's manager – I came along with her to sign off your report.'

I had a sudden flashback to the short, dark-haired woman who accompanied Sylvia to my house one morning, shortly before my brother's stroke. Was it only a month ago? It seemed much longer.

'I'm afraid I have some bad news,' she said. 'There are some concerns about gaps in your report. It can't go to the Approval Panel as it is.'

For a moment, I held my breath and said nothing. Then I flew off the handle, terrified my chances of adoption were being taken away. 'It's because I'm a single applicant, isn't it,' I spat out.

'It's nothing to do with that,' Elaine protested, but I would hear none of it. Finally, she revealed it was to do with a disruption. 'It happened to a couple on Sylvia's caseload and we're re-visiting some of her clients to ensure nothing similar occurs again.'

Slowly I began to calm down.

'We're not singling you out. It's just that there are some similarities with your case,' she continued. 'Don't worry, though, there's a way round it. But I'll need to make a second-opinion visit, in order to fill in the gaps in the report.'

'But the Approval Panel's only two weeks away,' I wailed.

'I know, but we have enough time – just. We'll simply add my second-opinion report as an addendum to the report Sylvia wrote. But I *will* need to call on you as soon as possible.'

When I put down the receiver, I vaguely recalled Sylvia telling me about a disruption – there had been a three-year old boy she thought ideally suited to a single adopter, but who was given instead to a couple. 'It didn't work out…the boy was sent back…'

I could hardly believe this had happened. I rang Molly who immediately reassured me, though she stressed how crucial it was to make clear I was *completely* child focused: 'Don't let them think you're more interested in your own needs.'

I inwardly shuddered for I recalled a friend once having told me that his ex-wife had apparently been turned down in the adoption process for that very reason.

'They were intelligent and articulate like you,' Elaine began, the next day, in an effort to explain why my case had raised alarm bells. 'The husband finally admitted that adoption had never felt right to him, that he had just gone along with it to please his wife, and hoped his attitude might change. He said, when he saw the child for the first time, he'd frozen on the spot. It just didn't feel real. And when the little boy refused to settle and be cuddled the first night, panic set in. The next morning they took him back.'

'I want to apologise to you,' Elaine said, 'for signing off Sylvia's report.'

I, too, apologised, for having lost my temper the night before. And then, without delay, we began going through her list of concerns in the report.

'First, we're not sure that you have any real awareness of the types of children in care. Did Sylvia make it clear?'

I had a flashback to the conversation in my sister Molly's kitchen: 'Did you mention Nana's neighbours to the social worker?'

'Yes, she did,' I told Elaine. And I explained, once again, that my family origins were not well-heeled, that my Nana had lived in a council house in a poor area of Cardiff, and that my father had left school at 14. 'My sister's a health visitor and has always discussed her caseload,' I added. 'In addition, her experience of adopting from abroad hasn't always been easy...'

'So you're aware the child will never be an Einstein?'

'Yes. Sylvia went through that with me, and it doesn't matter to me.'

'There's a comment in her report about the importance you place on manners,' she continued, looking doubtfully at me now. 'The children we place don't come from homes where they're taught manners.'

'Yes, I know but surely they can learn? I had to learn manners when I was a child. I think they're important because they teach respect and consideration for others – my mother always said that she might have had six of us but she could always take us anywhere in public.'

'I see…this is beginning to make more sense now. But the report also states that you might find it difficult parenting a child during adolescence…'

'I didn't say that,' I protested. 'Sylvia once asked me how I would deal with a teenager who was on drugs and I said I would find it difficult – but wouldn't anyone? I also said my first port of call would be my GP.'

'So what would you consider to be the difficult challenges that an adopted child might bring' Elaine asked.

'Extreme behavioural problems,' I replied, on the hop.

'But all of our children have behavioural problems – what do you mean by "extreme"?'

'I mean behaviour more challenging than the usual tantrums, something that might possibly go on for months or years.'

'We also need some clarification on the subject of significant relationships you've had,' Elaine now said.

Once again, I told her of the same relationship I had gone over months before, with Sylvia.

'So you *have* had a significant relationship!' she exclaimed.

'*I* believe it was significant, but Sylvia said it wasn't – *because* I hadn't lived with him for several years or been married.'

Near the end of her visit, Elaine took me through the catalogue of available children, and this time all of them looked cute. I even felt a tremor of excitement as I flicked over the pages to see children with blond curls and toddlers with black locks, ginger-haired siblings with freckles and bald-headed babies with dimples. And, to my surprise, some were black or multi-racial, which I hadn't expected in Sussex.

'She looks cute,' I remarked, on turning the page to see a dusky-skinned little girl with a big, cheeky smile.

'Yes, but unfortunately, she's not available; she's part of a family of three,' Elaine told me.

'And he looks really sweet,' I said, pointing to a little blond-haired boy.

'That's Paolo – he's in foster care with the little girl you remarked on. He's half-Italian.'

'Isn't he adorable,' I murmured.

'He's still available,' Elaine smiled.

When Molly later rang to ask how it had gone, I told her about the lovely little boy with the cute little face and blond curls. 'He's still available,' I said, excitedly, my imagination running riot.

Molly sounded excited, too, and offered to accompany me to the Approval Panel. I told her there wasn't much point because Sylvia had told me the Panel would refuse to let anyone sit in on the session with me.

It never occurred to me that going alone might be interpreted by the Panel as lack of family support.

e-mail, 17 April 2004

Dear Mike

…Yes it would be very nice next Christmas to know how chilli is made to the tune of Los Bambinos…but who knows how my life might have changed. I am actually just coming up to the close of a long process of approval to adopt a child. He/she will be 3-5 approx, from this area and it could happen theoretically from Sept onwards. Let's just say I know it will be a massive life change but I'm quietly looking forward to it…

e-mail, 22 April

Subj: The Stork

Dear Beth

Good to hear the news about your upcoming parenthood. I suppose this has been in the works for some time and my earlier e-mail about how pets were more trouble than children had no effect on your decision. I admit I tend to overstate things at times. I believe the world could use a few more first rate citizens turned out by intelligent, caring parents. And if you manage to miss the diaper (nappy) business, all the better. I personally most enjoy children when they become verbal. But I figure I can tell you what you will be doing for the next 15 years or so. If you have any wild oats to sow, time to get moving, child…

So confident was I now of obtaining my approval that I began to tell more people about my plans: my brothers were delighted; neighbours told me it was the best news they had heard all year; my friend Cindy didn't express surprise at all, laughing: 'Beth, you were made to be a mother!'

I planned some last child-free holidays, too. I began to think about the city in Mexico that Mike had mentioned when we sat at that little pavement café, back in January…

e-mail, 16 May 2004

Dear Mike,

… Some years ago there was an article in a local paper that they were going to knock down a house Virginia Woolf had lived in

at the foot of the downs to make way for a landfill site...A friend and I rushed over on our bikes, it was a lovely day, and the tumbledown house was down a long lane, quite solitary but it had beautiful windows (which I think went to a museum) and a fox ran through the garden when we arrived. I found an old enamel jug which we christened Virginia's jug and I have it filled with dead poppy heads, totally worthless but lovely to me anyway...As things could well change for me in the autumn I hope to make a few trips in the summer and am thinking maybe of a couple of weeks in Oaxaca...

The Approval Panel was to be held in a large detached residence, on a leafy road in the suburbs, at the edge of town. I had done little preparation, save for my responses to some stock questions I had gone over with my sister. With the gaps in my report now accounted for, in my mind it was all cut-and-dried.

My primary concern, on the morning of my Panel – exactly one year after the preparation course – was what I should wear. Would make-up and jewellery look too frivolous, I wondered, before finally deciding to opt for just a little mascara and lipstick. And I put away the blouse with a slightly low décolletage in favour of one more primly cut. I was holding this blouse against me in the mirror when I heard a knock at the door. I glanced down at my watch. It must be Sylvia. She had rung the day before to suggest a last-minute get-together to ensure everything was in order, and to go through Elaine's second-opinion report.

'It *is* just a rubber stamp, isn't it,' I said to her as she came in. But Sylvia looked more serious than usual.

'No, it isn't a rubber stamp,' she told me. 'But don't be overly concerned. I wrote the report, so most of their questions will be directed at me. They usually only ask the applicant one or two questions at the end.'

Sylvia then sat down on the sofa and read aloud a few excerpts from the report, and from what she read to me it sounded fair enough.

'Could I have a copy?' I asked.

'No, you can't have a copy of this one,' she replied.

(In fact, I would not see a copy of this report for two years, hence I was unaware that I was indeed described as work-focused with no time for a personal life and – by the way – my relationships were *not* significant!)

When Sylvia arose to leave, I felt awful to see her black skirt covered in my cat's white fur, but was too embarrassed to say anything. After seeing her out, I began to feel jittery about the Approval Panel. I went into the kitchen to check the oven clock. Still an hour to go – I could really go a drink now, perhaps a nice glass of wine to give me some Dutch courage. But I had none in the house, and all I could see in the fridge was a bottle of champagne left over from Christmas. No, I can't. But why not – it's a special occasion isn't it? In the solitude of my kitchen, therefore, I popped the cork and wished myself luck. Before long, one glass had turned into two and suddenly, not only was I feeling tipsy, but there was a danger I would miss the train. What if they guessed I had been drinking, I thought, horrified, as I rushed to clean my teeth. Would champagne smell on my breath, I worried, as I scrubbed away – imagine being turned down as an alcoholic!

I rushed then to put on my primly cut blouse, and skirt of suitable length, slammed the door behind me and tottered on high heels down the high street to catch the train.

Twelve grave-faced people looked up at me as I entered the meeting room. If I had not sobered up by then, I surely did now. They were sitting at tables arranged in a square, at the top end of which, facing the chairperson, were two empty seats. Would this be my last supper, I wondered, as I sat down with Sylvia and nervously listened to the endless round of introductions. I smiled back at the smug-looking, middle-aged adopter and equally smug-looking, middle-aged adoptee, the seemingly disinterested doctor and the legal adviser, the intense look from the social services representative; and I acknowledged the jolly twinkle in the eye of the elderly, male councillor.

Then, without warning, the chairperson began and I was subjected to a barrage of questions that Sylvia had promised would be directed at her. How will you make the drastic change to motherhood? Will you be able to manage your lifestyle changes? What sort of mother do you expect to be? Are you aware of the types of children in care?

Although I gave the stock replies I had used many times before, for some reason *today* they sounded peculiarly hollow.

I was then asked a number of social-worker-type questions for which I knew there were stock social-worker-type responses, but I was feeling even more nervous by now and struggled to enunciate them.

'Have you read any books on adoption?' the adoptive mother then asked me.

'No, I haven't,' I replied, 'but I've read all the extracts that Sylvia gave me.'

'But why not?' she persisted. 'Don't you think it would be a good idea to read up as much detail as possible before you adopt?'

I did not have a leg to stand on now, just a pair of wobbly knees. I wanted to respond that I had had enough of reading about the grieving process, about abandonment and loss, about behavioural issues that might crop up in teenage years. I had had my fill of their doom and gloom and worst case scenarios. *No*, I simply did not *want* to read a book for fear it might put me off adoption altogether. I mumbled something apologetically; it was met with a frown.

Then the subject of my Glyndebourne lodger was raised. I

had told Sylvia of my intention to let out my basement studio during the summer opera season, but she had mentioned child protection issues if there were another person in the household (especially given that social services would be unable to vet someone from overseas) and I offered to cancel my plans. But Sylvia had insisted, saying, 'You can't put your life on hold, entirely.'

'You're aware, aren't you, that you won't be able to have a stranger living in your house when a child moves in?' barked the adoptee.

'Yes,' I replied meekly, and mumbled something about the Glyndebourne season finishing in August. I felt like a schoolgirl made to stand in the corner for not having learned her French verbs.

And then, I was stunned to hear the word 'fostering' uttered. It came from the social services representative who had so far kept quiet. 'Have you thought about fostering first to see if you actually like the experience of looking after a child?'

I've had it! I thought. *I'm not going to be approved.*

I started to open my mouth but Sylvia, for the first time, interrupted. 'No,' she stated firmly, face flushed. 'Beth wants a family; fostering is a career.'

The chairperson asked if there were any more questions from the Panel members. There was a moment of silence and it seemed the proceedings were over. I felt totally dejected. Then, I heard a voice; it came from the chair to my near right.

'Yes, I have one. Tell me about Benny.' I looked up with astonishment at the red-faced, cheerful local councillor, only there because the rules required at least one man on the Panel.

There was a hush in the room as the others looked at him, too, and then they turned their attention back to me. Oh, Benny! I could have sung for joy. For ten minutes, I finally was able to speak from the heart. I spoke about Benny, the little schoolboy in the reading programme, and his effect on me – and how, I hoped, I had affected him. I was moved by my words and I believe the Panel was moved, as well.

When I had finished, the chairperson said, 'It should take us 15 minutes or so to make our decision.' She indicated for me to leave the room.

I smiled at Sylvia as I left, but felt concerned to see such a sad expression on her face.

Outside the meeting room I sat on the edge of a chair, alone except for the tea-lady setting out cups and saucers.

'Can I get you anything,' she asked, but I smiled and declined.

Did she know my life lay in the balance, I wondered, as I sat there, my eyes on the ticking clock. Did she realise that within 15 minutes, my future would be decided and I would know whether I was to become a mother?

Finally, the door opened and out came Sylvia and the chairperson, talking quietly. They approached me, and the chairperson then announced with a smile, 'Congratulations! The Panel has approved you for adoption. You should receive official written notification from the Director within two working days.' I was filled with elation.

The chairperson excused herself and walked away, and Sylvia said, 'I must admit, I thought you'd lost it when they mentioned fostering.' Benny, it appeared, had swung the day. 'It was like that moment in *Billy Elliott*,' she laughed, 'when it looked like he'd failed his audition and someone asked him how it *felt* when he danced…'

'How *does* it feel?' I thought with a smile the next day, as I began my journey into work. Unfortunately, I experienced yet another terrible commute. These incessant late arrivals and cancellations had become more than I could deal with and I was seething when I finally logged on at my PC. I began to consider my situation seriously. The newly arrived project manager would certainly be building his own team at some point – so with my adoption approval in hand, why not call it a day?

I took a deep breath, and finally took Sylvia's advice. I handed in my notice.

The Tuesday following the Approval Panel, the telephone rang just as I arrived home from work.

'I'm just ringing,' Sylvia told me, 'to let you know what the next steps in the process are.' A few moments of silence followed. 'That's strange,' she said, finally. 'I can't find the official notification from the Director. Have *you* received anything through the post?'

'No, I haven't. Is there anything to worry about?' I asked, feeling somewhat uneasy now.

'I don't think so, just an admin issue probably. I'll chase it up for you and give you a ring back tomorrow.'

Sylvia called me the next morning, at work. 'I'm afraid that the Director has refused to go along with the Panel's recommendation,' she told me. 'It's not an outright no,' she emphasised, quickly, 'but rather a *deferment*.'

My boss was sitting near me and it was difficult to express my anger. But angry I was. Livid might better describe me when Sylvia told me that the report apparently contained too many question marks.

'What question marks?' I snapped, trying to keep my voice as low as possible.

'She's queried your lack of mothering ability – the fact that you've looked after your nieces isn't enough proof. And the fact that you've never had a significant relationship.'

'But I believe I have had a significant relationship,' I spat out.

'*My* definition of "significant" is whether you've been married or lived with someone for a period of years,' she repeated, coolly. 'And because you haven't had one, there's

72

concern that *you* might be unable to attach to a child; that it could be to do with your childhood.'

I was speechless. Affronted, too; affronted at Sylvia's use of the word 'attachment', the word that had been discussed at length in the prep course and drilled into me during the countless home visits: 'It is essential that the child form an attachment or the matching will fail,' they had repeatedly stressed. The irony of it now was that it was my *own* ability to attach that was being questioned.

'You'll need to have some more home visits,' Sylvia continued, as though she were suggesting I take a few more days' holiday.

I could not believe my ears. 'Will this mean going through another Approval Panel?' I asked when I finally found my tongue.

'Yes, it will.'

'This process is going to last for ever!' I exclaimed as loudly as I dared. 'That'll be another six months of visits.'

'I'm not sure how long they'll take,' she replied. 'Nothing's been decided as yet. But I did tell them it wasn't fair on you if *I* did the additional sessions; they'll be appointing someone else.'

I glanced over to see whether my boss had any idea what was going on. How ridiculous, I thought: one minute I'm handing in my notice and he's offering his congratulations about the adoption; a day later, everything has seemingly fallen through. I can hardly go back and ask for my notice back – 'I thought it over last night and I no longer want to adopt...' *At least*, I thought with relief, *he had seemed keen about my offer to work part-time until he found a successor.*

'You've let me down,' I hissed to Sylvia. I then told her I would need time to think about whether or not to pursue the whole thing after all.

She asked me, quite simply, to give her a call if I decided to call it a day.

I cancelled my jog and instead walked in a daze down the Jubilee Steps and along the Thames until I reached the Ropemaker's Park. There, I sat for a long while on a bench, in a state of disbelief, watching the toddlers running around in the playground opposite. I felt as though the words *Not Good Enough to be a Mother* were already branded on my forehead.

One thing *was* certain, I decided, thinking back to Sylvia's words: I would certainly *not* be calling her to say I had given up. All the same, I thought of the alternatives if I were *not* approved... Yes, I thought, other doors, perhaps, lay ajar. And slowly, I realised, it would not be the end of the world if I were not approved. *Almost*, but not quite.

I sat there, in the quiet, looking at a mother push her child on the roundabout.

At the weekly project meeting, later that afternoon, I noticed the head trader drawing a gallows and hangman on his notepad. The stick figure, I guessed, was the outgoing project manager, now going through his latest plan.

One good thing had come of all this, I decided. By handing in my notice, I had finally begun to wean myself off the City and the commute.

As the head of risk management prattled on, I wondered about my chances of a foreign adoption. If only I had gone down that route in the beginning, perhaps the approval process would not have been so stringent – I might have avoided the entire obsession with significant relationships *and* even be approved for a baby or a toddler. Then, a horrifying thought occurred to me: what about all those people I had lately told of my adoption plans! What if I did fail and they were to learn I had been turned down by social services as being unfit to be a mother. Not least, what would I say to Mike? What would he think of *me*?

I watched the head trader complete his picture with a noose around the project manager's neck. I felt strangled, too.

I rang Molly as soon as I got home that evening. She was shocked at my news and immediately asked on what grounds social services had deferred me.

'They've queried my lack of mothering experience, for one.'

'You did tell them that you were practically a second mother to Caryl, didn't you?' she asked.

I thought back to my sessions with Sylvia and said, 'I'm not sure that I did.' My stomach was churning.

'Well, it would take at least two years if you chose to adopt from abroad instead,' Molly told me. 'And I'm not sure it would even be possible if you don't get through the approval process here.' I was numb. 'But I really don't believe social services would waste their time and money putting you through more sessions and another Approval Panel if they had any serious doubts about you,' she encouraged. 'And, who knows, the timing might be in your favour and you might end up with just the perfect child.'

e-mail, 13 June 2004

Dear Beth

...I plan to be in Oaxaca sometime in August as well, but am hazy on the dates at present... if our dates happen to overlap, I'll take you to a few of my favourite restaurants and show you where Malcolm Lowry got drunk on mezcal...

A letter from social services dropped through my letterbox on a sunny Saturday morning. A new social worker, Allie, had been assigned to me. She would conduct four additional home visits in June and July, covering my childhood, my mothering skills and my significant relationships. The letter further stated

75

that a second Approval Panel would be held *no later* than September.

I felt, on the whole, encouraged.

But when, a day or two later, Allie rang me at work to set up the home visits and I enquired whether deferments were common, she replied, 'They're *very* rare. I've only heard of one other case and they were a couple.'

I slunk guiltily back into my office chair on hearing those words.

The Allie now perched on my sofa in a hot, sun-washed sitting room, was totally different to how I had imagined her. She seemed warmer, had tousled hair and an impish grin, and immediately instilled in me a feeling of confidence.

Sylvia had accompanied her to do the formal introductions and she immediately apologised for 'letting me down', as she put it.

I accepted her apology, no longer harbouring ill feelings, and I said as she left, 'Sometimes you look back and realise that things often happen for the best.'

The session had just begun when Allie interrupted me suddenly, 'Your sister's a health visitor!'

'Yes,' I replied, puzzled at her obvious surprise.

'I didn't know that. I'm sure it's not documented anywhere in your report or file. I'll have another look, though, just to be sure…' she said, thumbing through some papers on her lap.

'I made it clear to both Sylvia *and* Elaine,' I replied tartly.

'Oh, I'm sure you did,' Allie responded quickly. 'But the fact that she's a health visitor should have been highlighted in your report. It's absolutely crucial information: you have a *ready-made* support network, and it's on your doorstep!'

'I know, I could never understand why it didn't seem to carry any weight… Actually, one of the things that bothered me was, what sort of meals to make when I have a child. Molly advises her families about meals that are nutritious but

cheap and she said she'd write down a few menus for me…
You'd think that would be the last thing I'd be worrying about
wouldn't you?'

Allie laughed along with me and made another note.

'Molly often talked about the types of children on her
caseload,' I told her. Then, remembering my sister's advice, I
added, 'And my grandmother lived in an area of Cardiff that
became quite rough when a number of dysfunctional families
moved in. I wasn't aware quite how dysfunctional until
towards the end of Nana's life when she began to talk a lot
about the past. One day, she mentioned Gaynor, a fifteen-
year-old girl we often saw when we came back to visit at
weekends. Gaynor was great fun, and it was a huge shock to
all the family when we heard she was pregnant. We were told
the father was a boy we'd seen her talking to when she took us
swimming. All these years later, my grandmother revealed to
me that the culprit was Gaynor's own father.'

'Her *father*?' Allie interrupted.

'Yes, I couldn't believe it.'

'But this is important information,' she said, jotting it down
furiously. 'It demonstrates that you *are* aware of the seamier
side of life. How old were you at the time?'

'I would have been about ten. Her father was an object of
fun to us because he wore a very obvious wig. He once came
round with a camera and asked my sister and me if we'd like
our photo taken. Molly was wearing a pair of denim hotpants
I'd made her from a *Woman's Weekly* pattern. In the photo he
took of us in Nana's garden we're giggling at his wig. But
looking back, it's all a bit creepy… The mother never got on
with poor Gaynor. Now, I realise, it's probably because she
knew what was going on but did nothing to prevent it.'

'Didn't your mother think twice about letting you and your
sister associate with this family?' Allie asked, to my
amazement.

I quickly blurted out a few words in Mum's defence, then thought to myself: *you can't win!*

'Sylvia told me one of the reasons I was turned down was because I had no mothering experience, but I was practically a second mother to my little sister,' I informed Allie. 'I was fourteen when my mother told me of her final pregnancy. She hadn't been well and had been to see the doctor. "We're going to have a little one," Mum said.

'A little what?' I had asked.

"A baby!" she said. She looked delighted, but initially, I wasn't at all happy; I was a teenager *and* one of five children – what would my friends say? My father wasn't happy about it either at first.

'My mother hid her pregnancy from the neighbourhood,' I continued, to the sound of Allie's laughter. 'Mum said it was because of another mother's reactions when one day, obviously pregnant, she picked up my younger brother from school. The woman looked at her and said, "When are you going to stop?" Mum later told me she felt terrible and she practically became a recluse for the rest of her pregnancy.

'When Caryl was born, we visited Mum in hospital on Christmas Day and took her a big stocking we'd helped Dad fill with gifts.'

'So your father came around in the end then?' Allie enquired.

'Oh yes!' I smiled. 'Mum would take Caryl out in a beautiful, high navy pram and simply introduce her as the "new arrival". I didn't tell my best friend at school either until after she was born. I just introduced her as my little sister when she came round to the house. She didn't say a word. So I was a second mother to Caryl until I left home at 19 – I wonder now if that's why I didn't exactly rush into having my own family.'

'I'm sure it had a lot to do with it,' Allie agreed.

'I decided not to go to university. Ever since I was 14, I had wanted to join the diplomatic service, having seen an advert in the newspaper. I even wrote and asked if I should join at sixteen but they advised me to stay on at school to do my A-levels. My teachers weren't happy about my not going to university – it was almost unheard of. I did a two-year RSA Diploma in Languages for Business at the local polytechnic instead and lived at home.'

'So you must have had a happy childhood then!' Allie exclaimed.

'Yes, I did,' I replied, puzzled at her statement. 'There were the usual squabbles with my siblings, of course, but I was happy – and very happy to have a little sister. We all were. I remember how Caryl once got into Mum's make-up bag and she had all this lipstick and eye shadow on her face. It was a mess but I was amazed to see how she'd applied it all in the right places. Her little face looked so worried when she saw me. I just laughed and she opened her arms to give me a hug. And when I travelled with the Foreign Office, later, she would put little things into my suitcase, like a little china rabbit or a pair of her hair bobbles. I would only discover them when I unpacked...'

e-mail, 17 July 2004

Dear Mike,

...You were right to prompt me about finishing the Alexandria Quartet... Just superb books. You could talk about them for hours. I love being back on that island where Darley's writing at a table near the oleander bushes and the child is dozing, and I loved the way the young Mountolive burst in on the Quartet

with such élan and freedom. This was a book after my own heart really, with the memories it brought back of the Foreign Office in London, Westminster and diplomatic life abroad… I booked my flight last weekend and am leaving on 22 Aug coming back two weeks later. I contacted the Aurora Hotel in Oaxaca twice by e-mail with no results…so I checked the Posada del Centro website and have since received two prompt responses and it seems I have a room…

At the close of the final home visit, Allie told me that she felt she had enough information to write up a new report, and confirmed the date of the next Approval Panel in mid-September.

Strangely, I was feeling even more tired now than when I had been working full time – and rather than feeling elated at my greater freedom, instead I had been shaken to realise how long I had been going up to the City, and how much of my life had gone by.

When I chanced upon a newspaper article, in which Paddy Ashdown encouraged people to visit Bosnia, I decided to book a few days' extra holiday.

The evening before I departed for Sarajevo, I celebrated my birthday with Molly, Tom and my two nieces on the beach. We shared a picnic, swam in the warm sea and watched the sun set. It was blissful and, over a glass of wine, we discussed the fact that by my next birthday I would probably be celebrating with *my* child.

My niece, Poppy, then asked her Mum excitedly if it would be a boy or a girl.

'Well, ask Beth yourself,' Molly smiled.

'Auntie Beth, will you be having a boy or a girl?' Poppy said, shyly.

I said that I didn't mind either, but that I expected it to be a boy. Social services had told me that as most prospective adoptive mothers wanted a girl, there was always a surplus of boys.

Later that week, whilst meandering through the tiny alleyways of Sarajevo, I noticed a cross-stitch kit displayed in a shop window; it was of a Muslim girl kneeling on a brightly coloured prayer mat. I stared at it and decided to go into the shop and buy it – for at that very moment I was certain I would be having a little girl.

e-mail, 13 August 2004

Dear Beth,

...I arrive in Oaxaca on the 23rd, 9:30 pm-ish. If you choose to switch hotels, I might mention that I like the beer and peanuts at the Bar Jardine, a sidewalk cafe on the southwest corner of the zocalo. (The cathedral and the Marques del Valle hotel are on the north side of the square.) Marimba bands play there several nights a week. It is said that if you sit at the Bar Jardine long enough, you will eventually see everyone that is in Oaxaca stroll by...'

Mike later told me of the anxiety he had felt when I first mentioned my desire to visit Oaxaca, and possibly to meet him there. He had been contentedly planning a move to Mexico, to live on his own, to watch the ocean and write. But after our meeting and long e-mail correspondence, his plans seemed in danger of being turned on their head. Why should I make such a long trip? What were my expectations, if any? Did I simply want a travel companion or was there more to it? On the one hand, he said he was fearful of becoming involved at all; but on the other, he found the idea intriguing. Above all, he hoped I was not looking simply for a holiday fling, something frivolous to fit in before the adoption. He later laughed and said *that* outcome would have been shattering to his romantic nature.

I saw Oaxaca as the icing on the cake of what, I assumed, would be the last opportunity for travel for some time ahead. It sounded exotic, and I feared that if I did not go there this summer I might never have the chance again. But I also wanted to be there with Mike. When he told me that he had booked his flights, I hoped we would fall in love.

Mike later told me, he had already fallen a little in 'something' from our e-mails.

Journal entry

Oaxaca; 23 August 2004

One thing I didn't want to do when Mike arrived was to blush and of course this I duly did. It was lovely to see him and we sat for a few hours at the Bar Jardine drinking wine and beers and talking. And he gave me two delightful books: Eudora Welty's Collected Short Stories and Thomas Wolfe's Look Homeward Angel…Then at midnight or just after, we strolled up the Alcala which was almost completely quiet and saw the museum, the cathedral and the old viaduct. One or two clubs were open. It was a still, warm night…

We later revealed to one another that if things had not worked out in Oaxaca, we each had an escape plan: Mike would simply return home and forget it had all happened; I would fly to Puerto Escondido, on the Oaxacan coast. But from that first breakfast that we ate under the colonnades of the La Primavera restaurant on the Zocalo, we rarely spent a moment

82

apart. I fell in love, giddily so; I stopped writing in my diary and left a number of straw sunhats that Mike had bought me, in a variety of taxis and buses. There were few tourists around in August and it felt like Oaxaca belonged to us. We walked for hours around the town, with its brightly washed walls; listened to the street musicians; lunched at Mike's favourite restaurants, and drank margaritas by the poolside.

At some point towards the end of our holiday, we discussed the future. Mike said he would like a child with me, but I knew that, at 47, it was already too late. Besides, since Allie's recent visits and her words of encouragement about the forthcoming report, my confidence about my approval had been renewed; I was committed to adoption and felt comfortable with that commitment. We discussed the timing of the adoption and guessed that it would probably require a year for the child to settle in before the three of us could think of being a family. Mike hoped it would be a little girl; he thought it intriguing that he might be a father again in his fifties.

It was strange being in Oaxaca alone on my last day. Mike had already left early that morning and the town felt alien in his absence. As I sat on the balcony of the restaurant Like Water for Chocolate, where once we had watched a light summer rain fall, I opened my diary in an attempt to fill in all those missing days. But I found it hard to remember their sequence so instead, I entered a brief comment and made a drawing of my (third) straw hat, which lay on the table.

Journal Entry

Oaxaca; 6 September 2004:

How funny life is. Suddenly this most wonderful man is in my life at the point I had decided that having such a person was no longer a priority.

e-mail, 6 September 2004

Dear Beth,

*I arrived home this afternoon having left a significant portion
of myself in Oaxaca…no parting should be made at six am. I
feel like something is totally incomplete and I have been out of
sorts all day long and am afraid it will extend longer. It has
never been harder for me to leave a place than today… At
9.30am as I was over the Texas Gulf coast I knew you were
most likely at La Primavera with your fruit plate and coffee,
tipping the marimba players and that I was alone and headed
in the wrong direction entirely…'*

e-mail, 7 September 2004

Dear Mike

*..I am so glad I made it to Oaxaca, there were several times I
thought about not going but I was, I suppose driven* ☺

On my return, I rang Molly and announced, 'I've fallen in
love!' She was delighted. I told my mother, too (who only then
admitted how afraid she had been that I might return
disappointed). And, over the garden wall, I told my next door
neighbours Jo and Ann who exclaimed, 'We're *so* pleased for
you!'

When I met my friend, Ruth, for lunch later that week, she
said I had been driven because I was looking for the father of
my child. I replied that if that was so, it was certainly on a
subconscious level.

Amongst the mail awaiting my return was a package from

Amazon containing the book *The Primal Wound*, recommended to me by social services and from which I had, up until now, only read extracts. I now intended to read the entire book in the next couple of weeks.

For there still lay an obstacle ahead in my quest to become a mother...

The only difference *this* time, I thought, as I dressed for the second Approval Panel, was that Molly was coming along to provide some moral and *evident* support, and I was wearing the silver ring with blue lapis stone that Mike had bought for me in Oaxaca; I wondered, paranoically, whether the social services representative might seize upon it. Otherwise, I was dressed exactly as for the first Approval Panel in May.

The chairperson and the Panel members looked exactly the same, too, except on this occasion there were smiles all round as I entered the room.

The chairperson quickly apologised for having hauled me there twice: 'We now have a much better understanding of you.' She next congratulated Allie on such a clear and concise report. 'This meeting will take more the form of a discussion,' the chairperson confirmed, as we then addressed my understanding of, and observations about, *The Primal Wound*.

'I realise how far I've come in the year since Sylvia gave me that first extract from the book,' I told them. 'I was frightened by what I read then. *Now*, I'm no longer afraid of some primal bond; in fact, in a lot of ways it makes sense... For other reasons, too, I find the book fascinating. I recognise all sorts of people in it: my adopted nieces, one or two friends and relatives...' And though I did not tell the Panel this, I also saw myself in it: my inability sometimes to end a relationship, and my need for approval. It was wonderfully ironic: because of a Panel member's suggestion that I buy a book to understand more about my prospective child, I also understood more about myself.

At the end of our discussion, the adoptive mother beamed and suggested I take 'a jolly good holiday' before I became a mother.

'I certainly intend to,' I replied, and everyone laughed.

Finally, the jolly-faced Councillor asked about Benny.

I replied how disappointed I had been that Benny, because he had gone up a year, was now excluded from the reading scheme. I said I had gone over especially to say goodbye to Benny and had told him that I would be adopting a child, although I wasn't sure that he really understood what I meant.

e-mail, 16 Sept 2004

Dear Mike,

I had my Panel sitting yesterday and was successful. Actually, they said it was unanimous and they told me not to worry about the Director's approval this time. It was assured. After the initial feeling of being very nervous, I enjoyed their questions. Molly was sitting outside and said she became very anxious because I was in there quite a while. She burst into tears when they told me I was successful. I thought I rabbited on a bit too much at times but they said how interesting I had been in my responses and a rather elderly councillor on the Panel said he wished he was between the ages of 2 and 5...'

Allie told me in mid-October – a month after the successful second Approval Panel – that, as of then, there were no suitable children available. I was disappointed but, after so many months engaged in the adoption process, I had begun to resign myself to the snail-like pace things undoubtedly would take. Mike and I, therefore, decided to take advantage of the delay and booked flights for a long Christmas holiday together in the Yucatan.

Allie later agreed (though I still had not mentioned Mike) that I needed a holiday. She said I had been through a lot lately – the adoption process, getting over the years of full-time commuting, and my brother's illness.

When I said that, as a single adopter, I expected it would be a while before I was matched, she looked puzzled.

'On the contrary, you'll make an ideal parent for many of the children on our books.'

Cycling up on the Downs one afternoon, I stopped to watch a flock of birds circling above me as they prepared for migration. It was already dusk and the sky was pale pink. I recalled the e-mail that Mike had just sent; he said how beautiful fall was in Texas that year, and I thought how, at that very moment, albeit on different sides of the world, we were both enjoying our autumns. Distance notwithstanding, I felt blissfully content.

Since Oaxaca, Mike and I had begun to telephone one another with some frequency. It was a little strange at first; the many differences in language and humour caused some misunderstandings and confusion in those early days. Mike later would recall to me how insecure I had seemed following Oaxaca, as though I thought he might leave me at any moment. I remember feeling as though I were in a dream, or in a bubble that might burst; I had wanted to keep the memories of the holiday in a neatly packaged box.

In one e-mail, Mike admitted that although he loved hearing about the whole adoptive process, at times he worried that he 'might simply fall from sight leaving barely a ripple on your seemingly well-planned and organized life...' Though he did add, 'When we're together it all just feels so right, so perfect and like it will go on forever...'

Journal Entry

Christmas Day 2004, Chabihau:

Stormy all day, rough sea. Drinking homemade daiquiris and listening to a CD of Dylan Thomas reciting A Child's Christmas in Wales. Fried fish for lunch a lady in the village prepared for us, with onions and tomato salad and boiled potatoes, and a bottle of Herzegovinian wine that Mike brought. Pecan cake for dessert. Later, a rainbow over whole of the sea into the village. Walked to see storm damage further up the road by the bird reserve...tide very high in evening, afraid the sea would come up as far as our house...

After a few days spent at Mike's home in Texas, to relieve my jetlag, we flew to the Yucatan where we stayed in a tiny village about an hour's drive from the capital, Merida, and so remote that we didn't hear about the tsunami in Asia until several days after it happened. I later worked out that, coincidentally, the sea began to come right up to the beach house on the evening of Christmas Day at the exact time the tsunami made its strike.

It was the perfect place to unwind and England seemed very far away. Hardly a car passed through the village and we were the only tourists for miles around. The villagers were very sweet to us. One day, when I was feeling unwell, the lady in the grocery shop – just a wooden shack really, with only a few bunches of bananas and some packets of rice and beans – asked after me and said to Mike that she hoped I would be well soon...

We would talk for hours, gazing out at the palm trees swaying in the breeze, sipping at lime daiquiris, lolling on hammocks that swung gently on the verandah, or walking along the beach looking for shells. At lunchtime, we would ride a couple of ancient bicycles to a tiny restaurant in a nearby village.

The evening before, at midnight, we watched the villagers quietly celebrate Christmas in the small church and then we walked around the village, quiet apart from the occasional sound of a dog barking, beneath a vast night sky filled with stars.

e-mail, 12 January 2005

Dear Mike,

> *...Allie called, asked after the hols and asked how I was placed now, i.e. did I feel ready to go ahead. I said I had been waiting for her to get in touch with details of a suitable child. She didn't commit, just said she would be in touch soon...*

Thousands of miles away from the Yucatan, on a cold, wet January day, a fire crackled noisily in the grate as I told my friends Nigel and Anna about my little Christmas idyll. Looking out of the window onto the other side of the street, I could see a row of lime trees swaying wildly in the wind and was reminded of that Christmas night when the sea had swept up onto the beach. I told them, too, of my e-mail invitation to visit Puerto Vallarta; my chance meeting with Mike there; our months' long e-mail correspondence, and subsequent meeting in Oaxaca.

'It's difficult to imagine now,' I said, 'but if that e-mail hadn't been sent, I would never have met Mike at all.'

'It's serendipity,' Anna announced excitedly. I saw her eyes light up; it gave her hope, too, I knew: out of the blue someone might turn up for her. Nigel simply grinned.

'Did Nigel tell you he was my referee for the adoption?' I asked Anna.

'No, he didn't,' she laughed, looking over at him. 'He's very discreet.'

'Do social services know about Mike?' Anna asked, as Nigel went up to the bar.

'No, I haven't told them,' I replied. 'I was approved as a single applicant and Mike and I agreed I should complete the adoption as a single applicant. We don't want to do anything that might jeopardise it – that's our first priority; our relationship has to come second.'

In fact, there would be many times when I wished I could tell Allie about Mike, because the relationship was certainly significant, in *my* terms, by this point. I was totally convinced of Mike as a person, and his commitment towards me; and given the many things he had told me about his children, I just *knew* he would be a wonderful father.

With hindsight, I believe Allie would have viewed the relationship as significant, too; in fact, my gut feeling at the time was that, ultimately, she would have been delighted for me. But I did not dare say anything – not only because of the deferral and the convoluted process I had hitherto undergone, but because of their reaction to my Glyndebourne lodger. I was in no doubt that introducing someone new, someone from outside the UK, into my life would only result, at minimum, in another long delay and, at worst, in no adoption at all. In fact, so concerned was I that someone from social services might spot me with Mike, I suggested we delay any visits of his to a later time, when I was further along in the approval process. Thus, our only meetings had been in Oaxaca, Texas and the Yucatan; the rest of the time we had only our e-mails, precious as they were, and the telephone.

'Have you any idea on the timing of the adoption?' Anna now asked, as Nigel brought back a round of drinks.

'No, I don't. All I know is that it'll be a call out of the blue...'

On a Friday afternoon, at the end of January, I returned home from work to find a message on my phone. It was Allie saying she wanted to talk to me; she was out of the office until Monday and would ring me back then. I had a feeling that this was it and felt a tingle of excitement run through me. I could barely wait until Monday. I immediately rang Mike but his daughter and her husband were staying with him and he sounded distracted.

First thing on Monday morning, Allie rang. She told me that a child on their books had just been approved for adoption. 'She's four-and-a-half and has had a very stable foster placement for more than two years. She's half-English, half-Bangladeshi – is that OK?'

'Of course,' I replied, excitedly.

'My only concern,' Allie said, 'is that a lot of the info on her Form 'E' (a social services form filled out for each child in care: it includes a child's personal details, education, placements since birth, profile by foster carer, etc) seems quite out-of-date. I'll see you get a copy of it and you can look it over.' She went on to tell me a few more details, though stressed that I should restrict the news to only one or two close family members: 'I've had experience of cases where family members and friends have turned against prospective adopters for not accepting a certain child. People can make unfair judgments without knowing the full facts,' she warned.

I felt very excited and immediately rang Mum and Molly to tell them the news. Due to the time difference, I did not ring Mike until later. He sounded shocked at the suddenness of it all. I experienced a mixture of excitement and apprehension as

I held the receiver, as though the alarm clock had just gone off and I was about to embark on a long journey.

The following day a large brown envelope arrived in the post. I was somewhat wary, given all the negatives social services had emphasised over the months, and consequently I quickly scanned the Form 'E', noticing that direct contact with the birth family was not recommended; I was encouraged.

After my cursory look, I was relieved that everything appeared straightforward. I decided it would now be safe to read it through once again – but slowly this time, to take it all in. It still sounded good!

The foster mother's profile of Mattie was particularly sweet: she wrote of a smiling little girl coming into her room for her morning cuddle, and having cereal and juice for breakfast (except on Sundays when it was scrambled egg and bacon). And how she loved to cut, stick and draw on the kitchen table for the rest of the morning, then play out in the sandpit or help to collect the eggs and change the horses' water.

It was a little confusing, however, because there were no dates on either the Form 'E' or the foster mother's profile. *She's starting ballet classes after Christmas*, the foster mother had written. How lovely, I thought, imagining her in a tutu doing pliés and arabesques – but hang on: did that mean she had been doing ballet for a year, for two years, or was just about to start?

There was no photo either, though this was not unexpected: seeing one too soon, I had been told by social services, might cloud your decision.

Allie came round the next day to discuss the Form 'E' and the prospective child. 'I'm afraid the bit about direct contact is out-of-date,' she told me immediately, effectively taking some of the wind out of my sails. 'Her social worker wants direct contact with the siblings, as well as with the mother, grandmother and aunt.'

'It sounds more like a foster placement than an adoption,' I said, in frustration.

'Weren't you aware that direct contact is the norm for an older child?'

'No, I wasn't. No one ever mentioned it.'

'I don't know what to think,' Allie said. 'I assumed this had all been discussed with you.'

'I've decided then that I want a younger child with *no* direct contact,' I blurted out. 'And anyway, I always felt I was bamboozled into putting down an age range I never wanted.'

'If it's a younger child you want, that needs to be made clear. We do need to get it right…although – and I don't mean to be rude – at *your* age, we're not going to be offering you a baby.'

As I sat there, feeling frustrated and perplexed, a remark my sister once made now echoed in my mind: 'Don't be too rigid about age, you might turn down the *perfect* little four-year-old.'

'I just don't understand why so much contact is always being laid down,' I protested, 'I'll never feel like she's my own.'

'It's whatever is felt to be in the child's best interest,' Allie explained. 'But we *can* negotiate the amount of contact with the child's social worker – it's quite usual to do so.'

'Is it really?'

'Yes, we're always doing it.'

This was sounding better. I began to calm down.

'And you're not legally obligated to adhere to the contact arrangements after the adoption order's gone through,' Allie added.

'Have *you* met her?'

'No, I haven't, but I've heard so many amusing stories about her that I'm probably biased. She sounds a real character. She's very pretty and she's got big dark eyes and this mop of dark hair.'

And just as Molly had predicted, I immediately began to build a relationship with this little girl. 'I must say I do like the sound of her,' I then said.

'Are you changing your mind?' Allie asked, looking at me curiously. 'You came out so much against having an older child. It doesn't mean you'll have to wait a long time for a younger one, there are plenty now on our books.'

I insisted that I wanted to learn more about *this* little girl. Allie still looked doubtful, so I repeated my sister's remark to her.

'I agree with your sister,' she said, after some hesitation. 'Then Toby, the child's social worker is the key. I'll set up a meeting for the three of us.'

'Do you have a photograph of her?' I asked, as Allie was on her way out.

'No I don't, but I'll ask Toby to bring you one.'

e-mail, February 2005

Dear Beth,

Just a word to let you know I was thinking of you and hoping that all goes well with your meeting (tomorrow) today. I am confident it will, and you'll be another step closer to having the attic room soon occupied by a lovely little one. I will be so pleased for you when this is all realised. It makes me smile to think about it. I will call later in the day to get an update if it is convenient...

'I came a little early,' Allie announced, when I opened the front door. 'I wanted us to have a few words on our own before Toby arrives.'

We went into the kitchen to have a coffee.

'Have you had more time to think about the child?' she enquired.

'Yes, I have and I feel very positive on the whole. I have a good feeling; I had it the moment I saw her notes, in fact.'

'That's good,' Allie said, 'but my boss is still concerned as to whether you'll be happy with the match. Nothing will be held against you if you *do* want a younger child. Your reaction bothered me during our last visit. At one point, you seemed so certain you didn't want an older child.'

I calmly told Allie that I had given it a great deal of thought and that, on balance, I liked the idea of a child young enough to still be going to nursery, yet old enough for me to have some time for myself.

'Well, I have some good news and some bad news,' Allie said, looking serious. 'The good news is that we have some updated information about the father. There's been a DNA test and the father named in her Form 'E' is *not* her biological father.' (This was good news because of the negative history of the presumptive father.) 'My boss, however, told me last night that Toby has already passed on the Form 'E' of this child to a couple.'

I could not believe it. What chance would I, a single person, have against a couple? I knew it was too good to be true.

'Why is he bothering to come round then,' I asked bitterly. I felt my lower lip tremble and realised I was close to tears. We had by now moved into the sitting room and I was sitting in the armchair, feeling very alone. Allie, on the other hand, seemed peculiarly detached.

'Would it bother you if this didn't work out?' she asked, regarding me closely.

'Yes, it would,' I exclaimed, 'and I know I won't have a chance against a couple.'

'That's not necessarily the case. A single applicant can have strengths a couple doesn't. For one thing, the child only has to bond with *one* parent. Let's just see what Toby says when he arrives.'

When Toby greeted me with a big smile, I reluctantly offered him a coffee, thinking how two-faced he was. I couldn't contain myself any longer: 'Allie told me that you've sent the details of this child to a couple, too!'

'No I haven't!' he protested, looking straight at Allie, and was adamant that he was considering no one else at this stage.

'But my boss told me this morning you'd sent out the Form 'E',' Allie said.

'I haven't.'

Was he lying, I wondered. But at the same time, I felt a huge sense of relief.

'I've heard all about you from Allie,' Toby said, turning back to me, 'and I've read all the notes. But I needed to meet you myself and ask you some questions and get a feel as to whether you'll be a good match for Mattie. I've spoken to her foster mother and she feels positive about what she's heard, by the way… '

Toby then asked to see the rest of the house, especially where Mattie would sleep.

'This'll be good for her when she's seven or eight,' he said, dismissively, when I showed him the spacious attic area of bedroom, playroom, bathroom and two gabled windows. 'It would be best if she slept close to you in the beginning; it'll all be very strange for her.'

My heart sank for I had always imagined a child up in the attic rooms, even when I still thought I would have my own. It was the nicest part of the house with its glimpse of the sea to the south and the tip of the Downs over the rooftops to the north. 'And if she does move up here later on,' Toby continued, 'you'll find yourself having to change the colour scheme to pink!'

We went back downstairs to have a look at the study next to my bedroom, which Toby suggested I convert into a bedroom. I inwardly groaned as I looked at the bookshelves in my study packed with hundreds of books, and my PC on the large desk. Where would I put it all, I thought to myself, with a feeling of panic.

'I'd like to make another visit in two weeks,' Toby told me. 'That'll give you time to reflect, let everything sink in. And I'll try to make a video of her before then.'

'Could I have a photo meanwhile?' I asked. Toby looked at me blankly.

'Didn't you bring one with you?' Allie said.

'No, I assumed you'd already provided one. I'll put one in the post.'

After they left, I pondered whether Toby was going to post the photo by first or second class. When nothing arrived the next morning, I worried that it might have got lost.

For two long days, I waited.

e-mail, 15 February 2005

Dear Mike,

Mattie does look very cute. She has big dark eyes and short thick hair cut into a sort of bob, about as long as the bottom of her ears. It was strange but it was like looking at someone a little similar to me. She is a nice size, I have the feeling she likes her food. I have occasionally had a look at the photos and they always make me laugh a little.

Mattie's photo finally arrived on Valentine's Day, in a brown envelope. I spotted it as soon as I arrived home from work.

I took the envelope from the hall, where the postman had left it earlier that day, and held it in the kitchen for a moment before ripping it open. Here is the face I will know for the rest of my life, I thought, as the pictures fell out.

There were three different poses, all printed on A4. I stood there transfixed. For years, I had imagined a little mirror image of myself. For years, I had imagined a little me. And here was someone – someone *else's* flesh and blood, even – who reminded me of myself as a little girl; especially in the photograph where she was looking at the camera out of the corner of her eye. In another, she looked rather coy, and in the last, she was the feisty little girl I had been told about. In all of them, she was smiling. She was a beautiful child, adorable.

I placed the three photos in different parts of the kitchen so that I could see her whilst I cooked my evening meal. It was as though she were in the room with me. I laughed out loud, as I poured myself a celebratory glass of wine.

If the essence of my future daughter began to emerge in my kitchen that Valentine's Day, then my sympathy for her mother began to emerge a few days later, in the same building where I had attended my prep course, almost two years before. Here, I was encouraged by social services to read all the available files about this little girl and her birth family.

The word 'relentless' came to my mind as I read through the pages and learned more of a mother, who from a young age had already begun to buckle under life's burdens. She was born at the same time as I joined the Foreign Office. She married and gave birth to the first of her three children at the time my sister Molly adopted her first child.

The mother only knew the father of her third child – my future daughter – for two months, December and January, at the changeover of the millennium. He was someone who had been supportive and caring towards her at a difficult time, a time when her abusive husband was in and out of her life.

Two years later, as the birth mother became more mentally and physically unwell, social services placed all three children in foster care, the youngest separately. She, Mattie, came to Jenny's (her foster mother) with a *Thomas the Tank Engine* balloon, a black plastic bin liner stuffed with clothes, and a dummy. At which *exact* time Molly was picking up little Mei from the orphanage in China and I was re-contacting social services, firmly committed to the idea of adopting a child.

Jenny's was not meant to be a permanent foster placement for Mattie, but her mother's health worsened and attempts to find an adopter, or foster carer, to take all three children failed. Mattie stayed on at Jenny's for two full years and developed a secure, loving attachment.

In September of 2004, when I was finally approved for adoption, social services made the decision that it was in the child's best interests that she be adopted. That was when those photographs were taken, the ones that arrived on Valentine's Day through my letterbox; the time I had my first sight of Mattie in her little smocked dress.

e-mail, February 2005

Dear Mike,

I woke up at 5am for a while…I did suddenly feel rather overwhelmed but that is always the way I think at that time in the morning…I do feel quietly happy about it all. It is so nice also that you came into my life at this particular time. It really feels like it was all meant to be…we must get some little cowboy boots for her one day…

I had just taken the leek and potato soup out of the fridge

when I heard a knock at the door. It must be my friends, Matt and Janet, coming for lunch, I thought, placing the quiche in the oven.

'Here's a photo of her,' I announced excitedly, as soon as they entered the kitchen, Matt carrying a bottle of wine. 'Isn't she cute?'

'She's lovely,' they both said, in turns, obviously pleased. 'Do you know what nationality she is?' Janet asked.

'She's half-Bangladeshi,' I replied, surprised at her question because I had not noticed much difference in skin tone.

'I *thought* she looked Asian as soon as I saw her,' Janet announced.

I took a second look at the photo. Funny, when I had told my boss about my news, *his* first question, too, had been whether she was white. And come to think of it, Allie did keep emphasising that she was quite dark, obviously to ensure it did not matter to me.

'Funnily enough, I have an olive skin tone myself and as a child, my brothers even used to call me 'Paki' to tease me,' I laughed, and we chatted for a while about those pre-PC days of childhood.

I served Matt his bowl of hot soup first. I was pleased with the recipe, one from my beginners' Cordon Bleu book. 'This is delicious,' he said and then, for some reason, began to explain to me that in the Sixties many people had decided the world was not one in which to bring up children: '*We* made a conscious decision not to have children.'

'That's not true,' Janet retorted, face flushed. '*I* wanted children but you never did. You told me *I'd* have to take care of them *myself* if I had them.'

'No, I didn't!' Matt protested. 'I don't remember saying that at all. *Actually*, I would have quite liked a child.'

Matt was the youngest of ten children, and a late child at that (his mother was 48 when she gave birth), so it would not have surprised me if he had been cool about the idea of having children. Though I always found it interesting how often women would go along with what their men wanted…I know I never would have.

'Do you think the quiche is cooked enough?' I asked Janet, holding the hot dish before her, sensing some wounds had been opened. 'It's already been in a long time.'

'I'd keep it in a bit longer. It needs to be a little browner on top, though it smells delicious.'

'What we've found anyway,' Matt said, 'is that out of all our friends and acquaintances, the *only* couples who've stuck together are those *without* children. All the others got divorced. So we probably made the right decision.'

The conversation turned to the safer subject of books, as I served the quiche. Both Matt and Janet were avid readers and we could easily spend an hour or two discussing our favourite titles. On this occasion, however, I felt unexpectedly tired, content to let them do most of the talking.

Listening to the pair chatter on, I recalled one afternoon during which a group of us, all women, had gone out for a walk along the river. We had all taken turns holding the lone mother's baby as we sat there in the long grass, chatting. I remember thinking how pleasant it all was until the mother announced suddenly, 'What a waste of womanhood,' and she looked around at each of us. Her comment made me stop for a moment. I was happy enough, wasn't I? Then, I realised, perhaps she was right.

'I've made an almond and apple pudding for dessert,' I announced to my guests, as I cleared the table. 'I'm not sure how it's turned out, though. I haven't made it before.'

Oh dear, I thought as I placed the pudding on the table, *I hope it's not a disaster!* Then, I caught sight of my new daughter smiling at me from the wall, and I smiled back.

When Allie came round the following week, she asked, 'What did you think of the photo of Mattie?'

'I think she looks lovely!' I beamed.

'You don't mind that she's quite dark?'

'No I don't, actually.'

'Are you still feeling positive about her?' Allie asked. 'You can still back out, you know…there are plenty of other children we can match you with; there's no pressure.'

I was feeling a little irritated with Allie, for once again offering me the opportunity to back out. In my mind, there was no doubt at all – so how could it not be obvious to her, too? I told her I was overjoyed, and had even been buying toys – there was a little wooden cooker in a toyshop down the road that I'd deliberated on for ages before finally going in to buy it.

'We'll have to check whether Toby's *still* positive, too, then,' she said, with what I interpreted as a doubtful tone.

I was taken aback upon hearing her words. Images of that perfect couple once more flashed into my mind. They *had* been sent her picture, after all. I was *certain*.

'The problem *is*,' Allie continued, 'my boss said that the child has been asking for both a mummy and a daddy…I don't think it's anything to worry about, though. Toby's assigned her a play therapist to work through any issues.'

'But she *might* have a daddy one day!' I exclaimed. 'Just because I'm single *now* doesn't mean I won't meet someone in the future.' And she *will* have a daddy one day, I wanted to shout out loud. It occurred to me how terribly ironic this all was becoming – Mike was secretly waiting in the wings and I was about to be turned down because I was single. *Should I own up to her? Oh, if only I could! But what would she say if I did? Someone who lives in Texas? Get real!* 'Don't misunderstand me,' I told Allie, 'Just because I'm adopting as a single applicant doesn't mean I think it's ideal for her *not* to have a father. But I know, even on my own, I'll be perfect for her.'

I've already formed a relationship with her, I wanted to cry out. My lower lip began to tremble.

'Does it worry you then, that it might fall through?' Allie asked, studying my expression.

'Yes, it does! I feel very sure about her.'

Once again, I felt all alone; alone and battered by this seemingly endless process.

'Then it's important I push for Toby to arrange a meeting with the foster mother as soon as possible. Jenny will be able to give you far more information about what sort of child Mattie is.'

e-mail, February 2005

Dear Beth,

I have the picture of Mattie you sent on the drop-leaf walnut table and every time I walk by, which is pretty often, I get another look. She really is an adorable child. I must commend your taste. I can hardly wait until she is ensconced in the attic bedroom along with her little library and toy collection…with Mama Beth hovering about and making leek and potato soup every little bit. Sounds lovely to me.

I was in a state of barely controlled excitement when I at last heard Mattie's foster mother Jenny's knock at the front door. But I was nervous, too, and rather fearful that I might not measure up, or that she might think my home – and me – too posh.

My worries were quickly dispelled, however, when I saw the fresh-faced, rosy-cheeked farmer's wife on my doorstep. Jenny was a few years older than I had imagined. At least Mattie would be used to having someone with a few grey hairs.

'I hope you don't mind – I had to bring baby Charlotte, too,' Jenny laughed, as I showed her into the hallway where she parked the pram.

Those net curtains opposite will really have something to twitch about now, I thought to myself with a chuckle. 'How long have you been looking after the baby?' I asked, as Jenny sat on the sofa, bottle-feeding Charlotte, who gave a gurgle of contentment. I thought how much warmer, how much fuller my sitting room suddenly seemed.

'Not long. Her mother's still in hospital and doesn't want to know her.'

I watched the baby, feeling a momentary regret at not having the chance to adopt one so small. 'How adorable she looks.'

'They'll be coming to take her away next week to join her siblings in their foster home. I'll really miss having her,' she smiled.

Jenny took out a small package from her bag. 'Here are some photos of Mattie we've just had done in a studio.' She handed me the small album, which I eagerly took. But when I looked at the little stranger's face, I experienced a feeling of shock.

'She looks different than in the photos Allie sent me,' I blurted out. My mind whirled. She had looked so cute in that little smocked dress. In these photos, I thought with a growing sense of panic, she looked much *older*. And her face looks different, too. This is not like the same girl! I felt my stomach sink and hoped it did not show. I glanced up to see a look of concern on Jenny's face. For a moment, I had been oblivious to the fact that she was still there. 'I had a photo from Allie which shows her in a smocked dress,' I explained. 'She was sitting on a sofa.'

'That was taken last September,' Jenny said, 'when they decided to put her up for adoption.'

Last September! But that was six months ago. Did children

really change so much in a few months? Why *hadn't* I insisted on a two- or three-year-old? I again was experiencing one of the emotional 'downs' now so familiar to me. There isn't anything I can add to this little girl's life, I thought. Why on earth doesn't she stay with Jenny, with whom she has obviously enjoyed a strong bond? I felt unnecessary.

'She's pretty, isn't she?' I said, trying to put a positive tone in my voice though to me, it sounded hollow.

'Yes, she is,' Jenny said warmly. 'She's a lovely child.'

Then, something of the sadness of all this struck me: I, whose existence the little girl was not even aware of, could at any moment simply turn her down. Yet she herself had no say in any of it. I began to recall the nice things Jenny had written about Mattie in the Form 'E'.

'So what's she like?' I asked, in an attempt to recapture my excitement.

'She's a sweet, loving little girl,' Jenny replied, 'and she likes a lot of cuddles...'

'But wouldn't she miss living on a farm?' I said, thinking how far removed was my townhouse on a busy street.

'Oh no,' Jenny responded quickly, 'I know she'll love it here. It's what she needs. And she'll be perfect as an only child... She *can* be a pickle sometimes, though,' she laughed. 'I keep telling her not to do anything she shouldn't because I've got eyes in the back of my head... I think she believes me, too,' she chuckled. 'She's been in foster care far too long, longer than is good for her.' Baby Charlotte was now sound asleep and Jenny removed the bottle. 'I feel sorry for Mattie. She's seen so many *other* children come and go. Now the last one, her little friend Paolo, has left, too. She got on so well with him. It upset her to see his new parents come to the house each day during introductions.'

'Did you say Paolo? Isn't he the little half-Italian boy with blond curls?' I had a sudden flashback to my second-opinion visit with Elaine, our heads huddled together looking through the book of available children. It occurred to me *then* that Mattie was the dusky little girl with the big cheeky smile I had commented on.

'Yes, that's right,' Jenny said. 'I'm so pleased for him; he's got lovely parents. Mattie misses him terribly. She's been asking me when she'll be getting *her* new mummy.'

'But isn't she bothered about not having a daddy?'

'No, she said she doesn't mind so long as she has a granddad. She's never had a granddad.'

'She can definitely have one of those,' I said, with a smile. My moment of panic was now over; Jenny had made me feel necessary again.

'Jenny, I'd like to ask your advice on something. I want to show you the attic bedroom I've prepared for Mattie. Toby wants me instead to convert the study into a bedroom so she'll be nearer to me. I'd like to know what *you* think.'

After looking the room over, Jenny told me that she knew Mattie would love the bedroom in the attic, not least because of its adjoining bathroom. 'She's always had to share our bathroom with so many foster children,' Jenny explained, 'I know she'll love having her very own! She's enjoyed having her own bedroom lately, too.'

I then decided to stick to my original plans, with a contingency of using the study next to my room as her bedroom if Mattie appeared in any way perturbed. Nonetheless, I was anxious as to what Toby would say about my decision.

'Mattie does like to keep busy,' Jenny chuckled, as she now pushed the pram towards the door. 'She's a very active little girl.'

'She's not hyperactive, though, is she?' It had been on the tip of my tongue to ask earlier, but I had felt embarrassed to do so. I had to know. There were so many TV programs about hyperactive children – ADHD, they called it now – who apparently drove their parents wild.

'Oh no, she's not hyperactive,' Jenny said quickly. 'She's just a high energy child.'

'Did she know you were seeing me today,' I asked, finally.

'I'm not supposed to say anything until your match has been approved,' Jenny laughed, 'but Mattie knew something was up this morning. She's *so* excited.'

Dear Beth,

...Please don't take the warnings that all the social workers are doling out too much to heart. It's part of their job to do so but the things they are warning you about don't necessary apply to everyone... I know everything will be just fine. Put the apprehensions away and enjoy the possibilities of the wonderful new life that is opening for you...

Dear Mike,

...Mum actually said today she, too, can't see anything going wrong. She, like you, thinks Mattie will fit in just fine. I think the social workers have to keep emphasising the worst just in case you turn on them afterwards and say you weren't warned... The mound of negative info they feed you can sometimes be overwhelming...

'I haven't heard from Toby, yet,' Allie told me, a few days later. 'He *still* hasn't signified his agreement to our going ahead.'

Allie and I were standing in my kitchen, and I, once again on edge, feeling as if my whole world were crumbling. 'Why has it been allowed to go this far then? I've even met her foster mother. I think it's unprofessional...'

'So you're feeling quite sure about Mattie, then?'

'Yes, I'm *quite* sure,' I answered between clenched teeth. 'And I *hope* Toby is sure, too,' I added. 'He said he'd try to make a video and bring it along.'

Allie and I took our coffee into the sitting room to await Toby's arrival. I sat on the edge of my chair, feeling anxious. I thought of all the social services' preaching I had heard over the years, about the need to empathise with one's future child. Had they ever shown any empathy to me? I felt even more anxious when I looked at my watch and saw that Toby was late. Then, just a few seconds later, I heard a knock at the door. I dashed to the door, and there he was, grinning, and – yes! – Toby was carrying a small package.

As I watched the video, I saw the little girl I had seen in the photos that had arrived through my letterbox. *This*, I knew, was my daughter. But all the while I sat watching, I felt Allie's eyes glued to me, studying my every expression. I was still on trial. How I wished I could be alone and unobserved. I endeavoured to keep smiling and emitted the odd 'ooh' and 'aah' at appropriate intervals. At the same time, I felt strangely voyeuristic as I watched. Mattie – she was certainly very cute and bubbly – was showing Toby her numerous cuddly toys (*Where will they all go, I wondered*), toys, I assumed, from people who were important to her, but strangers to me.

'Let's go back downstairs now,' Toby was saying to her.

'No.' She laughed, refusing to go.

She looked so settled there, I thought, as they descended the stairs, Mattie now pointing out baby Charlotte to Toby. I thought of the close bond she had already built with her foster mother, and again felt like a peeping Tom as Mattie picked up her doll and started rocking it in imitation of Jenny who had just picked up the baby. Where did I fit into all this? Even if I did want her, would she really want *me*? She looks like a lot of work, I thought, finally, all that chatter and vitality. Was I ready for my whole life to be turned over? I realised I had become rather quiet so emitted another 'ooh'.

When the video ended, Allie addressed Toby: 'Beth was saying earlier how she feels very positive about going forward.'

'Good,' Toby said, with a smile, looking up from the TV.

'She wants to know if *you* are happy to proceed, too.'

'Yes, I'm keen,' he said, 'and so, too, is Jenny. I wanted to give you time to let it all settle in,' he continued. 'I didn't want to pressurise you. It'll be a big change. She'll keep you very busy, and there'll be lots of washing and ironing to do.'

So Toby, too, is giving me the chance to opt out, I thought. I looked over at him.

'According to the play therapist, there are no issues about a daddy,' Toby continued. 'But the male role model *is* important. Make sure you put plenty of photos of Granddad and Uncle Tom in her album.'

At the doorstep, later, Toby hung on a while after Allie had left. 'I *do* feel positive,' he told me. 'I believe it'll be a good match. I'm very pleased.'

'I'm pleased, too,' I said, as he shook my hand.

That was just what I needed: an affirmation from social services that I was doing the right thing. We heard the sound of a car horn and both looked up.

'That's Uncle Tom,' I laughed, waving at my brother-in-law as he drove by. 'He's one of the male role models.'

Later that day, I took the video of Mattie round to my parents' house. What would they think, I wondered, as it began to play.

'She looks like a bundle of fun,' my father said immediately.

'Oh bless her,' said my mother. 'Who could resist her?'

e-mail, 4 March 2005

Dear Mike,

Must say I had a nice feeling putting my coat on the rack for the last time this morning. Someone on the train next to me took out his laptop and I do find the noise intrusion nowadays irritating – thudding down on keyboards, yelling on mobile phones, hearing other people's music blasting out over their headphones... When I first started commuting nearly 17 years ago there was just the sound of chatting...people used to moan incessantly about the poor train service; now no one talks at all. How times have changed...and everyone is carrying huge bags of gym gear and shoes now – I nearly had someone's backpack smack my face this morning when he took it off the rack, with complete disregard as to who was behind him. In my day, men carried a briefcase that only held a newspaper and some sandwiches. Well, I think I deserve a good old-fashioned moan on this my last day of commuting...

Like an automaton, I arose at the usual hour the following Monday morning and travelled up on the usual train to London for an art exhibition.

It had been strange standing there on the platform in my casual clothes, seeing all the familiar faces, shoulders hunched. And later, in a long queue outside the Tate, I began to wonder what on earth I was doing there, too. Instead of having lunch after the exhibition and shopping at Liberty's, as I had planned, I caught the first train back home.

I decided to ring Kath during the first week of what I saw as my maternity leave. Latterly, she had not been replying to my e-mails, and when I had gone over to see her, the church had been strangely empty. During my last week at work, I had gone to look for her, only to find someone in her office, sorting through her papers. He told me that Kath was very ill, that her cancer had gone to her brain. He gave me her address and phone number.

When I rang, I was much relieved that Kath sounded glad to hear from me. I told her how she had kept me going during a difficult period, both at work and at home.

'I'm pleased to hear that,' she said, and then told me she had almost completed the story for her grandchildren. It was, she said, keeping her alive.

I mentioned Mattie's imminent arrival.

'She'll be beautiful,' Kath said, adding that her sister was married to an Indian and that they had beautiful children. She asked after Mike, too.

Her last words to me were, 'Enjoy your life.'

That same week, over dinner, I told some local friends my adoption news.

'I'm surprised you don't want a baby,' one of them commented.

'Me, too,' the other, Cindy, agreed. 'Won't you mind missing out on the baby stage?'

'I'm not particularly bothered about having a baby,' I replied, 'and anyway, I was never that desperate to go through the baby stage or pregnancy.'

'But you're pregnant already!' Cindy announced. 'Only it's better: you won't have the stretch marks!'

I hadn't experienced the nine months of gestation either, a time that allows one to adapt and a time in which one's body undergoes significant changes. Although a number of years had passed by since I made that first phone call to social services, there had been so many ups and downs along the way, so many delays and disappointments, that only from the day Allie rang with news of Mattie did I allow myself to accept the fact that it was *really* going to happen… And now, in only a matter of weeks, the stork would be dropping off a ready-made four-year-old.

e-mail, 28 March 2005

Dear Beth,

...I am very much looking forward to seeing you again. In some ways, it does seem the time of our separation has passed speedily, and in other ways, it seems far too long. I suppose it depends on how I feel and what is going on at the moment. It has helped to speak with you on the telephone a good deal and my being vicariously involved with watching little Mattie come into your life is definitely a plus. But I sometimes fluctuate between being very excited for you and feeling like I am missing out on so much, and certainly to miss much, much more...

I began to alter my home for the new arrival. I cleared out redundant furniture, switched stuff around, bought children's things and gave the house a spring clean. And for the first time in years, I also had an opportunity to hear the birds sing, see the clematis come slowly into bud outside my kitchen window, and the Judas tree break into its sudden splash of purple flower. It was time, too, to put away my Cordon Bleu and dust off my Delia Smith; time to bake bread and pastries, cookies and hot-cross buns; time to take out my knitting needles – unused for years – only this time to make *child-sized* sweaters.

'You're looking well,' Allie would tell me on the occasional visits she was still bound to make. Later, she confessed, she feared I was enjoying my new-found freedom from work far too much: 'I half expected you to tell me you'd decided not to go ahead with the adoption – especially when you mentioned your holiday.'

Mike had earlier suggested two weeks together for a pre-adoption break. He offered to come to England, but I was still a bit paranoid about someone from social services spotting him in my immediate vicinity, so instead I chose to visit him in Texas.

In Fort Worth, we went shopping for children's books – Mike particularly wanted to buy Mattie *Anne of Green Gables* – visited museums and art exhibitions, and then drove south to Austin where, on a warm sunny evening on the patio of our hotel, and feeling very nervous, I met one of Mike's lovely daughters. The patio was full of people talking about the film scripts they were writing, politics and the college basketball playoffs. I felt quaintly British because everyone had trouble understanding my accent, which pleased Mike who could now point out it wasn't only he who had difficulty in this regard.

We then travelled through the Hill Country, to the west of Austin, where we saw peach trees about to blossom, Texas bluebonnets which looked like large grape hyacinths, and a mass of other wild flowers in bloom. And then, via San Antonio, to the Texas Gulf coast where we spent much of our time simply walking along the beach, eating boiled shrimps with cold beers or having a game of pool in one of the little funky beach bars.

But thousands of miles away from my home, I was finding it difficult to unwind. I was still experiencing an occasional thought about the Adoption Matching Panel, scheduled for a fortnight after my return. And on my mind, too, was the prospect of the subsequent two weeks of introductions I would have to go through, prior to my daughter moving in.

'You were pretty distracted during the visit,' Mike recalled later. 'Of course, there was so much about to change in your life.'

Things were changing in the lives of my future daughter's birth family, too. They, at the time, were planning a farewell party for Mattie, knowing some of them might never see her for years to come, if ever.

As Mike and I sat on the rocks of the breakwater, chatting and looking at the rolling waves of the Gulf, I wondered how Toby would inform the birth mother of the adoptive match, and what a difficult task that would be for him. I was thinking, too, about his meeting with the extended birth family to discuss the changes in contact arrangements. And whilst I was drinking pina coladas and eating key lime pie at a restaurant near the beach, I knew that Jenny, that very day, had taken my future daughter for a trial at the nursery school just down the road from where I lived.

'There was this little girl who showed a lot of interest in Mattie,' Jenny told me when I arrived home. 'Mattie liked that and when I picked her up later in the day she mentioned the little girl, saying how nice she was, and that she had skin the same colour as hers. I wasn't supposed to,' Jenny chuckled, 'but I couldn't resist it. I told her I *thought* she might have just met her new cousin.'

My new *daughter* had not only been in the very town where I lived, but she had also visited her new nursery school and met her new cousin! I was excited, but at the same time felt somewhat daunted. My life, as I had known it for so many years, was coming to a close… And a new life, for both Mattie and me, was about to begin.

e-mail, April 27 2005

Dear Mike,

Just to say our match was approved today. Actually Allie and Toby seemed more nervous than me. Some of the questions were directed at them, some at me. They were both delighted afterwards. Molly and I then drove along the promenade of Eastbourne and had tea in a small tearoom at the foot of the Downs in a place called Litlington. There was also a small shop there and I bought a very pretty skirt and top.

I do feel so much better now that this is happening. I have my meeting next Wednesday to agree the introductions schedule. Mattie had her last day at her old nursery this week where they had a little send-off for her. And her maternal family had a party for her and wanted to take lots of photos. Toby told me that Mattie, after a while, said she was fed up of having to smile all the time and had had enough of having her photo taken.

I have now come home and have just run a bath. The sky was blue all day today...

Part Two

Our Story

Bluebells lined the lane – I thought that a good omen – and it had stopped raining. I had forgotten that traffic could mount up at Windmill Corner, and was feeling a little agitated for I feared I might be late. Nonetheless, I stopped the car, re-arranged my hair in the mirror and then smiled as I put on some lipgloss. It was like being on a first date.

As I drove up the bluebell-lined lane, I saw chimney pots on top of what looked like a farm cottage. That has to be where she lives, I thought excitedly. I glanced at my watch again; I would be there right on the dot, or at worst a minute or two late. I hoped they were not worrying that I might not turn up.

I saw Toby first. He was standing at the end of the lane, waiting for me.

'Hello, I'm the stork,' he said, as I climbed out of the car. 'There she is,' he smiled. I followed his gaze and saw a little girl walking towards me. She was crossing the small patch of grass in front of the farm cottage, hands in her jacket pockets. I waved at her, and she waved back. I could see she had pigtails and that on the pocket of her pink jacket was imprinted a large letter 'B'.

'Hello,' I said as we stood in front of each other, 'you're such a tiny tot!' How she must have felt, I cannot imagine, looking up at her new Mummy.

'I remember that bluebells lined the lane, and I was worried I might be late,' I would often tell her later.

'You *were* late,' she would reprimand me…'Five minutes.'

'No I wasn't,' I protested, 'and if I was, it was only by a minute.'

As I gazed at her little face, all lit up, I thought how much she *always* loved hearing me recount the moments of our first meeting.

'Do you remember what my first words were?' I would ask her.

'You're such a tiny tot!' she would reply, laughing.

'Yes, that's right, and I asked you what the letter 'B' stood for.'

'For "Barbie".'

'Yes, and then *I* said: "I think you should have a letter M on your pocket: M for Mattie."'

'Shall we go in for a cup of tea?' Jenny, her foster mum, who had now joined us, suggested that day. And for the first time, Mattie and I walked together, hand in hand, across the grass. We walked through the little white gate and into the cottage, to a sitting room packed with toys and pictures of the children whom Jenny had cared for over the past twenty years.

Mattie and I sat together on the settee, looking at one another adoringly, like two lovers. And I noticed other things, too, that day: the slight hint of red in her dark brown hair, her perfect, little white teeth, and how she made a grab for the chocolate cakes that Jenny brought in with the tea. Both of us were oblivious to Toby sitting opposite us, observing, and I did not even notice he had slipped away until Jenny suggested we all go outside.

Mattie and I collected the eggs from the hen house that first morning, picked cow parsley for the horses and she gave me a pheasant's feather for her new granddad. I remember how she chatted and laughed, and the proud look on her face when she took my hand and introduced me to the grooms. 'This is Beth, my new mummy,' she told them.

But later, back in the farmhouse, she suddenly let go of my hand and re-sought Jenny's, and I was reminded that my daughter and I were, after all, strangers.

At the pre-set time of my departure, I was upset when Mattie began to cry. 'I've waited a long time for her,' I heard her sob, as she hid her face in Jenny's neck.

'I've waited a long time for you, too, Mattie,' I said softly.

'Did you hear that?' her foster mum said, repeating my

words to her. Still holding the little girl, Jenny said quietly to me, 'She thinks you're not going to come back.'

I tried my best to reassure Mattie, but by then I was both mentally and emotionally exhausted, and – I admit – a little relieved to get into my car and drive away: I needed time on my own to reflect, to absorb it all, I realised, as I drove down the lane away from the farm cottage with its chimney pots. I wanted to be back in my own house, to see my garden, stroke the cat and open a bottle of wine. I then recalled that my mother was coming over for dinner that evening, a pre-arranged date made only a week ago – seemingly a lifetime ago – when I had no idea it would be the evening of the first meeting with my new daughter.

Allie, my social worker, phoned first to see how things had gone, and I poured out my entire day to her. And later that evening, when my mother arrived, I did the same with her, too.

'So when will Mattie be moving in with you?' Mum asked.

'Not for another two weeks,' I replied, and showed her a copy of the so-called 'introductions schedule' prepared for me by social services. This outlined the fortnight of to-ing and fro-ing between my home and her foster home in order to meet and get to know Mattie and to gradually take on the day-to-day tasks of her care – including nursery runs, outings, making occasional meals for her, bathing her and putting her to bed, visits to see her new home and visits to meet her new family members.

'It sounds like a very tiring two weeks for both of you,' Mum said.

Was it *really* only yesterday that social services, Jenny and I had met to agree the introductions schedule? We were all of us squashed together in a room packed with toys.

On Day 1, I was to meet Mattie at her foster home; day 2

would again be at Jenny's; on day 3, Jenny would bring her round to my house for tea. On day 4 I would breakfast at Jenny's—

'What time will breakfast be?' interrupted the social services manager, with a chuckle.

'Six o'clock,' Jenny laughed, before conceding that she could stretch it to seven.

How about eight? I wanted to suggest, but I kept quiet.

Eventually, we completed the schedule up to and including day 13 – the day Mattie would move in with me.

'Is everyone happy now with the agenda?' the social services manager asked.

'It's fine with me,' I said, though already feeling exhausted just by the sound of it.

'OK then I'll type it up and send it round by e-mail later… Now does anyone have any objections to kicking off tomorrow?'

Tomorrow? I nearly fell out of my seat. I had assumed they would at least give me a few days to become mentally prepared. I looked around at everyone huddled together on the brightly coloured sofas, hoping in vain that one of them might suggest a delay.

'Is Mattie ready for tomorrow?' I asked Jenny, feeling a little unsure myself.

'Oh yes, she already knows about it! She's *so* excited.'

Toby then asked for the photo album, which at their suggestion I had prepared for Mattie. It was a small Chinese one with a carved wooden cover that my sister Molly had given me years before. 'I'll just show her a few photos of her new home, at first,' Toby said, 'so she doesn't get overwhelmed.'

I then handed a small cuddly white bear to Jenny; it was tucked inside a little embroidered bag I had bought in Oaxaca. Allie had suggested that I choose two similar toys and photograph one, in this case the cuddly bear's twin Black

Bear, in various rooms of my house for Mattie, the idea being that Mattie would bring White Bear to meet Black Bear on her first visit to her new home.

The photo of me in the album, posing in front of a large, scarlet camellia bush, had been taken the previous weekend at my eldest brother's 25th wedding anniversary celebration. They had had a large barbecue out in their garden and everyone had asked lots of questions about Mattie. My sister-in-law's mother even offered to knit her a little cardigan.

'I always recommend that the new parents go out for a nice meal the night before introductions begin,' Toby had said, as I made to leave the room. 'It's a special evening, because your life will never be the same again.'

e-mail, 5 May 2005

Dear Beth,

I am so glad that you and Mattie have at last found one another. When you were telling me about your meeting I was extremely moved. I must either be a sentimental sort or very much in love. Maybe a little of both. I think it is wonderful what you all are going to do for one another's lives… I definitely would like a schedule of the coming days because there seems to be lots happening…'

'Mattie was very upset when you left,' Jenny told me as soon as I arrived the next morning. 'Then she found your scarf. Did you leave it by mistake? She took it to bed with her and hasn't let it out of her sight since. She woke up this morning at five and came into our bedroom to talk about her new mummy and how pretty you were.'

123

Mattie then dashed into the room and hugged me, my scarf wrapped around her little neck.

We spent another glorious, but for me emotionally taxing, day together. Pottering around the garden, Mattie told me all about Ruby and Sam, the two foster children with whom she shared Jenny's home, and later we had fish pie for lunch in the farmhouse kitchen.

In the afternoon, as my departure time neared, I asked her, 'Do you want me to leave the scarf again today?'

'I want you to forget it again,' she replied.

The next day, a Saturday, Mattie, scarf wrapped around her neck, White Bear and Jenny arrived at my front door.

Nervously, I had been putting some finishing touches to ham sandwiches, because Jenny had told me that Mattie liked ham. I also had made, and iced, some fairy cakes for I remembered how she had made a beeline for the cakes on that first day. It was a beautiful day and I laid the patio table, thinking Mattie would enjoy eating outside.

'Yuk,' she said when she sampled my homemade bread, before grabbing another cake.

'Shall we go and see where Black Bear is?' I suggested when she made to eat a third.

'I won't come up with you,' Jenny announced, in a gradual move to vacate the central role.

I was alone with my new daughter and White Bear when we climbed the stairs to meet Black Bear. 'There he is!' Mattie immediately cried out, spotting him on top of the pink patchwork quilt that my auntie had made for her – although Black Bear was soon forgotten as she made for the window, fascinated to see the lamp-posts, rooftops and chimney pots on the other side of the street. She spent a few moments ensuring she could open the window because she would 'need air' and then worked out how to climb onto the high antique iron bed, huge in comparison to her own tiny one. She also checked that she could turn on the taps in the bathroom.

Mattie then went into her playroom where I had put a doll's wardrobe and dresser that my father had made for me one Christmas, many years ago, along with the little wooden cooker I had found in the shop down the road. But most of all, Mattie seemed to love the little desk, an old oak one full of crayons and pens. I had intended to move it out but fortunately, my mother urged me to keep it.

'Toby's downstairs!' Mattie suddenly cried out as she played with her dresser. 'I'm only teasing,' she then giggled and told me to go back downstairs and join Jenny because she wanted to make tea for us.

'Will she be OK up there on her own?' I asked Jenny when I came back down to the patio. I felt rather anxious.

'She'll be fine.' Jenny smiled.

Ten minutes later, Mattie appeared with a tray filled with toy cups and saucers and little toy packets of food and plastic fruit from a set I had bought in Woolworth's.

'I love my new mummy, but I love you, too,' I heard her tell Jenny as she poured us a pretend cup of tea. It was a first indicator of the emotional conflict she was to feel. Otherwise, Mattie seemed to be very much at home. *I* was the one who found it hard to relax. Was I saying the right things? Was I being affectionate enough? What was Jenny thinking?

Months later, when I asked Mattie what *she* had thought when she first saw her new home, she replied, 'I remember the cakes – I took some back for Ruby and Sam – and best of all I liked making tea.'

'I remember you came to breakfast one morning at Jenny's,' Mattie once recalled, 'and we had scrambled eggs and bacon, and you came to wake me up, and then we went to the bluebell wood.'

What I would have given, by then, to have had that Sunday

to myself, for I was physically and emotionally spent. But it was breakfast at Jenny's so I had dragged myself out of bed at 6am, and driven over to the farm cottage to wake Mattie up.

The smell of scrambled eggs and bacon met me when I arrived at the front door, 15 minutes late. As I entered the house, I heard the sound of giggles and someone running up the stairs.

'She was so excited about you coming early,' Jenny laughed. 'She's been awake since five and now she's gone back up to pretend that she's still asleep.' Jenny then added, 'Try to do her hair for her if you can, she won't let me any more!'

Mattie giggled as I pretended to rouse her in the tiny bed. She then said, 'Good morning, Mummy!' She was calling me Mummy a lot now, I thought, as I helped her dress. And I was both surprised and chuffed when she let me do her hair, which I tied into pigtails.

When we went down to breakfast, large plates of bacon and scrambled eggs awaited us, and a mug of steaming hot tea for me.

It was damp and drizzly when we set off, out on our own for the first time, headed for the bluebell wood, the first stop on our itinerary.

In the first ever photo I took of Mattie, she has on her little red cagoule, underneath which you can just see her light-blue, smocked summer dress and her pink wellies. And, of course, my silk scarf is wrapped around her neck. 'I want to look like you,' she had told me as we set out. So there she is in the photographs, scarf around her neck, standing in a sea of bluebells, at first looking coyly at the camera, and then her usual cheeky self as she sits on a tree-trunk looking like a pixie – just before she tells me she is fed up with having her photo taken.

'Do you remember anything about our trip to the bluebell wood?' I later asked her.

'Yes,' she replied, 'I remember you took photos of me and I didn't want to go far.'

'That's right,' I said. 'Why didn't you?'

'Because I had to walk back.'

I asked if she remembered two old ladies who came up to us as we were leaving. They had asked if she'd enjoyed the wood, and whether she knew that deer and foxes lived in it. Mattie had said that she thought there were only bluebells in the wood, but that she'd also heard the birds tweet. 'Yes, and they tweet even louder on Sundays, one of the ladies told you,' I reminded her.

I honestly would have preferred a return to Jenny's at that point, to have a quick cuppa and then leave, but I was bound to follow the itinerary, which meant a visit to an animal sanctuary that Mattie knew well. She seemed bored there so I suggested seeing the geese by the lake, confident they would re-engage her.

'I don't want to, they frighten me,' she said, sulkily, as we approached the lake. I couldn't understand why Mattie was no longer the fun-loving girl of the previous few days.

'There's nothing to be frightened of,' I said, shortly before letting out a scream as one of the geese came up and oinked at my behind.

'I want to go home,' Mattie scowled humourlessly. And on returning to the car, she refused to get in. 'I want Jenny to come and pick me up.'

I noticed, with a sudden shock, the tears rolling down her cheeks. I felt terrible. What had I done wrong? I spent a few minutes trying to coax her into the car but she stubbornly refused, accusing me of being a fibber and that if she got in the car I would not take her back to Jenny's. I quickly glanced around the car park: *what must everyone be thinking? It must look as though I'm trying to abduct her!*

'Come on,' I urged, 'if we don't hurry our lunch will get

cold.' Only when I told Mattie that I could not call Jenny because I did not have my mobile phone on me, did she finally climb into the car.

Mattie was silent the whole of the journey back, refusing to speak, whilst I drove on feeling like a child molester, dreading what Jenny would say.

Just as I feared, upon our return Mattie burst into tears and immediately rushed into Jenny's arms. I was frantic, trying to imagine what might have gone wrong whilst Mattie continued to ignore me throughout lunch.

'She's just overwhelmed,' explained Jenny, who hugged her tight. 'It's a lot of change for a little girl.'

A simple and obvious explanation. Why hadn't I realised? Perhaps, because I was feeling overwhelmed, too. I was nearly on the verge of tears myself, desperate to escape. But there were still three hours ahead of us.

'She's having one of her turns,' I heard Jenny say quietly to her husband, Jack, who had come in for lunch.

What did Jenny mean by 'one of her turns'? I began to panic. Was I being hoodwinked, somehow? Were social services just trying to lump me with a difficult child?

'How about a drive around the estate in the Land Rover after lunch,' Jack calmly suggested, and I felt a surge of relief now to have the rest of the day laid out. Little Ruby and Sam came along, too.

'Just ignore her if it happens in future,' Jack said in his gruff but kindly way as we all left the house. 'She's a good girl; she gets over things quickly.'

It had stopped raining and was fast becoming a lovely May day. I began to feel better. Mattie was feeling better too, it appeared, chattering and even smiling at me as we bumped around the estate, spotting hares and Canada geese and counting the steers against the gentle backdrop of the Downs...

'Mattie, do you remember the time when you didn't want me to drive you back to Jenny's?' I asked her, months later.

'Yes,' she replied.

'Why was that?'

'Because I loved Jenny more than you and I didn't know you then, but I love you both so much now.'

Later, during my introductions review session, the social services manager told me, 'You handled that very well.'

'Yes,' Jenny agreed. 'The worst thing would have been to give in to her – you were right not to call me and instead insist on bringing her home.'

'But I had no choice,' I laughed. 'I was telling the truth – I didn't have my mobile on me.'

I confirmed how well Mattie was getting on at her new nursery school. The teacher had told me how lovely she was. It was generally agreed that the introductions were going swimmingly and I sat there feeling on top of the world, until Toby burst my bubble.

'She's regressing in her speech,' he announced.

I recalled Toby mentioning this on the first morning that Mattie and I met. His statement had bothered me at the time: did she perhaps have some mental deficiency; was she not quite what she seemed?

'I'm probably over-analysing,' he then said, no doubt sensing my concern. But his comments still played on my mind and after the review session, I called my sister.

'It's quite normal,' Molly said, 'Poppy even does baby talk occasionally and she's nine.'

The play therapist, who was helping to resolve any issues Mattie might have prior to moving in, would later confirm that I had no need to worry about her speech regression. 'She's a sweetheart,' she told me.

Just three simple words, but how they made a difference!

Mattie was obviously a special child, but I still needed occasional confirmation of it.

Dear Beth,

I know you have another full day ahead of you, so I'll be somewhat brief. I just want to say how much I have enjoyed talking to you lately. If possible, all that has been going on in your life makes me feel even closer to you. I do hope you are feeling the same way. Initially, when I heard about the adoption, I was pleased for you but figured that there likely would be no space for me in your soon to change existence... Anyhow I think I was wrong. Somehow, I believe all these changes have strengthened things between us. I could be wrong but that is how I feel anyhow. I think I love you more than ever, and can see us all together somewhere living happily ever after...'

There were still six days of the introductions period remaining before Mattie would move into my home. Six more days of doing two or three trips back and forth, nursery runs, bath and bedtime sessions and making meals; six more days of outings – including tea at her new cousins' house and, the next day, with her new grandparents; six more days of Allie and Toby's phone calls and visits; six more days of practically living in someone else's home.

After years of work and the five-year plans that had previously dominated my career, I was now looking no further than the end of each day. I became focused on each departure time in the schedule, calculating in advance how long I had to go before I could retreat home with relief.

There was light at the end of the tunnel, however: Day 9, my day off.

e-mail,13 May 2005

Dear Mike,

…Here are a couple of photos for you… I do already miss Mattie a little and it is only 9.30! I have just put those books of yours in her cupboard. I'm sure her little collection will grow quite quickly and she is eager to join the library. I remember how exciting I used to find that… I do love talking to you about Mattie so am glad you are not bored ☺

With love (I am getting ready for my bike ride). You have really helped make all this so much more enjoyable for me…

The moment I woke up on Day 9, I knew it might be a difficult day for Mattie. She had seen her new mummy each day, without fail, for eight consecutive days. So, the evening before, I had left a little gift and card with Jenny so that Mattie would have something from me the next day. I also wondered whether to call her when I awoke, but in the end I did not, fearing a phone call might unsettle her. Truth be told, I did not really want to call. For *one* day, I wanted to retreat into my familiar nest, and I was looking forward to doing normal things.

Paradoxically, I was struck by how everything *was* going on as normal when I walked out onto the busy high street. Did those people walking up and down on their way to the shops or to work, see that there was something different about me now? Could they guess my news?

I spotted someone waving at me on the other side of the street. 'Hi, how's it going?' he asked, crossing over. He was the partner of one of the women with whom I had commuted.

We had crossed one another's paths recently whilst out on our mountain bikes and it was then I had told them my news. Liz had been especially interested and asked lots of questions.

'It's going really well,' I now replied. 'My new daughter will be moving in next week.'

'Better you than me,' he grinned. 'You must be feeling really nervous about it all.'

'No, not really, she's a lovely child… Maybe it'll give Liz ideas,' I added as an afterthought, semi-seriously.

'Oh no,' he replied, looking shocked 'I can't see her doing that… A puppy might be nice though,' he said, scuttling off.

I carried on down the high street, now anxious to make the most of every free hour of my 'holiday'. Even shopping in the supermarket seemed a treat. But I began to tire, and was tempted by the thought of my sun-lounger on the patio and the luxury of simply doing nothing. And although I enjoyed myself on my free day, from time to time I wondered what Mattie was up to, imagining her clutching at my scarf.

The next morning, when I went round to the cottage to pick up Mattie, Jenny said, 'She found it very unsettling yesterday. It was strange for her not having you around. She wouldn't let go of your scarf all day long.'

I felt a little guilty, for I had enjoyed my day off; I feared I had not missed Mattie sufficiently, although I was very anxious to see her little face and smile once again. But when she ran into the hallway to greet me, my heart dropped when I saw how she was dressed – and today of all days.

'I told Mattie the top and trousers were just perfect to meet her new Chinese cousins in.' Jenny laughed as, with dismay, I looked at the over-sized, black baggy trousers and maroon, mandarin-collared top that would not have seemed out of place in a Bruce Lee film. It was Mattie's hurt feelings I feared as I thought of the lovely clothes her cousins, no doubt, would be wearing when I took her round for tea that afternoon.

As soon as we got back to my house, I checked through one of the suitcases of clothes I had brought over from Jenny's. I was relieved to find, at the bottom, a nice pair of jeans.

'Jenny wanted me to wear these to meet my cousins,' Mattie protested, although she readily agreed to put the jeans on when I said they were more appropriate for riding her Barbie scooter.

How proud of her I was, as she rode down the road to Molly's house. This outing also gave Mattie a chance to have a good look at the town in which she was to live. Would we see anyone we knew, I wondered, excitedly. We soon bumped into a neighbour who lived opposite and who owned an antiquarian bookshop in town.

'Hello,' he said, looking really pleased. 'Is this your new daughter?'

I introduced them, and Mattie promptly asked him where he lived.

'I live over there in the pink house,' he replied. 'You must come over for tea.'

'We'd love to, but today we're on the way to my sister's so Mattie can meet her new cousins.'

'Oh, how exciting for you!' He beamed down at her.

We said our goodbyes and further down the high street, we were looking in the window of a toyshop when, 'I've got other cousins called Scarlet and Jude,' Mattie suddenly announced.

I looked at her with a feeling of shock, naively having imagined she would have already forgotten her old life, given that her future with me now looked so promising. The thought occurred to me as to whether she missed them. I did not dare ask.

'I remember thinking how sweet she was,' my sister Molly told me, later. 'Poppy was mesmerised by her and I noticed the immediate bond between her and Mei; it was uncanny.'

The two little girls hugged that afternoon as soon as they saw

133

one another, having already become acquainted at nursery school. But I noticed how Mattie's eyes took in at a glance Mei's beautiful, beaded T-shirt with a large cat on the front. She even refused to take off her body-warmer, although it was a warm afternoon. I made a mental note to get her a T-shirt like Mei's.

When Mattie openly admired the little pair of pink, plastic high-heeled play shoes that Mei was wearing, her new Uncle Tom asked if she would like some, too. 'Yes,' she replied, expectantly, at which he left and then returned with a huge pair of his muddy garden boots. Mattie looked at him askance for a moment and then burst out laughing.

'Uncle Tom's a big tease,' I laughed.

Tom came over to me at one point and said how interesting it was that Mattie spoke with a south London accent. I had been a bit surprised, too, but simply assumed her birth family had spoken that way. I thought it amusing that of all the things I had imagined before I met Mattie, I never wondered once about how she might sound!

Poppy later told me how shy Mattie had appeared on that day, and how at first she wanted to hide behind me. And I recalled then how her little face soon lit up at the sausages and chips and chicken kebabs for tea, and even more so at the chocolate and vanilla ice cream cones for dessert. And that, as the children ate, a pecking order began to take shape. At one point, Uncle Tom told Mei not to take more than one sausage at a time, whereupon Mattie seized her new cousin's hand and forced one of the sausages out. An amused Tom noted, in a low voice, that Mattie had obviously helped Jenny with the other children in the foster home.

After tea, Auntie Molly brought out some presents for Mattie: a large box of coloured Play-doh – Mattie exclaimed excitedly at the huge assortment of colours, saying they only had pink and green at Jenny's – a book about a lost rabbit, and a tiny cuddly rabbit to accompany it.

That night when Jenny greeted Mattie at the cottage door she told her, 'Your eyes are shining. You look so happy.'

It was good for me, too, to hear those words.

Jenny told Mattie to go and clean her teeth. She then handed me a box; inside was a little gold chain, engraved with the words 'Special Daughter' – a gift from Mattie's mother to her daughter on the occasion of her farewell party. 'Mattie broke it in anger, soon after she was given it,' Jenny said, 'but I managed to mend it. Keep it safe for her; I'm sure she'll appreciate it one day.'

'What do you remember about the day you first went to Auntie Molly's for tea?' I later asked Mattie.

'I remember that Scooby and Doo [the dogs] kept walking around me,' she said, 'and I remember the broccoli had stalks on it.'

I told her *my* main recollection was when I looked over at her standing on the patio, alone for a moment, taking it all in. 'Then you looked up at me and smiled, and came to stand near me.' It was just like when my cat Tibbles came and curled around my legs, I remember thinking at the time. 'And Uncle Tom took the *first* photo of us together, that day,' I said.

It's one of my favourite photos. In it, Mattie is wearing orange hair-bobbles with dalmation dogs on them. And you can see the little dimples in her cheeks as she smiles, and her mauve body-warmer is covered with chocolate ice cream stains.

e-mail, May 2005

Dear Beth,

...I looked again at the photos you sent me and enjoyed them

once more. What a lovely child. And what a lovely mum, as well. In one, Mattie is looking toward the camera, and in the other she has her eyes cast toward her new mummy. I don't know whether you noticed it or not, but it was very sweet. Take a look if you have time later. You both appear very happy...

Later, as I looked back and reflected on those two long weeks of introductions, I at times forgot how often I felt like a spare part, how uncomfortable I felt intruding in someone else's home. And how guilty I sometimes felt at taking Mattie away. I forgot, too, that at the same time that I was becoming a new mummy, I was also slowly losing my old self, losing my identity as 'me'. I was taken by surprise when Jenny once asked how I was faring. Was I a player in all of this, too? Wasn't it all about this little girl? Of course, I told Jenny that I was fine.

I remember how I would sit down in the farmhouse kitchen, where the kettle was always on the boil, and be waited on for half-an-hour. I remember the fish pie Jenny served at lunchtime, the slice of iced cake and the boiled egg and soldiers for tea. And I remember how her husband, Jack, would pop in unexpectedly to give me some rhubarb or a pheasant, or simply pass the day. At those times, I could simply let go for a moment in what was, in truth, an exhausting and emotionally draining two weeks.

'You'll miss Mattie after all this time, won't you?' I had asked Jenny at the introductions planning meeting. But she had simply brushed away my comment with a laugh. *I expect she's used to it,* I thought – and wasn't it her job?

It was after a conversation with my social worker, Allie, that I gave Jenny more consideration. 'Some time should be allowed for grieving,' Allie had said. It was not Mattie she was talking about, but Jenny. It was one of Allie's bugbears that foster parents should be given time to get over their loss, too.

For Mattie, a delightful, fun-loving and affectionate little girl, had lived with Jenny for more than two years.

I recall how Jenny began to snap a little at Mattie towards the end of the introductions, and how she seemed less enamoured at my traipsing through her house. 'Doesn't it seem a long time to you?' she asked. 'It's far longer than normal; I think they're being unfair on you…and Mattie's been with me too long, more than is fair on her.'

Mattie's behaviour – generally excellent – was becoming more challenging as she sometimes tried to play Jenny and me off against one other. 'There are so many changes,' Jenny said. 'It's a bewildering time for her. She's finding it difficult managing her loyalties.' She explained how especially difficult the previous few months had been for Mattie, due to the birth mother rarely attending the scheduled contact sessions with her children: 'Is it a Mummy day today?' Mattie used to ask, and, 'Is Mummy going to come today?' Whenever the birth mother didn't turn up, Jenny had suggested that Mattie telephone her instead, but she would say, 'The battery's gone in Mummy's phone so we can't.'

'I was hoping Jenny could be my mummy forever,' Mattie once told me. And only later, when I had some distance from it, could I look back and wonder how Mattie – such an engaging child, full of vitality and always with a big smile – must have felt during those two weeks of introductions. I was so overwhelmed myself, I just assumed she was taking it all in her stride. But one morning, Jenny mentioned to me that she again had shown Mattie the photo of her new cousin Mei, inserted in the little photo album I had given her. Mei is lying down on the sun-lounger in my garden and laughing up at the camera. 'It always brings a smile to Mattie's face,' Jenny said. 'I bring it out now and then when it all gets a bit much for her.'

Jenny's words took me aback, for Mattie always appeared so

happy to me. But how *must* Mattie really have felt sitting opposite me – a near stranger – at meal-times; being taken to nursery school by me; or accompanying me on some little trip? How did she feel being fed and bathed by me? What did she think seeing her little friends at her nursery school for the last time – the school she had been attending since she was nine months old? And how did Mattie feel, saying goodbye to the farmhands, especially old George at the dairy shed who had named a calf after her and who popped a bottle of fresh milk into my hand as he bade her farewell. Or seeing her new nana and granddad for the first time?

We bumped into them unexpectedly, the day before our scheduled meeting; they were on their way to visit Molly and had let themselves into my house to drop something off. Mattie giggled when she saw them in the hallway, so I assumed she was excited – what child would not be to have such a lovely new granddad and nana?

The next day, Mattie and Dad were sitting together on the garden bench; it reminded me of the scene in *The Godfather*, the one in which Marlon Brando is playing with his grandchild. 'You'd think she'd known him forever,' Mum said, as we watched them through the kitchen window. 'Mattie has already brought some joy into our lives, and she's bringing Dad out of himself, too.' We had been discussing my brother's illness, and how difficult a time it had been for them dealing with the aftermath of his stroke. Later, Mattie helped Granddad wash the car and then she helped Nana to bring in the washing, noting to me afterwards how Nana always left a few clothes pegs on the line.

Years later, when I spoke of that afternoon in terms of it being their first meeting, Mattie reminded me of that initial impromptu meeting in my hallway. 'I was scared,' she said. 'I never saw them before.'

'It's all gone really well,' I told the social workers gathered at the final review session, the day before Mattie was to move in.

Everyone agreed, and Jenny said that Mattie had particularly enjoyed spending a whole day with me, on our own, at my home. 'She mentioned that you hoovered the room; she liked that,' Jenny chuckled.

Everyone laughed and I felt myself go red.

'I think she liked it because it made you seem more *ordinary*,' Jenny explained.

The manager confirmed that I was to pick Mattie up from her nursery school later that morning, make her some lunch and then take her to Jenny's for a farewell party and her last night in her foster home. The next morning, at 9am, I would collect Mattie – and the last of her toys – and bring her to her *new* home.

'You do, of course, need to tell us if there are any significant changes in your life over the next few months,' the manager said.

'What's your definition of 'significant'?' I asked wearily, at which everyone laughed.

Allie came by that afternoon, just before we left to take Mattie to the farewell party. 'I can't believe it,' she said, smiling in disbelief. 'You in your new role as Mum. You were always so much the career woman before…You two look so natural together.'

And it did seem very natural. Allie and I chatted on until I glanced at the oven clock and realised with horror that Mattie and I were going to be late.

As we all dashed out of the door, me carrying the large flowering fuchsia that Mattie had chosen as a farewell present for Jenny, Allie called out, 'You might even think about having another!'

At the farm cottage, Jenny quickly ushered Mattie in as I uttered an apology for being late. I was the unwanted one now

– unwanted by both Mattie and Jenny, who were obviously looking forward to the party and their final hours together. The only evidence I had that the farewell party had occurred was a piece of cake Mattie handed me the next day. When I asked about the party, a while later, all she said was, 'I had a watch and lots of cards and one was from Paolo.'

On the morning Mattie moved out of her foster home, I remember Jenny coming out of the farm cottage as soon as my car drew up. She was carrying the few remaining toys from Mattie's bedroom (henceforth to be occupied by Ruby), and a bag of Mattie's clothes from the day before, which she had washed and pressed. But there was no sign of Mattie and I began to feel anxious. Jenny went into the cottage to fetch her.

A few minutes later, they both came out smiling and looking relaxed, I thought. *I* felt very tense. Jenny told me that her daughter, Sam, was going to wave goodbye, too, but from afar, as she had been crying in the kitchen all morning. It was only then that I realised how attached Jenny's daughter was to Mattie. (Sam often helped with the cooking, Mattie later told me.)

As I started up the car and looked around to wave goodbye, it was only then that I saw the tears in Jenny's eyes and the sadness on her face, as she stood close by the car. I looked around at Mattie then, sitting silently in the back seat. I saw that she, too, was wiping a tear from her eye. If I had not looked around at that moment, I never would have known.

Soon, Mattie and I were driving off, past where Toby had stood next to his car on that first day of introductions, to the spot where the bluebells began to line the lane.

'Jack said he would wave goodbye from the bedroom,' Mattie called out suddenly, and I slowed the car down for her to look round. 'There he is!' she exclaimed, and she waved at him whilst wiping away another tear from her cheek.

Soon, it was only possible to see the chimney pots of the cottage, until they, too, disappeared.

The end of Introductions may feel like the end of the process. Actually it is just the beginning.

Preparation Course notes

Mattie wore a white dress, the day she moved in. There she is in the photo I took, lying on the sun-lounger, looking up at me with that big, joyful smile on her face. She is wearing her best dress – a beautiful one trimmed with broderie anglaise – and a coloured bead necklace and the new Barbie watch that Jenny and Jack gave her at her farewell party. Her hair is in pigtails – or pinkies as she calls them – tied with lime-green hair bobbles with dairy cows on them, and behind her is the blue of the catmint blossom.

On that first full day together as mother and daughter, I felt a mixture of elation and relief. As I watched Mattie lying on the sun-lounger, chasing Tibbles around the garden, eating her tea or busying herself with her dolls, I marvelled at the fact that she was finally here. The adoption process, which I had initiated four years earlier, was much closer to completion. Done was the hectic to-ing and fro-ing of the introductions period. At last, Mattie and I were allowed to behave like a normal family.

That evening, as planned, I rang Jenny to inform her that Mattie was doing well, had gone to bed at seven – her usual time – that she was already sound asleep and that things could not have gone better.

'Jenny's having a shower,' Jack said, when he finally picked up the phone, adding that he was relieved to know things had

141

gone OK. 'You'll find you'll have no problems with her,' he told me, 'and it's not often she has a bad night.'

'We look forward to seeing you both for tea next month,' I said, before replacing the receiver.

I rang Mike later. Our e-mails, by this point, had just about stopped; I knew Mike had loved receiving them but there was now so much going on in my life that it felt like an effort even to log on. Besides, we were by now speaking to each other on the telephone at least twice a day. Mike, however, said he would continue to send an e-mail now and then, to read when I found the time.

e-mail, 17 May 2005

Dear Beth,

I hope everyone in your household had a long and restful sleep. It sounds like yesterday went very well. And thanks, so much, for keeping me abreast of it all. I know it was exhausting, but probably a bit exhilarating, too… I have thought of you so many times the last few days. Please, do enjoy your day and your time with little Mattie.

On her first day waking up in her new home, Mattie came down to my bedroom and merrily chimed, 'Good morning, Mummy!' She straightaway climbed into my bed and cuddled up to me. It was just before six and she seemed totally at home. I felt very happy. We chatted for a while and Mattie didn't mention Jenny at all; I felt relieved that she didn't appear to be missing her foster mother. She soon complained of being hungry, though, and insisted that we get up for breakfast. After I made her a boiled egg and soldiers, we went up to her bedroom where she washed her hands and face and cleaned her teeth. I felt very motherly, and took great delight in helping her into the pretty new top and leggings I had bought in the children's shop down the road. I then brushed her hair and fastened a pretty slide in it.

Later that morning, Mattie and I went out to the same children's farm we had already visited once during introductions. But this time, I took photos. Lots of photos.

There she is, standing in front of a large pigpen, laughing at the camera in her new pair of cool-looking sunglasses. She looks quite a different girl to the Mattie in outsized clothes whom I took to nursery school during introductions.

The next morning, a nursery school day, I thought how adorable Mattie looked in her new pleated skirt and spotted blouse, with her hair neatly tied back into pigtails. You could tell that she was proud of herself. It was a special occasion for both of us – the first time I was taking her to school from her new home. At the same time, I felt slightly apprehensive because *this time*, I was totally on my own.

Upon our arrival, the first thing Mattie did was to seek out her cousin Mei and give her a hug after which, like two little sumo wrestlers, they took turns lifting one another up. This was to become part of their morning ritual. I then kissed Mattie goodbye. Just like on those mornings during the introductions period, Mattie never looked back once we had said goodbye.

When I left the nursery, shutting the heavy, wooden doors behind me, I was surprised by the sudden wave of loneliness that washed over me. My first instinct was to ring Mike but, I calculated, it was only three in the morning in Texas and I thought better of it. My friend James lived close by; we did not see much of one another nowadays but as it might be his day off, I decided to pop in for a chat.

James's sister, Denise, greeted me on the doorstep. She was

down for the weekend, she told me, welcoming me into the tiny sitting room where they were in the middle of eating a late breakfast of homemade bread and strawberry jam.

'You *do*, you look radiant,' Denise told me.

I sat down, hardly able to contain myself. 'I've just dropped Mattie off at nursery and I had to come and talk to someone,' I said, as James handed me a large mug of tea. 'Things couldn't be better.' I told them that Mattie had been with me two days now and was sleeping well and eating her meals. 'She's settled in beautifully and seems so happy.'

And it wasn't *only* me who was looking radiant these days, I thought. Mattie too, seemed to have a glow, at times acting like a moonstruck lover. She had taken to writing 'Mummy' and 'Mattie' on her drawings, which she then fastened with Sellotape to her bedroom and bathroom walls. She began to place photos of Mummy around her room, too. One in particular she liked, had pointed it out to me upon seeing it in my study: I am standing, arms folded, in a deep green wood full of bluebells. How would I have felt if someone had told me when that picture was taken, just before I delayed the adoption process, that three years later my daughter would be hanging that photo above her bed? And at night-time, Mattie would always ensure I had a little pretend meal left beside my bed on a red lacquer tray I had given her. It was the last thing she did as part of her going-to-bed ritual, along with drawing another picture with the words 'Mummy' and 'Mattie' written on it, which she would leave on my bed.

I felt like a queen bee in James' sitting room that morning, regaling them with my good news, feeling rather pleased with myself.

'It makes me think of doing something like that myself,' Denise said to me, as I babbled on like the four-year-old child I was adopting.

144

'Why not?' I gave her a few encouraging words of advice as James looked on, grinning.

Later, stepping out of their sitting room straight into the street, I again felt that strange wave of loneliness flood over me. I decided to walk the long way back, passing near the nursery where Mattie was no doubt drawing more pictures for Mummy. I glanced down at my watch and saw that it was already approaching eleven. Allie and Toby both had advised that for a while, Mattie should attend nursery mornings only and I only had an hour to go before picking her up. I wondered what we should do after lunch.

I walked through the town gardens. The bulbs were out in full bloom, their colours a wild frenzy against the duller hues of the castle above. I passed by the Judas trees where some toddlers were playing, took the exit by the auction rooms, and then climbed one of the narrow alleyways that led up to the high street where, I noticed, they were preparing for the lunchtime rush in the Turkish takeaway.

Most adopted children form attachments to their adoptive mother. This is a kind of emotional dependence, which may seem crucial to their survival. Bonding, on the other hand, may not be so easily achieved...

The Primal Wound

Social workers' home visits were to continue until such time as the adoption order was granted, and Toby, as Mattie's social worker, was scheduled to come first.

When we had attempted to find a mutually convenient time the week before, I protested that Toby's suggestion would conflict with Mattie's lunch. 'That's OK,' he replied, casually, 'it'll be good to see how she's getting on with her eating.'

But Mattie fidgeted a great deal during her meals – something Jenny had warned me about – and, largely unable to use a knife and fork, she often ate with her hands (something I had not expected). During each meal time, as a consequence, the floor around her feet was splattered with food. I even caught Mattie, on occasion, letting drop a vegetable she didn't like – in the same way she would sometimes pour her glass of water into the sink when I wasn't looking (I would get her to drink her water in the end by having a competition to see who could drink the fastest!). So I feared that Toby's presence might be disruptive and that any resultant misbehaviour on Mattie's part might reflect poorly on my parenting abilities. Above all, I wanted everything to appear *normal*.

So I decided to break the routine and bring forward lunchtime, planning it carefully so that by the time of Toby's arrival I would be clearing away the dishes. But after only three months away from the office, I had already forgotten that the best plans allow for the unexpected. I failed to anticipate that Toby, who was usually late, might turn up early.

Damn! I thought as I headed for the front door, 15 minutes before our agreed time.

'I just need to take some bread out of the oven,' I announced, rather flustered, as I re-entered the kitchen, Toby on my heels. Now this should impress him, I decided with satisfaction, as I put two crusty loaves onto the cooling rack, the aroma of homemade bread immediately filling the room. But Toby, plainly uninterested in my baking efforts, had caught sight of Mattie eating outdoors and was already stepping out onto the patio.

She was seated at the small, cast-iron garden table in the

shade of a large sun umbrella, wearing the brightly coloured plastic apron she had brought with her from Jenny's.

'Hello Mattie,' Toby said.

Mattie actually seemed pleased to see him and I breathed a sigh of relief. *Now, please sit still and stop fidgeting whilst you finish your lunch,* I silently pleaded, as I watched them from the kitchen. I was dismayed by the dull, floppy appearance of some French beans that lay languidly on Mattie's plastic 'Princess' plate, but Mattie's table manners, I noted proudly, were much improved. And in contrast to the previous occasions I had seen Mattie in Toby's presence – when she would either babble incessantly or simply ignore him – my new daughter chattered, ate and laughed naturally, just like any other four-year-old. Indeed, with only a little coaxing on my part she even finished her beans and ate her fresh fruit dessert – my insistence, I decided, befitted a firm but fair mum.

I joined them at the table and Mattie immediately announced, 'I love you, Mummy'. She then jumped onto my lap and gave me a big hug and a loud kiss on the cheek. As she did so, I noticed, she cast a triumphant look in the direction of her social worker. Though my cookery skills that day might have suffered some schoolgirl errors, my new daughter's sales skills were the work of a professional. I beamed at Toby, who sat there smiling against the backdrop of my neighbour Cicely's hanging hydrangea.

'I can see she's happy – you can tell it immediately,' Toby said to me in a low voice, 'so there's no need for me to stay long.' He then stood up and said, enthusiastically, 'But I *would* like to go up to your bedroom, Mattie, before I go. Can I see it again, this time with all your toys in it?'

'Actually, I asked Jenny about the bedroom,' I nervously informed Toby, 'and she was adamant Mattie would prefer the bedroom in the attic.'

147

'Oh really?' he said, a look of surprise on his face.

'And she's been fine up there, but if there are any problems later I can always set up a bed in the study next to my bedroom,' I added, anxiously.

'OK.' Toby nodded, to my relief.

Mattie then proceeded, gleefully, to lead Toby into the house and up the stairs. I, all the while, kept a guilty distance behind them – guilty not only because of the location of Mattie's bedroom but because I was thinking, too, of the pile of old toys stashed away in the basement.

In my eyes, Mattie was my four-year-old *newborn* and I wanted her on her own – not in the company of all those playthings I first had caught sight of in Toby's video back in February. The memories associated with her old toys were one thing, but there was a practical issue, too: where would they all go? How I had groaned inwardly, each morning I had arrived during introductions, to see yet another mound of cuddly toys, another pile of books, another stack of dolls waiting for me outside the farm cottage. I dared not refuse them, recalling how disparagingly Jenny had spoken of another adoptive couple who left all their child's toys behind; *and*, I had gathered from Jenny, many of these toys she herself had bought for Mattie from charity shops. So I concocted my own strategy. Back home, after sorting them, I carried a sizeable selection up to Mattie's room whilst the rest, bagged like a dead body, I hauled down to the basement boiler room and covered with a large shroud-like blanket.

'She seems to have settled in well up here,' Toby said as he looked around the room, making no reference to the toy pruning that had taken place. 'Just try not to make too many rules for her,' he added, not for the first time, as we made our way back down the stairs.

'What are you doing?' Mattie later asked Toby, when she saw him writing on the back of his hand.

'I'm writing down the mileage so I know how far I've travelled today,' he replied. 'I'll be going now. I'm glad to see you've settled in so well, Mattie, and I'll be back to see you in two weeks.' Toby then turned to me and asked about the play therapist and I said she was due the following day. 'The summer hols will be a good opportunity for you to get to know one another better and to bond,' he added, as we saw him out.

What are you talking about? I felt like saying to him. *Mattie and I have bonded already. What more is there to know about her? What more is there to it?*

One week after Mattie moved in, I had no idea that I was enjoying the honeymoon phase of this adoption or, for that matter, that I was in a honeymoon phase at all. I had somehow forgotten Allie's warning of a time during which the child might be compliant, careful to be on their best behaviour – ensuring, above all, that they will not be sent back. I was therefore unaware that I was being wooed by my attentive, thoughtful and considerate child. What's more, she was obviously very bright, very pretty and impeccably well-behaved. The whole thing seemed like a piece of cake.

Even if I *had* recalled Allie's words of warning, I doubt I would have felt they applied to me. Mattie seemed almost the model child: one who went to bed on time and had an undisrupted sleep (there had not even been any bedwetting). And she was a child who enjoyed helping around the house – wanting to wash the dishes, clean and help me cook. She even exhibited the sense of humour most women require from a mate. Mattie was my secretary, too, dashing to answer the phone, engaging the caller in conversation whilst I completed some task in the kitchen – though, granted, she *would* get upset if I got to the telephone first. And it *was* true, she displayed some attention-seeking behaviour if I talked on the phone, in her view, for too long. But otherwise, I hardly heard her complain. Only her chatter and laughter and her beautiful four-year-old's singing voice filled the house.

Later on, I would recall Allie telling me that being on one's best behaviour was tiring, that it would not last forever and that as a child grew in confidence they might begin to act out. 'That's when they might start to test you,' she said, 'to see if you still love them no matter what they do.' But during our honeymoon, and in the first glow of motherhood, I would almost certainly have discounted her words. Allie, surely, was talking about those difficult children with behavioural problems, those other children about whom we had spoken on the prep course and during the home visits. Mattie – a seemingly perfectly adjusted child who had benefited from a stable and loving foster home – was, I was certain, not the typical child from care. She was happy, loving and confident – and, moreover, very resilient.

It never dawned on me that, unfamiliar as both of us were with our new roles, we were in fact playing the part of affectionate yet distant relatives paying an extended visit – careful of our ps and qs.

If Mattie was the compliant daughter, I was on my best behaviour, too. I was the eager-to-please Mum, re-learning dishes I had not made since school cookery lessons as I strove to improve and increase my repertoire in a constant bid for her approval. I was the over-the-moon Mum when Mattie deigned to nod her approval after trying a new dish. I was the deflated Mum, crestfallen if I made the gross error of adding salt to her scrambled egg. And I was the earth mother I once vowed I would never be – for here I was making homemade bread, cake and biscuits, and knitting a sweater. I was the woman who could do it all, even finding time to complete a short story about my recent trip to south Texas, which I *somehow* fitted in, helped no doubt by my obsession with routine.

'Adopted children thrive on routine and consistency,' Allie had frequently told me. Now, I realised, I thrived on them, too. I became focused on the kitchen clock, constantly darting glances at it whilst rigorously adhering to the timings of those routines: morning snack around 10.30am; lunch no later than noon; afternoon snack at 3pm; tea at 5; bathtime at 6; story no later than 6.45; bedtime at 7. The whole thing was a doddle, I thought, and I scoffed as I recalled Toby's words about the summer holidays and bonding. There was no doubt in my mind that my new daughter and I had attached beautifully.

But 'attachment' – a term often used in the same breath as 'bonding' – was relatively straightforward, I would discover later, when I sought out my copy of *A Primal Wound*. 'Bonding' was not.

Bonding, in reality, had just begun.

'She's grieving,' my daughter's play therapist announced, following their session together.

I was just taking a tray of homemade hot cross buns out of the oven, thinking how nice it had been to have an hour to myself, when Fiona uttered those dreadful words.

Grieving? I could hardly believe my ears.

'Mmm, they smell good,' Fiona said as I put the buns on the cooling tray.

Grieving? I felt as though my whole world had come to an end.

'I'm delighted,' Fiona added quickly, catching my expression. 'When I visited her at her foster home, she displayed no signs of sadness at the prospect of leaving. That isn't normal for a child who's spent more than two years in a very stable environment. I was concerned she might have been in denial.'

I had a sudden flashback then to something Allie had once said: 'I've been told Mattie's very excited about her adoption and can't wait to move in,' she had smiled encouragingly. How delighted I was at hearing her words – I was accepted already. But afterwards, I recalled how excited *I* was as a child at the prospect of moving from Cardiff to the Midlands, and how short-lived that had been.

'It's a very good sign,' Fiona said. 'And certainly nothing to be concerned about,' she emphasised, picking up on my disquiet.

'So it *is* quite normal then?'

'Yes, she's grieving normally,' this kindly, soft and cuddly-looking woman of generous proportions reassured me. 'There's nothing to be worried about.'

But how could I not have picked up on it myself? I fretted. I looked at my little daughter as she entered the kitchen, her little face smiling up at me, and I felt rejected. All the while Mattie had been living with me, she was grieving for someone else! And not only that, the cat was out of the bag – what would Toby and Allie say when they heard the news from the play therapist?

When Toby had suggested that Mattie have play therapy, to help with her feelings and apprehension about separating from her foster carers and commencing a new life, I had been surprised. *This happy, confident child needs a play therapist? Come on!*

'He's singling you out again as a single parent,' Jenny had scoffed at the time.

But my sister, Molly, though voicing some surprise at my news – play therapy was expensive, she said, and therefore usually only offered to disturbed children – advised, 'If I were you, I'd make the most of it; if there's any issue that might need to be resolved, that can only be good for her – and good for you, too.'

Whether play therapy was to be good for Mattie was not uppermost on my mind when Fiona had arrived for the first session at my home; all I was focused on was the thought of a glorious hour to myself; and for Mattie – about whom I sometimes felt guilty at not being able to offer a gaggle of siblings as companions – an ideal playmate for the afternoon.

'She's settled in so well,' I had told Fiona earlier, 'and she's hardly mentioned Jenny, apart from the occasional reference.'

But I, seemingly, had forgotten not only about bonding, but the grieving process, too. Gone from my memory was that session on abandonment and loss that we'd covered during the prep course, more than two years earlier. I had forgotten, too, my sister's warning that I must be prepared for the child's sadness when they first moved in, how they might weep inconsolably for their foster carer at night. But that was what foxed me: Mattie had not cried or shown any distress.

Fiona and I continued our discussion in the kitchen whilst I gave Mattie a snack. 'Children often get hungry following a session,' Fiona acknowledged with a smile. 'We played a lot with the babies and her nurturing skills are excellent,' she informed me. 'If children have good nurturing skills there are unlikely to be any real issues later. I don't think we should need any more than three or four more sessions.'

Fiona then laughed out loud to hear Mattie call me a 'billy billy' when I dropped something on the floor. 'That's one of the terms we've made up,' I explained, as Mattie and I laughed, too. 'A "billy billy" is even sillier than a silly billy. It's like we have our own language.'

'That's good,' Fiona said, still laughing, as Mattie now pulled a face.

'I often forget that she's only four; she's so mature in some ways,' I said.

'Yes, she is. But never forget her real age,' she advised. 'That's essential... And how are *you*?'

It was a question that took me by surprise – much in the same way as Jenny's identical question took me by surprise

153

during the introductions period. And just like that surreal introductions fortnight, seemingly in the dim and distant past – although in reality ended only a week ago – I felt strangely detached. Why was Fiona asking after *me* – was it not Mattie on whom she should be focusing?

'I'm fine,' I replied, not daring to admit how much I welcomed the hour's respite. And I refrained, too, from telling her that for the first time in my life I often felt as though things were out of control – my thoughts darting off in a dozen different directions at once, always at the beck and call of this demanding, inquisitive and very active child.

'She'll keep you busy,' I remembered Toby saying after we watched his video back in February; and it had soon become apparent that Mattie was not a child who enjoyed an hour on her own, colouring. Worse still, she had taken to following me round the house of late, even calling for me frantically if she did not know immediately where I was (so going to the loo provided no break for me either!).

It recently dawned on me that I was finding it difficult to relax, at times in a state of near panic. I was constantly planning the day ahead, and the day after that, and it was not only activities for Mattie I was planning but the day's menus, too, though often, when we returned from the supermarket, I would discover I had not bought the right things. And everything we did together took an age, so the only way I found to manage time was to work out how long it would have taken me in my old life, and then multiply it by three.

'It's all going really well,' I said, as I accompanied Fiona to the door.

'Sometimes the play therapy brings out feelings which might result in some acting out later, or she might have a disturbed night,' she warned me.

I picked Mattie up and we saw Fiona off. I felt as though we were two castaways as we waved her off into the distance.

e-mail, May 2005

Dear Beth,

...I know things will only get easier with time. In a few weeks both of you will be old hands together. It sounds like you are making the transition to a new home a smooth and loving one for Mattie. This is so very important for a little one who has unfairly received some hard knocks from life. Things are looking good for her now, I am happy to say. It must have been nice for you to have come to bed and found the little note and a late night snack. What a sweet and thoughtful child...

I groaned as I looked at the clock on my bedside table. It was only 5am when Mattie tumbled into my bed for her usual morning chat, cuddle and tickle. She had recently asked me to tickle her under her chin and on the back of her neck. It made her happy, she said, no one ever tickled her before she came to live with me. But still groggy, I knew that '5am' was not what Jenny had put in her notes. This was different. She clearly stated that Mattie awoke 'between 6.30am and 7am.' I moaned inwardly and thought that at least I didn't have a commute ahead of me, though I was already exhausted at the prospect of another long day ahead.

This morning, my new daughter did not shout out her usual 'Good morning, Mummy!' to awaken me. There was no chatter, no request for a tickle, no insistence that I get out of bed to prepare breakfast. All I heard was the faint drone of traffic outside as Mattie curled up quietly in my arms. It was still dark in the bedroom, only a glimmer of early morning sun peeping in around the sides of the blinds as I lay there, hoping to enjoy my warm bed for a few minutes longer. She was so quiet, I assumed that she had gone back to sleep.

After a short while, I raised myself to look down at her. I could see that she still had her eyes open, but that her face was turned away. That's strange, I thought, Mattie always complained about that. 'I like to see your face,' she would say, putting her hand on my chin to turn it round to hers.

'Are you OK?' I asked, wondering if she might be ill. But she remained motionless and said not a word.

Only when I raised myself still further, did I see the tears sliding silently down Mattie's cheeks.

'Are you sad about something?' I asked, anxiously.

She nodded her head.

'Did something make you sad at nursery school?'

She shook her head.

'So what are you sad about?' I asked, gently, but she remained silent. 'You can always tell me if something makes you sad, I won't mind, whatever it is.'

'I miss Jenny,' she said, and then began to cry out loud.

It was five minutes past five in the morning, and never had I felt so desolate. I tried to comfort her but I was dumbstruck: Mattie seemed so self-possessed, always with a happy smile on her face – and shouldn't the play therapy sessions have sorted out her issues to do with grief? I racked my brains, as I lay there, certain it must be my fault that she was missing her foster mother still. Her words had felt like a kick in the stomach to me. They were frightening. This child lying by my side might be living with me against her wishes. Mattie continued to sob.

I hadn't denied her her links with the past, I thought, my mind now in overdrive. So many times, we had gone through her photos: Mattie in the policeman's hat; Mattie splashing about in the paddling pool; Mattie playing in the mud in the farmyard; Mattie in her little wellies on the shingle beach. So often, she had shown me those photos – bittersweet for me because I had missed out on her as a two- or three-year-old. And bittersweet because of the poignancy of that big smile and of her over-sized clothes, of the little smiling faces of her playmates who months – maybe even years – before had moved on to their own new mummies and daddies. Perhaps Mattie had sensed my occasional irritation at the constant harking back to her past, my envy of Jenny who had been the one to share in those years, not me? *But surely, I haven't revealed my feelings?* I thought.

Outside the bedroom, the sun continued its rise on a world that seemed far removed from the grieving inside.

Mattie had a beautiful bedroom and playroom, even her own bathroom, I reasoned, as I compared my house to Jenny's. What's more, she was already enjoying a social life that she could never have dreamed of a month before. And what about her lovely new Auntie Molly and Uncle Tom, her new cousins, and the fact that for the first time in her life she had a granddad…?

But this wasn't a farm, I thought, as I lay there feeling depressed. There were no eggs to collect here, no horses to feed cow parsley to, no fellow foster children with whom to eat cornflakes in the morning, and to play with. There was no Jack for her to tell off for smoking his pipe, or to accompany on his tractor… Above all, there was no Jenny: Jenny who had cuddled her, bandaged up her scraped knees, tucked her into bed; Jenny who to all intents and purposes had been her mother. My new daughter was missing her mother…and, I realised, I was merely a stranger. Was her attachment to Jenny too strong to make the break?

As I lay there feeling rejected, I wondered whether Mattie wanted to go back to her old home. I looked down at her little face and noted with relief that she was no longer crying.

'I want to phone Jenny,' she announced.

'You'll be seeing her soon; they're coming over for tea in a few weeks,' I replied, now alarmed at the thought – the last thing I wanted was for Jenny to know that my daughter wanted *her*, not me. Not least, if Toby and Allie knew, they might over-analyse the situation and – who knows?

'I want to phone her now,' Mattie persisted. But almost immediately she complained of being hungry.

That's a good sign, I decided, and suggested we get up for breakfast. *It must have just been a momentary feeling of sadness she's experienced – the cry's done her good.* But nothing could have prepared me for witnessing my new daughter's grieving firsthand.

I still felt shaken as I buttered her toast in the kitchen downstairs.

'Are you all right, Mummy?' Mattie asked as she always did, in the early months, whenever she found me deep in thought.

'Yes, I'm fine,' I replied, 'I was just wondering what you wanted on your toast.'

Later that night, I thought with satisfaction how smoothly the rest of the day had passed, and how Mattie seemed once again to be her normal self. I fell into bed with relief at the thought of having some time just for me. But as I put my head on the pillow and lay there in the dark, I realised it would only be a few hours before Mattie would once again awaken me from my sleep.

'She moved in two weeks ago,' I told my friend, Cindy, whom I ran into outside my house, after dropping Mattie off at nursery.

'Yes, I know,' Cindy replied. 'I bumped into Molly in town last week and we had a chat. She said how well it's going for you both.'

The last time I had seen Cindy was three months ago. I had

popped in on her to give an adoption update, during a brief respite from rushing around local primary schools to secure a place for Mattie.

I had to admit now to feeling a little hurt that Cindy hadn't been in touch since – hard to believe that her name was one of those entered by my social worker on my support network diagram.

'Would you like to come in for a drink?' I suggested, though I would have preferred an invitation from her, just to have a break from my own four walls.

'I'd love to,' Cindy said.

As I later brought a couple of glasses of elderflower cordial out onto the patio, Cindy exclaimed, 'Gosh, Mattie's going to be doing three full days at nursery. Lucia only did a couple of half-days when she was little.'

'Well, Mattie seems to have settled in well – and she was anyway doing three full days all the time she was at her foster mother's,' I replied, on the defensive. 'Besides it's good for Mattie: she's got the company of other children and she needs the stimulation.'

'So how often does she see her mother?' Cindy asked.

'Not at all, at the moment, but her social worker wants them to meet once a year.'

'Only once a year!' Cindy looked aghast.

'Her mother often didn't turn up to their contact sessions,' I explained, 'and it was upsetting for Mattie...' But all the while I was babbling on, I thought, *What a cheek! What does Cindy know about Mattie's background – or about adoption at all, for that matter?* And why was I even discussing Mattie's business with someone who, at the end of the day, I realised, was only an acquaintance.

Cindy then launched into a discussion of her own problems and I suddenly felt depressed; and bothered, too, when I glanced at my watch and realised we had been talking for over an hour. Mattie was due out of nursery in 45 minutes – didn't it occur to her that this was my precious time alone?

I was finally seeing Cindy out when she caught sight of Mattie in a series of photos that I had stuck on the kitchen wall.

'She's very pretty,' Cindy said.

'Oh, thank you!' I beamed, proudly.

'She's *quite* dark isn't she?' she added, and I briefly explained Mattie's ethnic background.

Cindy turned to me and simply said, '*I* couldn't have adopted.'

e-mail, 28 May 2005

Dear Beth,

You sounded in much better spirits the last time we spoke…As a totally unbiased third party, it seems to me that Mattie is thriving with almost daily improvements. It, no doubt, is totally due to your superior mothering skills. I suppose for one that has been thrust in a totally new situation, sort of like being tossed into a rain-swollen river, it can, at moments, be unsettling. But from my safe perspective on the dry bank, it appears to me that you are Olympic material… So just relax, sweetie, I think you got the gig…

'What's that Mummy?' Mattie asked, pointing to an invitation card on top of the mantelpiece.

'It's an invitation to a neighbour's tea party in her garden. Would you like to go? There'll be plenty of cake.'

'Oooh, yummy,' she replied, rubbing her tummy with glee.

'I wonder if a tea party might be too much for her,' I later

160

remarked to Allie, mindful of her warning that in the interests of bonding and a need to keep Mattie from being overwhelmed, I should not introduce her to too many people too soon.

'If they're only neighbours and acquaintances, it shouldn't be too intense for her,' Allie said.

But will it be too intense for me? I later asked myself, when I rang to accept. Would we not be a spectacle on this, our first performance together, in the outside world? How would Mattie behave? Would we look like mum and daughter, or like two strangers thrown together? And what would they all say about us afterwards?

On the day of the tea party, my daughter showed an obvious preference for the chocolate cake *and*, to my surprise, for the attention of the entranced guests, preferring to chat to *them* rather than join me in the garden. I hung around a while, hopefully, then slunk out alone, feeling rather unattached, glad to finally encounter some familiar neighbours sipping tea on the lawn, all eager to ask me how things were going with the adoption.

'What does she call you?' asked a middle-eastern woman, whom I knew from swimming lessons years earlier.

'Mummy,' I replied.

'What should she call me?' I had asked Allie just before moving-in day.

'Take her lead,' she advised, 'however, it's not that usual for an older child to say Mummy right from the beginning.' But Mattie had been desperate to call someone Mummy ever since the autumn of 2003 – the time when her birth mummy had begun regularly to miss contact. 'Good morning, Mummy,' 'Hello, Mummy,' 'Are you all right Mummy?' she would say countless times each day, and had done so since the first day we met. My neighbour, Jo, would later laugh and say, 'We once counted how many times she said 'Mummy'.'

I was relieved when Mattie came out to join me in the garden, although it was not long before she moved on to chat to some other guests who, it appeared, were equally captivated by her. I stood there, watching her intently as I nibbled at my cake, as though observing a boyfriend chatting up someone else. Her treachery only worsened, however, when her nose began to run. I removed a tissue from my handbag but it was not to me she went for help, but to the nearest grown-up – and a complete stranger to boot. I put the tissue back into my bag and retreated into the house where I was relieved to see, finally, an open bottle of wine. With a warm glow, I thereafter passed the rest of the afternoon, grateful for any scrap of attention my daughter might send my way.

As Mattie and I were leaving that evening, we encountered my ancient and formidable next-door neighbour Cicely, a late arrival. 'Ah, so you're the noisy one,' she announced brusquely.

For the first time that afternoon, Mattie was speechless whilst I mumbled an apology for her unneighbourly loudness.

It must have been the previous Saturday that Cicely was complaining about. That was the day Mei and Poppy came round and Auntie Molly had stayed for a while to read them a story on the garden bench. It all seemed idyllic at first, but as soon as Molly left Mattie went berserk, shouting and running round the garden with Mei in her wake. She was particularly defiant, too, refusing to put down some long garden canes she insisted on poking into the kitchen. After I removed them, she ran through the house, making a hell of a noise.

'I can't stand it!' I had shrieked down the phone to Mike from the quiet of my bedroom, just as Mattie and Mei came charging in like two savages. 'It's a nightmare!' I told him as he listened patiently. 'My cottage pie! It's going to burn. I must go.' *My first cottage pie in twenty years!* I slammed down the receiver and ran down the stairs.

It was perfectly cooked, however, done to a tee. I proudly took it out of the oven and called the children in.

For the next 20 minutes or so, I had hovered in the kitchen throwing anxious glances in Mattie's direction, as though awaiting a compliment from a new beau. I had taken ages preparing the pie, following every minute detail of Delia's recipe. 'So is it OK?' I'd asked Mattie, tentatively, as she ate without saying a word.

'Mmm,' she replied, 'but the carrots are a bit hard.'

'It was lovely meeting Mattie at the tea party,' my neighbour, Jo, said to me a few days later, over the garden wall. Mattie was already bathed and in bed.

'I was thinking, it must have been interesting for you,' I said.

'It was churning. It brings it all back. Mattie reminds me of myself. I was exactly the same age when *I* was adopted. I remember standing very close to people, wanting to touch them, and chatting all the time.' Jo then laughed and said, 'She's lovely, but she'll wear you out.'

I felt numb, as I came back inside. Jo's well-intended words had disturbed me. For there I was, thinking everything looked normal. There I was, thinking that we looked just like any other mother and daughter. I felt as though someone had pinched me awake from my dream. What's more, it was Sunday evening and half-term – a whole week *without* nursery – was about to begin.

Dear Beth,

Sounds like you both had a fine day yesterday...obviously, things are going well in the adjusting to one another process. In visiting with you on the phone, you seemed very pleased and happy and had several sweet things to relate that Mattie had said and done. If you manage to write about it all, at a later date, you might want to invent some adversity to keep the reader on the edge of his or her seat...

It was Allie's first post-placement visit and I was making coffee when she asked, 'So do you think having a child will make it difficult for you to meet men in the future, that it might limit you?'

I replied, with what I hoped was a deadpan expression, that I did not believe so. 'Mattie's such a lovely child, I don't think it would put anyone off; if it *did*, they wouldn't be worth it anyway...I always somehow felt that adoption might lead me to that someone special.'

I saw Allie nodding approvingly. 'You'll need to think carefully how you introduce her to any new partner,' she advised.

'Yes, I know,' I said, putting Allie's coffee on the kitchen table as we both sat down. Deciding a change of subject was in order, I said, 'We've been sorting out some of Mattie's old clothes.'

'It's not a good idea to get rid of all of them immediately – she needs to feel there is some continuity with her old life.'

'I've kept lots of pyjamas and dressing gowns and all the underwear, and a few nice pairs of jeans and some pretty tights,' I acknowledged. 'But a lot of the dresses make her look like Grandma Walton – I don't want her to feel she's any different from the other children at nursery.'

'It *is* important that she fits in,' Allie agreed. 'To put it politely, Jenny does like to dress them in an old-fashioned style.'

I remember one of the times I had picked up Mattie during introductions. I thought how adorable she looked, even though her red pinafore dress and checked shirt were several sizes too large. *Now*, Mattie was my daughter and I wanted her to feel proud of herself, not self-conscious, and I wanted to feel proud of her, too. I had been to the children's shop down the road and bought her some more things, including a cat T-shirt like the one Mei wore on the day of their first tea.

'They're beautiful,' Mattie had exclaimed, when I handed her the bag. Irritatingly, however, whenever she dressed herself in our first six months or so, it was always the old clothes that she seemed to put on.

Mattie walked into the kitchen carrying a jewellery box from her bedroom. 'It's from Jenny,' she told Allie, as she wound the little key that started the music playing.

'That tune always makes me feel sad,' I said, as I felt my eyes fill with tears. Horrified I might cry, I quickly made a joke about 'Big Ears' having joined us and I told Allie that I knew Mattie had listened in on many discussions at Jenny's, of that I was certain; and those times when she was apparently paying no attention, she was actually all ears. 'That's why I often spell out words like b-i-r-t-h f-a-m-i-l-y.'

'You won't be able to do that for long,' laughed Allie

As Mattie worked through the contents of the jewellery box – coloured beads, little plastic bracelets, hair slides – I was concerned about her desire to show Allie something from her old life. Would Allie deduce from it that Mattie was not settling in?

Mattie then announced she had been unable to find her Noddy colouring book in her playroom.

A mistake I made in the early days was not keeping a few

activity things for Mattie in the kitchen. At that point, I was still making an effort to keep the house looking untouched. And although I wanted to show Allie I was the firm but fair parent who would not drop everything at their new daughter's beck and call, within moments I was traipsing up to the playroom to fetch her book.

Meanwhile, Mattie, ever artful, having worked out that whilst a social worker was around I was unlikely to remonstrate, had already laid out some paper on the kitchen floor along with the large bottles of paint she had brought with her from Jenny's.

'I love painting.' She beamed up at Allie.

Out of breath from having run all the way to the attic and back, I gritted my teeth, fearing I would appear too inflexible if I tried to prevent her doing so. *She's wearing one of her new outfits, too!*

I attempted a meaningful conversation with Allie whilst watching my daughter who, within minutes, was covered up to her elbows in paint and making handprints in every conceivable colour. I grew more and more stressed.

'We did this at Jenny's,' Mattie interrupted, as she made yet another print.

'Sorry Allie, what was that you just said?' I asked, in what I hoped was a cool, calm and collected voice.

'I asked how Mattie's enjoying nursery – is she still doing mornings only?'

'Yes, just the three mornings, but as she's settled in so well I'm intending to book her in for three full days after half-term.' I managed to refrain from adding that I could hardly wait. 'Jenny said that Mattie's been doing three full days since she was nine months.'

'Make sure she's ready for it,' Allie advised. 'She's had a lot of change in her life. You might try one full day first and see how it goes.'

166

'Yes, I will. It's a blessing she has her cousin, Mei, in nursery with her.' I mentioned the girls' little sumo wrestler ritual each morning, at which Allie laughed. 'I'll be taking her to the ballet next week,' I added, still observing the painting talents of my daughter. (At least it was keeping her quiet). 'I had a couple of opera tickets I booked months ago but they clashed with the introductions, so I changed them.'

'You've introduced her to so many new things, already, it'll really help you bond.'

'I've finished!' Mattie announced, finally, and I did my best to admire the coloured handprints and other strange-looking shapes. 'I tried to do arm prints, too,' she explained, 'but it was difficult.'

'How lovely,' I fibbed. 'Now, be a good girl and go out and wash yourself under the outside tap.' I quickly cleared away the mess from the floor.

'Mattie doesn't have to be present at our next meeting,' Allie then told me. 'It's Toby's job to check that Mattie is all right, whereas I come to see *you*. I just thought it would be easier for you if Mattie were present.'

You must be joking! I thought.

As we saw Allie off at the doorway, I picked Mattie up. 'I like picking Mattie up, and she likes to be picked up, too,' I said, and Mattie gave me a big kiss on the cheek.

'That's nice,' Allie said with a smile. 'You might find she'll regress a little at times; she might act more like a three-year old. But it's quite normal for adopted children, they're just catching up on the years they've never had. And you might find you like it, too – it's a chance for you to experience some of those years you missed out on with her.' Allie made her way to her car. 'Enjoy your half-term!' she called out as Mattie and I waved her goodbye.

Thinking about the half-term before me, with no nursery school to give me a breather, I became somewhat apprehensive.

And as I watched Allie drive up the road, I felt like one half of an incompatible couple marooned on a desert island.

Mattie had just come into my bed for her morning cuddle. 'I want a daddy,' she announced.

I froze when I heard those four words, uttered so innocently. For a moment or two, I was dumbstruck – and then fearful that if social services were to hear of it they might take her back. I decided to play things casually, and – without revealing the daddy card up my sleeve – said blithely that, perhaps, Father Christmas might bring her a new daddy. 'Do you think his sack will be big enough though?' I asked her.

'No,' she giggled.

Fortunately, the possibility of a bounteous Christmas seemed to satisfy her – though I would never have dared such flippancy if Mike had not been waiting in the wings. The rights or wrongs of adopting Mattie as a single mother had always niggled at the back of my mind; no doubt, a daddy would be a welcome addition for us both.

e-mail, June 2005

Dear Beth,

I do like to hear from you and get updates on what is happening in your new life. I know I am some great distance away but I feel ever closer to you and already believe I know Mattie. It does seem odd when I think about it. I would say my life has certainly taken a different direction since you strolled into it that fine day in Puerto Vallarta… I am so very pleased that you both have won the human lottery and ended up with the perfect person. Makes me believe that not everything is pure chance…

Half-term, Allie predictably had said, would be a good chance for Mattie and me to bond. But the weather was bad and, without nursery, Mattie lacked the structure she enjoyed. I missed the structure, too. What's more, Mike was away for a few days, attending his nephew's wedding; I always felt uneasy when he was away from home, as though the distance in miles suddenly doubled overnight.

Early in the week, I decided to take Mattie and Mei to the children's farm. Whilst they played happily in the barn among the haystacks and on the toy tractors, I settled down with a coffee and took out my knitting. I was touched when a friend of Molly's popped by the farm especially, to drop off a gift and card for Mattie. Half-term, I thought, despite the bad weather, was not going too badly, after all.

But on Wednesday, when Molly and I took the girls to visit my parents, for some reason I felt low. The plan was to have lunch and then take the children to a seaside play park. But on our arrival I became tearful and my mother and Molly ended up taking the children out on their own.

I was still in the garden, hardly having moved by the time they returned a few hours later. I burst into tears again.

'I know exactly how you feel,' my mother said.

What must have been going through Mattie's mind that day, I cannot imagine. On one occasion, she came up to me and just stared whilst I cried.

Later that afternoon, I mentioned to my mother that Mattie had asked once or twice if she could ring Jenny.

'What did Jenny say about her ringing?'

'I asked before Mattie moved in and she said that some of the children ring her when they first move in with their new parents and she didn't mind. She did say she had to put her foot down on one occasion though, when the parents of one little boy kept ringing every night. She let it go on for a month and then told the mother it had to stop.'

'I would let Mattie ring when she next asks then,' Mum advised.

The very next day after breakfast, Mattie said, 'I want to ring Jenny…You promised,' she added quickly, picking up on my hesitation.

'OK, but I'll need to get her number.' What would Jenny think receiving a phone call after only two weeks? I worried.

Jenny answered and immediately asked, 'How's Mattie?' It struck me, in an instant, that Mattie must have been constantly on her mind.

'She's settling in really well,' I reassured her, 'but she would like to have a word with you – would you mind?'

'No, of course not, it would be lovely to talk to her!'

Out of sight, lurking nearby in the kitchen, I listened as my new daughter chatted to her foster mum.

'Hi,' I heard her say, and then waited with bated breath, expecting her to tell Jenny that she wanted to go back. 'Jenny, Tibbles sleeps on Mummy's bed,' I heard her giggle. I stood there feeling a huge surge of relief. 'Mummy's knitting me a sweater with a cat on the front.' Now that really pleased me. 'Mummy made scrambled eggs and they were horrible – she put too much salt in them.'

'I made a mistake,' I murmured from my hiding place, unable to stop myself. There was worse to come.

'I want a daddy,' I heard her tell Jenny. 'Yes, but Granddad's not the same as a daddy,' she persisted.

What on earth would Jenny think now, I wondered, horrified, in my hiding place.

Mattie then asked Jenny if she could speak to Jack, too. 'Are you all right?' I heard her ask him. 'Are Sam and Ruby all right, too?'

That was part of her need to call, I then realised. It was part of the essence of Mattie: the need to know that everyone was all right. And finally, after what seemed like an age, but which was probably only 15 minutes, she put down the receiver.

Mattie then joined me in the kitchen, looking content. Life in her old home was going on as normal and Jenny was still there. I, on the other hand, felt a bit low.

I still was not feeling myself the next day.

'I wish I hadn't accepted the invitation,' I said tearfully to Mike, now back from the wedding. (An acquaintance had invited Mattie and me over for the afternoon.)

'Cancel it if you're not up to it,' he suggested.

'But it might do me some good to get out of the house,' I wavered, 'and it would be a chance for Mattie to get to know some children…'

But as I later sat in Gemma's garden, on an unexpectedly hot afternoon, I feared I had made the wrong decision. Her children seemed reluctant to play with Mattie, and the whole time I was on edge, feeling as though we both lay under a magnifying glass – two unusual specimens thrown together, our every move and mannerism under observation. Was Mattie acting normally in their eyes, I wondered, and was I acting motherly enough? How relieved I felt when Mattie came to sit on my lap, just like any other child.

'How's your fella?' Gemma suddenly asked, causing me to glance down to see whether Mattie had caught on. 'Oh, she won't know what I mean,' she laughed, 'that's why I said 'fella'.'

But I was relieved when Mattie jumped off my lap and ran to play on the slide, as the next barrage of questions was fired. 'Where do you think you'll live in the future – over here or in the States? What are you living on? When will you be going back to work?'

After I told Gemma I was taking a year off, her response was, 'So you're retired then?' Had she assumed I had been earning the sort of money City traders were accustomed to? *Is that what everyone thought?* I shuddered.

'No, I'm not retired,' I replied, 'I wish I were.'

How I wished, too, that I had brought a hat, as I began to perspire under the relentless sun. Was I supposed to go and play with Mattie, I pondered, when I noticed her on her own, the other children having gone in. Is that what any other mother would do? But I stayed put, feeling as though glued to the garden chair.

'No more, now,' I reprimanded Mattie, in a voice that reminded me of my mother, as she came and grabbed another handful of biscuits from the table. 'She has her tea at 5,' I explained, feeling frustrated that Mattie had not taken a blind bit of notice of my words.

'You'll have to be more flexible than that, Beth,' Gemma laughed, and I again was near to tears.

The next day, Saturday, we got out Mattie's 'Barbie' scooter and made our way down the high street, wending our way through the shoppers huddled around the stalls of the farmers' market. We were on our way to meet my friend, James, who had invited us for coffee at a nearby café.

I brought Mattie's attention to a llama whose neck, I noticed as we got closer, was being stroked by Liz, one of the women with whom I had commuted up to London years ago. Pleased to see her, and certain she would find Mattie delightful, I tried to catch her attention. 'Hello,' I called out.

'Hello, Beth,' she replied, absently. She gave Mattie only a brief glance before devoting her full attention to the llama, stood motionless in front of a group of writhing Peruvian pan pipers.

Perhaps she's just not interested in children, I decided, recalling her boyfriend's comment about her having a puppy.

'Look, there's James!' I announced to Mattie. I had noticed him waving at us from an outside table.

We joined James and he asked what we would like.

'What a treat to be waited on,' I smiled. 'Perhaps Mattie would like to go in with you and choose a cake,' I suggested, grateful for a chance to sit down and vegetate alone for a few minutes.

On their return, I pointed out Liz to James. She was now walking past us with her boyfriend in tow. 'It's strange but she didn't seem to want to talk when I took Mattie up to see the llama.'

'That's odd,' James replied, 'I'd have thought she'd like to meet her.'

Just as he spoke, Liz came over, on her own. 'You must be Mattie,' she said and soon she, too, became captivated by my daughter as they chatted for a few minutes. 'I must be going now, Tim's somewhere around,' Liz then smiled. 'I seem to have lost him!'

On our way back to the house, during a rest stop, I pointed out to Mattie, 'Look there's the train station!' How often, during all my years of commuting, I had stopped in exactly the same spot each evening to see the train trundle off, its passengers tiny black dots in the brightly lit compartments.

'I'm hungry, Mummy,' Mattie later complained, as we walked slowly past the kilim-clad Turkish takeaway where the smell of kebabs wafted out, making me feel hungry, too. Continuing our way home, something else other than hunger was nagging me now. I was a single mother. I had become the physical manifestation of those two words spluttered out with disdain by politicians.

'I wouldn't like to be a single mother,' I had once announced to my former running companions over dinner.

'But you *will* be a single mother,' one of them replied immediately.

'No, I won't, I've got Mike,' I retorted tartly.

But Mike was thousands of miles away, and despite the support he gave over the telephone, he was not here.

For the first time, as we continued our way up the high street, I empathised with the single parent's lot. It was the 'doing it all on one's own' – something that had been impossible for me to entirely comprehend before I became a single parent myself. Maybe I had just put on my blinkers in those pre-adoption days, when the grass on the other side of the fence seemed a deep shade of green. Taking your child to nursery school, cooking their meals, playing with them at bath time and reading bedtime stories – all sounded simply idyllic. Now, with all the other things added in – the washing and ironing, changing bedclothes, the shopping, cooking and cleaning, the gardening, the bonding (of course) and the apparent loss of your social circle, too…sometimes that deep shade of green now took on a dull hue.

'Write down all the things you like doing,' I recalled the social services manager saying at the start of my prep course – was it really two years ago? I had recently found my list whilst clearing out some old things:

- Having friends round
- Gardening
- Going out for a drink or dinner
- Reading
- Cycling
- Travelling

'You may as well tear that piece of paper up now,' he'd announced, triumphantly, 'because you won't have time to do any of those things, at least not for many months.'

But a lot of the things on my list I can do when the child moves in, I had thought at the time. I never dreamed when I scribbled the top item, 'Having friends round' that hardly anyone would be in touch. Apparently, I had been abandoned.

If I were re-writing the list today, it would not be a list of what I wanted to do, but rather what I wanted to be, and I would put just one word on that list: spontaneous. Spontaneity, I decided, was the primary selling point of a childless life: doing things at a whim, like putting on my cycling gear and going out for a ride on the Downs.

Half-term over, why did I feel so flat? My sister Caryl had come to visit and we were walking down the high street together, looking in at the shop windows, though none of them held any appeal for me.

'Do you remember us driving down from London the first day you moved into your cottage?' Caryl said, as we passed by the estate agency that had sold me the property.

'Yes, I do. I remember we bought fish and chips the night before and we ate them in the empty flat with a bottle of wine.'

'It was so exciting when we finally arrived,' she reminisced.

But the moment the removal van had arrived and I saw all the furniture and boxes stacked up, I had suddenly felt pretty low. And then one of my new neighbours looked over the garden wall and asked me if I was a career woman. 'My husband went off with a career woman,' she announced, whilst hanging some tiny clothes items on the line. 'He left me with our two daughters – you'll find this town is very focused on families and children.'

Caryl and I were now walking around the town gardens. 'The last time I walked through here was the first day I dropped Mattie off at nursery, just after she moved in,' I said. Caryl and I admired the bright primary colours of the perfectly matched tulips and other flowering bulbs, and the huge mulberry tree that would shed its luscious fruit later in the summer.

I looked at my watch. 'I'm always a little anxious as to how she'll greet me when I pick her up after nursery. I don't know why, because she always looks happy to see me. She usually runs up to me and likes to be picked up. It's probably just having had the half-term break that's made me feel like this.'

'Would you like me to stay and go with you?' Caryl suggested.

'No, I'll be OK,' I insisted, knowing she had a train to catch. But I felt lonely, again, as we kissed each other goodbye. And when Caryl turned around to wave one last time, as she passed by one of the large Judas trees, I became tearful once more.

By then, the hands of my watch had finally moved to twelve and I made my way to the heavy nursery doors.

'Mummy!' Mattie shouted, as the doors finally opened and a rush of children spewed out, my daughter amongst the first. She held out her arms for me to pick her up and I gave her a big kiss.

Mattie initially refused to take my hand as we started to walk up the steep, cobbled hill. And when she finally did so, she dug her little nails painfully into the palm of my hand. 'I'm starving!' she shouted out.

This reminded me of something my friend and erstwhile referee, Ruth, had related years ago – how abominable her own daughter could be after school. 'I put it down to a low sugar level,' she had said.

But I soon came to realise it was more than a blood sugar issue. Something similar was beginning to happen when Mattie came down to my bed in the morning: previously, all she wanted were cuddles and tickles, but now she wanted to 'fight' as she called it. 'Fighting' consisted primarily of kicking, which I assumed, at first, was her idea of fun. But when I once caught the look of menace on her face, I knew it was not all playing. Fortunately, this would only last a few minutes, long enough for her to get it – whatever *it* was – out of her system, and then things returned to normal. I hoped it was not *me* that she was fighting, but rather *someone* or *something* else. As a child who had had absolutely no control over her own life, perhaps she was fighting all of us, fighting the entire system.

Whatever the cause, I decided to keep this recent change in Mattie's behaviour to myself. It was troubling, but I already had other anxieties that I needed to get off my chest.

'She rang her foster mother during half-term,' I blurted out to Mattie's play therapist, a few days later.

Fiona appeared completely unfazed. 'She only wants to tell Jenny about her new life and how she's getting on,' she smiled, as I stood there in the kitchen, half expecting her to add the words 'silly billy' or even 'billy billy'.

I had debated as to whether to tell Fiona about the phone call, fearing it might get back to the social workers. Given Fiona's mild reaction, I decided to offload my other anxiety, the daddy anxiety.

'That surprises me,' Fiona said as I handed her a cup of tea. 'Not having a daddy didn't appear to be an issue when we discussed it earlier. I'll have another word with her.'

Mattie now joined us in the kitchen. 'Shall we go up to your playroom again, Mattie, or to one of the other rooms this time?' Fiona asked her.

'You could use the study if you want,' I suggested.

'Yes, the study,' Mattie announced, after a few seconds' deliberation.

'That's good,' Fiona said to me quietly, before they disappeared, 'because it shows she's happy to have the sessions in a room you both share.'

When Fiona reported back an hour later, she again said that there did not seem to be any significant issues for Mattie in not having a daddy.

Fiona must have found that out during all the shrieking and stomping on the sanded, wooden floorboards overhead. What had the painter, up on his ladder outside the study window, made of it all, I had wondered – especially, as Mattie had closed the curtains. For some reason she always preferred her play therapy sessions to be in a darkened room. Earlier, I had seen Mattie poke her nose out of the window and bossily tell the painter where he had dripped paint and which bits he still had left to do. 'She made me feel quite nervous up there on the ladder,' he reported later.

In some ways, Mattie's bossiness could be endearing. There were constant reminders from her to fasten your seatbelt or to shut the fridge door; in fact, she liked to warn me – everyone – about any perceived obstacle or danger. She was motherly with it, too: 'Put the scarf around you, Mummy, and go to bed straight after your bath,' she said once when I felt unwell. But I suspected that her peers at nursery school did not always take to her mothering!

'Mattie *is* a bit confused between your parenting and Jenny's,' the play therapist, Fiona, later told me... 'Jenny had different ways of doing things and different boundaries, too. For instance, you might give Mattie a choice of meals whereas Jenny didn't,' Fiona explained. 'But there's no right way of doing things, Mattie just needs to sort it all out in her head.' As Fiona spoke, I thought of the previous week when I had asked if Mattie wanted one fish finger or two for her lunch. 'You decide,' she said, with a shrug of her little shoulders and a look as though I came from another planet.

Fiona's words – unexpectedly – instilled in me a feeling of confidence. I constantly had been hearing how marvellous Jenny had been – and no doubt, she had. But how refreshing it was to hear that Jenny's way of doing things was not necessarily the Holy Grail of mothering.

'I do keep to quite a few of the routines from Jenny's,' I admitted to Fiona.

'That's good, though you might find you'll want to change them as time goes on and you become more used to one another.'

Change them? But I liked them as they were! Not just Mattie's life, but my own, too, now revolved around those routines. 'I want dinner,' she would cry out if I did not have her lunch on the table by noon, banging on the table with her little 'Princess' knife and fork. *And bedtime by seven, with the rest of the evening to myself? A godsend, and something I certainly needed.*

'She's gorgeous,' Fiona mouthed to me as I saw her out.

As we said our goodbyes, I mentioned that I would be taking Mattie up to London that weekend, to see a ballet.

'Good luck!' she said, with a knowing smile.

Around this time, Mattie abruptly announced that she wanted to use her birth surname again.

I had been advised by social services that Mattie should use my surname henceforward, except when filling in legal documents. Until now, she had seemed perfectly happy to do so, too, obviously delighting – or so I had thought – in the new name-tag produced for her at nursery school.

I experienced a brief sense of rejection at her unexpected request. But how would *I* have felt if I had been made to change *my* name at the grand old age of four?

As fate would have it, a parcel arrived for her that same morning from my youngest brother, Rees, and his wife. 'So, I suppose you won't want this parcel,' I said casually, 'because your old name isn't on it. Should I send it back?'

'No!' she squealed, once more fully embracing her new surname and tearing open the package. It contained a beautiful, bright pink, beaded fairy dress. Mattie quickly put it on and we immediately went out to the garden where I took some photos. In one of my favourites, she is standing next to

179

some deep purple irises almost as tall as she, hands on hips, wearing a feisty expression.

I later e-mailed the photo to some friends, to announce the arrival of the Wicked Fairy. I sent it to my former boss, too, and in doing so, for just a brief moment, felt a little wistful for office life and Canary Wharf.

e-mail, 10 June 2005

Dear Beth,

Today sounds like great fun for you all. A day in London, complete with ballet and no telling what else. If I were there, I would wait patiently in some nearby pub, drinking and visiting with the denizens and most eager to meet you all after the big extravaganza, and maybe take you out to dinner. Someday, maybe…

I had long deliberated as to what Mattie should wear on her first trip to London. In the end I chose a pretty, pink floral skirt I had bought in the sale in Gap. And on Molly's advice, I had packed plenty of snacks, as well as some lunch, and, of course, a spare pair of knickers, just in case.

Promptly at 11am, I shut the front door behind us and we set out on our major expedition, the first stage of which entailed a proud march down the high street.

'Hi,' called out an acquaintance, the husband of an artist from whom I had bought several paintings in my childless days. 'Is this Mattie?' he asked, as he stopped for a little chat. We soon waved him goodbye and were again on our way, and I recalled how a friend of theirs once told me that the artist feared losing her gift, if she were to have a baby.

'Look, there's the station!' I pointed out to Mattie as we rounded the corner at the top of the familiar, steep hill. She was becoming excited now. It was a big day for her: her first time on a train, her first trip up to London, her first ballet – and all of it with her *new* mummy. I was excited, too, for it was my first trip up to London in more than three months, and with my new daughter at that.

I was surprised, once we were ensconced in our seats in the crowded carriage, how remarkably unfazed Mattie now appeared to be. 'I'm hungry,' she announced, before the train even left the station, and she seemed more thrilled by the prospect of nibbling at one of the cooked sausages in my bag than by the train trip or the impending ballet.

Later, when Mattie refused to sit still during a journey that was punctuated with her persistent requests for another snack or a trip to the loo, I thought, this is worse than commuting. In the end, with Fiona's 'Good Luck' echoing in my ears and in order to have some peace, I agreed to Mattie's request that she be allowed to lie behind my seat (a place normally reserved for luggage) – I preferred that the other passengers judge her out of control rather than witness any open disobedience towards me.

At Victoria Station, I looked around eagerly for the No. 11 bus to transport us to Covent Garden via the Houses of Parliament and Big Ben – I was so looking forward to pointing out some London landmarks to my daughter.

'We're only running a limited service today,' a burly, red-cheeked bus inspector announced, handing a delighted Mattie a small union jack flag. 'It's because of the Queen's Birthday Parade,' he explained, 'a lot of the streets are out of bounds.'

Twenty anxious minutes later, the bus finally turned up and we rushed up the stairs to occupy the front seats. But as I was getting ready to point out Big Ben to Mattie, we came to a standstill and the driver announced he was behind schedule and unable to travel any further. *On this day of all days!*

Desperate, I hailed a taxi and Mattie and I fortunately arrived at the ballet in the nick of time.

I was pleased that I had opted for seats in the front row of the stalls, especially as Mattie seemed particularly excited by the orchestra. Moments before the lights dimmed, after making sure she was seated comfortably on her cushion, I turned around and with a swift glance took in the whole of the auditorium behind us. In that look, the previous 20 or so years flashed before me as I recalled some of the friends, partners and family who had accompanied me here. A hush came over the audience and I looked down at Mattie, thinking how amazing it was to be sitting here with *her*. It was our big secret, too: no one here had an inkling that we were a new mummy and daughter.

'There are going to be three short ballets,' I whispered to Mattie, her little face transfixed, as the curtains rose.

In the first, an extract from *A Midsummer Night's Dream*, Mattie was mesmerised at the dancers, dressed in pretty, diaphanous costumes, and she sat perfectly still – except for those times when she would look around and smile at me, or give me a hug.

But the second piece, a contemporary ballet to the music of Jimi Hendrix, sadly failed to engage Mattie, whose concentration had worn thin. I worried that she might be annoying the people behind with all her fidgeting and whispering. Things improved a little when I seated her on my lap.

During the interval, I drank a much needed glass of wine in the Floral Bar. 'Would you rather we go home now?' I asked, hopefully, as Mattie sipped at her fruit juice.

'I want to stay,' she insisted, surprising me.

'Then you'll have to sit perfectly still and quiet,' I warned.

We went back to our seats where I collapsed like a dying swan, fearing the worst. But as soon as the ballerinas, like a long row of fluffy ducklings, appeared on stage for *A Symphony in C*, Mattie, transfixed, sat perfectly still, except for the times when she would turn around – usually in the quietest bits – to give me a loud smacker on my cheek.

When I put her to bed that night, I breathed a sigh of relief, pleased that the day had gone so well.

For the first hectic months following Mattie's arrival, Sunday was a godsend. First, I would drop her off at Sunday school, in a church that Molly, Tom and their children frequented, and afterwards she would spend the rest of the day with them, at home, at the beach or park. Mattie loved it, and during a stressful and trying period for me, those weekly breaks were my salvation. What shall I do this Sunday, I would think, as I cleared out the dishwasher or did the ironing. Perhaps, I could take my bike out on the Downs, or I could have a nice walk; I might even drive down to the coast for a solitary swim. But some Sundays, when I felt particularly spent, I simply chose to do absolutely nothing, preferring to loll on the garden bench in Tibbles' silent and agreeable company.

The Sunday following the ballet was one such day.

When my sister brought Mattie home after a day at the beach, she refused to come inside and instead hid behind her Auntie Molly. I did my best to conceal my dismay.

'OK, don't come in then,' I finally said, thinking the quickest way to sort it was to call her bluff. But as I made to close the door, a realisation swept over me: she doesn't want to come back to me.

'Mei sometimes does the same thing to me,' Molly said calmly, making light of the incident. But I stood there, shaken. I had no cousin Mei or Poppy *here* with whom she could play. There was no equivalent, either, of an Uncle Tom. Who *wouldn't* prefer to be at Auntie Molly's?

Mattie finally acquiesced, but later that night, after I had bathed her and tucked her into bed, she petulantly announced, 'I want Auntie Molly to be my mummy.'

Those words cut me to the quick. I could not wait to escape from her bedroom.

'I've made a terrible mistake,' I gasped to Mike, as soon as he picked up the receiver and I recounted what had happened.

'Remember, it's been less than a month since she moved in with you,' he said. 'It's still early.'

'I know, but I can't stand it any more.'

'Do you think you've bitten off more than you can chew,' he asked gently.

'Yes, I think I have,' I admitted, and began to cry down the phone.

'I'll support you, regardless,' he said, 'but think about it carefully. It's not a time to be impetuous.'

'But she doesn't want to live with me,' I babbled on.

'She's just hurt your feelings,' Mike said calmly, 'it's *you* she wants to live with.'

I could not believe that it all had come to this – and only three-and-a-half weeks after she had moved in. Never would I have thought, during all those years I struggled through the adoptive process, that it would end up like this. Had I made a mistake? Now I knew why my single friends had not gone in for adoption. How I now envied them, having only themselves, or their partners, to think about whilst I was entrapped, suffocating, tied to the house, being followed around relentlessly – stalked – by a four-year-old. Now I knew why social services had carried on so much about the difficulties that would face me as a single adopter.

'And I did it all willingly,' I shrieked to Mike, 'like a lamb to the slaughter.'

All those times I had complained about the lack of statistics on disruptions – and now *I* might become one of those statistics, one of those who sent a child back.

Mike later recalled to me how helpless he had felt being so far away. If only he had been there, he could have done something, at the very least he could have held me. That was probably all I needed. He said he never believed that I would go as far as to send Mattie back. 'I would have supported you,' he told me, although inwardly, he said, he felt appalled at the prospect – not just at how it might affect me, but Mattie, too. And probably for her entire life.

Deep down, I knew, too, I could not send Mattie back. Rather, I felt resigned to my fate: I had made my bed and I had to lie in it.

When Mike and I came to the end of our two-hour long phone conversation, during which I alternately babbled and blubbered, another devastating thought struck me. 'Allie's coming to visit tomorrow morning!' I screeched. 'She's bound to guess something's up as soon as she asks me how things are going. I know I'm going to burst into tears.' I began to weep again.

'You'll be fine,' Mike reassured me, as we said goodnight. 'I'll call you afterwards to see how it went.'

As I ascended the stairs to my bedroom, feeling a little calmer, I realised what a relief it had been simply to admit I *might* have made a mistake. Even though I had no intention of sending Mattie back, the decision *was* within my control. I did have that option, didn't I? Just as Mattie must have felt helpless at the lack of control over her life, my own lesser loss of control had unnerved me, too. Would I be able to keep all this hidden from Allie, though, I wondered anxiously.

By my bedside, I found a card drawn by Mattie. She must have brought it down during my long phone conversation. There were two smiling faces and the words 'Mattie' and 'Mummy', covered with lots of kisses.

I lay in my darkened room, thinking, as I began to drift off to sleep. I thought about how I would feel if social services

185

were to tell me that the adoption could not go forward. I had to admit, in some ways, it would be a relief to have the house back to how it was…But would it really? How would I *really* feel knowing that the room above me was empty? How would I *really* feel without the chatter and laughter that filled these – for so long – empty rooms? Then, I knew. I could never abandon her, ever.

The next morning, I was still dreading Allie's visit, certain she would pick up on some bad vibes, so on her arrival I made a joke about feeling like a Fifties housewife and kept my eyes downcast as I finished sweeping the kitchen floor.

Sweeping the floor was a necessity for both practical and mental reasons. Over the weeks, my kitchen had slowly lost the minimalist look I had been so proud of, whilst more and more clutter (dolls, toys, and felt-tip pens without their caps) insidiously invaded it. But after I had swept the floor clean, I once more had the feeling that things were under control.

'How have things been for you?' Allie asked me.

'Fine, thanks.'

'And how's Mattie? Is she in nursery?'

'Yes, she is. She's fine, too.' I then mumbled, irritably, 'It's as though Mattie came out of a zoo,' as I swept some sweetcorn out from under her chair. 'She wasn't taught how to use a knife and fork.'

I then put the kettle on and, feeling comfortable that Allie had not suspected my crisis of the previous day, I decided to take advantage of Mattie's absence to discuss something that had been bothering me.

'Since Mattie moved in she's been making the odd comment about how she doesn't like the colour of her skin or hair. It never actually occurred to me that her skin is that much different to mine because I have an olive complexion… And she often says she's not pretty,' I continued. 'I keep

186

telling her how pretty she is and that her hair is beautiful, too. I tell her it's not black, but dark-brown with hints of red and gold in the sun. But Mattie insists it *is* black. She said, the nursery teacher told her so. The word "black" seems to carry a negative connotation in Mattie's eyes. She came back from nursery one day last week and said there were two "black girls" there and one of them was her cousin. It was the way she said it, too. I couldn't believe my ears. "Mei's not black," I told her, "she's just a slightly different colour to some of the other children. Children come in all colours." I realised Mattie must think *she's* black, too.'

'It's not normal for a child of her age to say those sorts of things, which are in fact racist,' Allie commented. After we had discussed it more, Allie suggested that Mattie might have picked this up from her biological family.

'I was surprised by how many brown-skinned dolls and books with brown-skinned children she brought with her,' I said. 'I decided to sift some of them out to achieve more of a balance.'

Allie agreed with what I had done. 'There still exists a lot of underlying racism,' she said. 'I once had a little boy on my caseload who tried desperately to scrub his black skin white…'

Mattie and I had recently met an acquaintance of mine on our way to the butcher's. With a nudge and a laugh, she asked me, 'Where did you pick her up from?'

You're talking about my daughter! I thought. But I didn't say it. I told her that Mattie was adopted and immediately I could have bitten my tongue. Why did I feel obliged to tell her anything?

'Where does she come from?' was a question that always surprised me. And because of its frequency, I sometimes caught myself wondering whether the person assumed she was adopted or suspected my liaison with someone of Asian descent.

'It's important to maintain her awareness of her Asian background,' one of the Panel members had advised at the adoption Matching Panel back in May. 'Have you read up on adopting a bi-racial child?'

'Yes, I have. I was given an extract to read.' I refrained from adding that I had not understood a word of the socio-speak gobbledygook. Neither did I tell them that although I knew the importance of maintaining an awareness of her racial background, I was not intending to ram it down her throat.

I brought up the issue of skin colour with Fiona, when she arrived for a play therapy session a few days later.

'We'll look at it as part of our play today,' she said.

As she and Mattie went up the stairs together, I heard her ask, 'How was the ballet?'

'It was boring,' I heard Mattie reply, assuming I was out of earshot in the kitchen.

'You horror!' I mouthed, and I picked up the sweeping brush again and tuned in to Radio 4.

e-mail, 13 June 2005

Dear Beth,

I think it is a good idea to not run the little thing off. Despite the tough moments, I think in the long run it will be very nice to have her around. Besides, who will care for you in your dotage?

As a brand-new mum with a ready-made four-year-old, I at times felt a bit of a fraud. I imagined that other mums were saying to one another, 'What on earth does *she* know about mothering?' Many of them had had years of bringing up children, years of knowing what children liked to eat, liked to wear, what to give them for tummy ache, what they liked to play with. I was different.

And most mums didn't have social workers in their lives, so when I received a call from someone announcing she was Mattie's health visitor, I felt quite excited: *all* mums were visited by their health visitor!

A tall, willowy blonde arrived on a Thursday afternoon. Mattie was delighted to see the smiley lady who had been her health visitor for the whole of the two years she lived at Jenny's.

'You loved having your height and weight taken, didn't you?' the health visitor remarked, as Mattie chortled with delight.

As I watched, I recalled the first time I bathed Mattie and how skinny her little legs were; and I also recalled Allie's remark, that if newly adopted children were doing well, they tended to blossom.

'Good,' the health visitor said, to my relief, adding some notes to a red book. 'She's put on a little weight.'

But once Mattie had been weighed and measured, she took no further interest in the visit and put on her *My Fair Lady* DVD. I thought about telling her to turn it off but decided to let her be.

'Will you be seeing Jenny soon?' I asked the health visitor.

'Yes, next week: I'm still Sam and Ruby's health visitor. I'm glad Mattie's doing so well. I can tell Jenny she's still the same Mattie; I know she'll be thrilled.'

I was pleased that Jenny would soon receive an update for I knew that she must have been dying to hear how things were going.

Mattie got up and went into the kitchen. I was about to get up myself to find out what she was up to when the health visitor said, 'Jenny did wonder whether Mattie would be having contact with her birth family.'

'At the moment, Toby wants contact with several members of the family,' I answered.

'Oh, I hope it doesn't happen! I know Jenny was unhappy with contact. She said Mattie never wet her bed normally, but that she always did after contact.'

The health visitor told me that she would not be paying us any further visits because Mattie would soon turn five. I was a little disappointed. She also said that she would be unable to attend the Looked After Children meeting to be held at my house the following week, but would send in a report that could be read out at the meeting. She assured me that it would be positive.

Mattie now appeared with a biscuit tin and this time I sent her back to the kitchen with it.

'I can see you're firm with Mattie,' the health visitor said. 'Jenny was very firm with her and it's essential with Mattie, because she can be very manipulative.'

Her words frightened me somewhat. *Had* Mattie been manipulative with me? I wondered.

Mattie soon re-appeared and I looked down at her angelic little features. Had she been hoodwinking me?

Until such time as I legally adopted Mattie, she was the subject of a care order and hence still 'looked after' by the local authority. The first Looked After Children (LAC) meeting was bound by law to take place one month after Mattie had moved in, and Allie had asked if I minded having it in my home. Although I did not much care for the idea of making umpteen cups of tea, I nonetheless wanted to appear willing, so I agreed.

In mid-June, six members of social services knocked at my front door, and the kettle was soon boiling merrily.

The first to arrive was a jolly looking 'letterbox lady', sporting a wide smile. She reminded me of Nurse in the Enid

Blyton books and I imagined her gently scolding the children for getting grubby picking blackberries for tea. Next, was a small, quietly spoken woman, assigned completion of Mattie's life history book. Hot on her heels followed the well-dressed and mild-mannered chairman. Finally, a few minutes later, Allie, Toby and Fiona arrived.

I emerged from the kitchen with the last cup of tea and announced, 'Mattie is represented today by her slippers.' I pointed to a pair of pink slippers from which Winnie the Pooh beamed up at us and a roar of laughter erupted. Although the ice was broken, I still sat uncomfortably on the edge of the last remaining chair.

Allie and Toby began by noting how well Mattie had settled in. 'She's thriving and continuing in her routines,' Allie announced, 'and Beth and Mattie have formed a loving, caring relationship.'

'Mattie is sleeping very well, too,' I added, as the chairman nodded his approval. 'She does occasionally wake up in the middle of the night, but after a cuddle in my bed she's happy for me to take her back to her own room where she immediately falls back to sleep.'

After more general discussion, Toby read aloud the health visitor's recent assessment.

The floor was then given to Fiona, the play therapist, for her assessment. 'I've seen Mattie four times now (including twice at Jenny's), and although she's shown some anxieties, most of the issues have been worked through successfully... I therefore expect the sessions to only be short-term – just until the life history book is completed at the end of June.'

At the mention of the life history book, I felt my hackles rise. The life history book is an account of an adopted child's life in words, photographs and documents; a chronological account designed to help the child understand and accept their past, and to aid in their bonding with the new parent.

191

The book was several weeks overdue – someone was supposed to have gone over it with Mattie *before* she moved in – and I was concerned that doing it now might cause Mattie distress. I was also worried because of how Mattie's father might be represented.

'Progress on the life history book is slow due to a variety of reasons,' the woman given its completion explained. 'Jenny has now sent me the photos I need for it but I still don't expect to have it completed by the end of June as previously agreed…'

'So when will it be completed?' the chairman asked.

'By the end of July,' she replied.

The chairman asked for that to be noted in the minutes and then began to move to the next item on the agenda.

'But who will you be saying her birth father is,' I quickly interrupted.

'Talik,' the woman squeaked.

'But *he's* not her birth father!' I exclaimed. 'And given his background, I would prefer he's not mentioned.'

'But she's always known him as her father,' she responded.

'And we can't leave the father out of her life history book,' Toby joined in. 'A child needs to know they have a father.'

'But he's *not* her birth father,' I repeated, 'and she hasn't seen him since she was two!' I could feel the colour rise to my cheeks. 'If Talik must be referred to, then I want a clear indication that he's Mattie's half-siblings' father, but not *hers*.'

'But we're respecting the birth family's wishes,' Toby explained, 'they don't want her to know the truth about her birth father until she's older, and *they* want to choose when she's told.'

What a cheek, I felt like saying: a cheek both on the part of Toby *and* the birth family.

Toby then said that he would explain it all to Mattie in a 'life letter' he would write, something for her to read when she was older.

'But she's *my* daughter now,' I insisted, 'and she's already suffering from confusion over who her real father is... What do you think, Fiona?'

Fiona, it was obvious, preferred to stay out of it. But she did say that whatever appeared in the life history book had to be the truth. 'I'll cover any confusion about her birth father in one of our play therapy sessions,' she said, adding that because the life history work was delayed she was willing to see Mattie until July, both to provide continuity and to go through the life history book at the time it was ready. I felt so relieved.

The chairman now addressed an equally contentious issue: direct (face-to-face) and indirect (written) contact with the birth family.

The extent of direct contact that social services required still frightened me, and I felt it made no sense. I had told the adoption Matching Panel members back in April that I *was* in favour of contact with Mattie's half-siblings, but that I did question direct contact with a mother who had often failed to appear at contact sessions during Mattie's foster years, causing her much distress. 'Quite,' one of the Panel members had responded at the time, 'there's no point in maintaining contact that is detrimental to the adoption.' I remember the surge of relief I felt then; finally, someone in a position of authority appeared to be of my view. But Toby (who was social worker to both Mattie *and* her birth family) had persisted that day and said, 'I'm happy to ring up on the day of contact to ensure her mother's got on the bus to attend the meeting...'

Now, just like that day, months ago, Toby was again pushing for direct contact between Mattie and her mother, grandmother and aunt. And I once more brought up the birth mother's failure to appear at contact sessions and the distress it had caused Mattie.

After some heated discussion, the chairman encouraged

193

Allie and Toby to present an agreeable solution at the next LAC review, three months later.

The meeting ended with unanimous agreement that Toby and Allie's home visits be reduced to one visit each per fortnight. (Hooray!)

The 'letterbox lady' was the last to go that day, and only after setting a date for her own visit with me the coming week. I groaned inwardly at the thought of yet another meeting with a member of the social services team.

The next week, as I handed her a cup of tea, this large, rosy-cheeked 'letterbox lady' ebulliently told me, 'The purpose of our meeting is partly to clarify my role. I facilitate and maintain indirect contact for all parties involved in an adoption placement. But only where there's an agreement, of course,' she boomed on. 'I'm like the postman in effect,' she laughed, 'I receive all the letters from the child and the birth family respectively and then pass them on at the agreed intervals…and copies of all letters and photos are kept on file until the child is eighteen.'

'Oh really?' I replied, stifling a yawn.

'Yes, that means the letters are always available to the child if for some reason the originals are lost over the years. It's all in the leaflet I'll leave with you.'

'OK,' I said, wearily, at the thought of yet another document to read.

'Now, the other reason for our meeting is to reach an agreement as to the actual dates for the letterbox exchanges between Mattie and her birth family,' she carried on.

'Yes, but why now if it's months away? We haven't even agreed to *direct* contact yet,' I pointed out, a little irritably – I had just received the record of the recent LAC meeting through the post and was astonished to read in it that I was 'against all direct contact'.

'We still need to get the letterbox agreement set up as soon as possible since I'll be needing to get lots of signatures...Now, let's see, when do you expect the adoption order to be granted?'

'I'm not sure – I suppose by the end of the year.'

'Good. So when do you think would be a good time for Mattie to write to her birth family? We advise that it's *not* around Christmas-time or birthdays, of course,' she chuckled.

'Well, how about March to be on the safe side, just in case there's a delay with the legal side of things,' I responded.

'March sounds good. So that means they will then be replying to Mattie in April.'

'But *will* they be replying? I understood that most of them didn't bother.'

'You're right, most of them don't – and it's important that Mattie doesn't have *any* expectation of letters. It can lead to feelings of rejection.'

But isn't no reply a rejection? I thought. I was getting confused by all this. 'Do the birth families like to receive letters, even if they *don't* reply to them?'

'Oh yes, they love to hear, and especially they love to receive a photo,' she beamed. 'But be careful' – I almost expected her to wiggle her finger at me – 'it's best not to give them a school photo or one that might indicate where the child is living.'

I began to feel rather anxious.

'Now, do you want to allow an exchange of presents and cards at Christmas and on birthdays?' she asked.

'I hadn't even thought about it...I don't know,' I hesitated.

'Most adoptive parents views those times as private,' she suggested.

'Yes, I think I would rather they were kept private, too.'

'Good. Well I think we're done then. I'll be drawing up the Letterbox Agreement in the next few days, but I'll need to get the birth family to sign it prior to sending it on to you.'

'Does signing mean it's legally binding?'

'No, it's not binding. It's all set out in this leaflet – but if you have any questions, do give me a call,' she said, merrily, packing away her things prior to departure.

e-mail, 26 June 2005

Dear Beth

It sounds like you are having some lovely times. Lovely times with a lovely mummy for Mattie. I hope to see you soon. I am starting to suffer a bit. It is a good thing I have been working such long hours...

The last item on the introductions itinerary – 'Tea with the foster parents' – had seemed such a long way off back in May. Now, on the morning of Jenny and Jack's visit, I awoke feeling apprehensive as to how Mattie might react to seeing them again – and also how she might feel saying goodbye once more. I then remembered that Poppy and Mei were coming round to play that morning; perhaps, that would take her mind off Jenny's visit.

Surprisingly, Mattie appeared to be very relaxed, and hardly seemed interested in the forthcoming meeting. *I* was the one feeling jittery.

When Mattie's cousins left shortly before Jenny and Jack were due, she disappeared upstairs to the loo.

On hearing a knock on the door, I called out 'Mattie, it's Jenny!'

When Mattie re-appeared in the hallway, not only were her shorts dirty from playing in the garden, they were damp, too.

'Oh Mattie, why didn't you change?' I said with dismay.

When I opened the door, Mattie rushed straight into Jenny's arms.

'I'm sorry she's a bit grubby,' I apologised.

'You're not grubby are you,' smiled Jenny, her attention fixed intently on Mattie.

Immediately, it became obvious how much the two had missed one another. And whilst they sat down on a floor cushion, canoodling like a courting couple, I was left to chat with Jack, a fellow wallflower. I occasionally cast a glance at the two lovebirds, giggling in their little love nest, but they only had eyes for each other. Jack tossed them a glance at one point, but he simply grinned at me raising his eyes to the ceiling.

'How about bringing in the fairy cakes, Mattie,' I suggested, and arose to make a cup of tea.

Mattie proudly carried in a plate of cakes topped with garish squiggles. 'I did the patterns,' she beamed.

'What! You decorated these yourself?' Jenny exclaimed.

'By the way, you're welcome to go up any time after tea to see Mattie's room,' I told Jenny and Jack. I recalled Jenny once having told me how important it was for the foster parents to have some time alone with a child in their new adoptive home.

Listening to them mount the stairs, laughing together, I felt like an outsider in my own home. I decided to put the tennis on – it was the opening day of Wimbledon – but it proved difficult for me to concentrate. All the time, I could hear the faint sound of laughter and chatter up in the attic rooms. What would Jenny and Jack think when they noticed that half of the toys were missing? What was Mattie saying about me? I remembered Jenny saying how *some* adoptive parents didn't like foster parents visiting the child in their new home. At the time I found it hard to believe. Now, I could understand it.

When they came downstairs a half-hour later, beaming, Jenny said, 'It's such a beautiful room. And Mattie seems so happy here.' I was very pleased to hear that.

Mattie, excitedly – and proudly, too, I was touched to see – then led Jack on a tour of the garden, which was dotted with treasured birthday and Christmas gifts they had bought for Mattie over the years: a beautiful 'Silver Cross' doll's pram (the matching cot was upstairs in Mattie's bedroom), a bike, a paddling pool, and her beloved 'Barbie' scooter.

Jenny stayed behind in the kitchen. 'So how have things been?' she asked, whilst I made another cup of tea.

'Everything's been going well,' I told her and was surprised to see the look of relief on her face. 'Mattie's settled in well and she sees a lot of her new cousins – they were around earlier.'

'Oh, that's nice! It's good they live so close.'

'She *has* been a bit defiant lately but I think she's testing the boundaries like any other four-year-old,' I said. I was harking back to what Fiona had told me, and I saw Jenny nodding her head in agreement.

But I refrained from telling Jenny how Mattie had begun to throw things down the stairs if she did not get her way. It shocked me when it started, seemingly out of the blue. I always insisted she stay upstairs until she had picked the things up and, luckily, it was never long before she got over whatever was niggling her, and did so. Even so, I found those moments of defiance unsettling. The honeymoon, it seemed, was over.

'And how are the meal-times?' Jenny asked eagerly.

'She's great now, she hardly fidgets at all.'

'Really? That's marvellous!' I felt a thrill at her praise. 'How did you resolve it?'

'I find that if I let her eat on her own whilst I potter around in the kitchen she eats well. But if I sit by her, she tends to chat and fidget and takes ages over it... By the way, I asked Mattie recently if there was any toy she missed and she said she'd forgotten to bring a big blue ball her old mummy gave her.'

'That's right, it must be in the garden; I'll keep it aside for her.'

'I've put a lot of her toys out of sight for a while,' I explained. 'There were too many to put in her room, but I thought that at some point, I'll ask Mattie to go through them and pick out anything she wants to keep.'

'That's a good idea,' Jenny said, approvingly. In fact, it had been my mother's suggestion that I do so, when I had voiced my feelings of guilt over my desire to weed them out.

'Jenny, please feel free to spend as much time as you like on your own with Mattie.'

'It *would* be nice to have a look at your garden!'

Another half-hour later, they all trooped merrily back inside.

'I'm starving – I want my tea,' Mattie announced.

'A hungry child is a good sign,' laughed Jenny. She then said it would soon be time for her and Jack to go.

'I don't want you to go!' Mattie cried out and ran to her.

'Do they still want her to have contact with the birth family?' Jack asked, as Mattie clung to Jenny.

'They do at the moment,' I said.

'We think it's best that Mattie sees little of her birth family now – better to wait until she's old enough to make her own decision. She'll have little in common with them as she moves on.'

Jenny once again said they had to get back to Ruby and Sam, their other foster children, but Mattie clung more tightly and began to sob. I stood there, feeling like a spare part as she cried in Jenny's arms. Then suddenly, to my great delight, she leapt down, said 'I'm hungry!' and ran to me to be picked up. Jenny looked pleased.

'Perhaps Mattie can come and visit you during the summer holidays – before she starts big school,' I suggested, as she hugged me tight. 'And it'll give her a chance to see Sam and Ruby again, before they leave you.'

'Yes, of course! That would be lovely,' Jenny agreed.

'I don't want her to go, Mummy,' Mattie sobbed, as Jenny and Jack said their goodbyes. But her few tears rapidly disappeared as soon as she started tucking into her favourite scrambled eggs (without salt) for tea.

With the benefit of hindsight, I'm sure it must have been a difficult day for Jenny, too.

e-mail, 25 June 2005

Dear Beth,

I am pleased the visit with Jenny and Jack went so smoothly... I do miss you a lot and can barely wait until I can be with you again... I hope I adapt as easily to England as you did to Texas and Mexico. It will be so exciting for me... I am still very much in love and missing you immensely.

Fiona rang, unexpectedly, that week, to cancel the next play therapy session. A few days later, an envelope, addressed to Mattie, arrived through the letterbox.

Dear Mattie

I am so sorry I wasn't able to see you last Wednesday. I was unwell and had to go home to look after myself. I am better now and looking forward to seeing you soon.

Love Fiona

'I don't want to see Fiona again, if she can't come next time,' Mattie announced, when she came into my bed for her early morning cuddle.

I explained to Mattie that it wasn't Fiona's fault that she had been poorly. But I, too, had been dismayed by the cancellation, which was followed by a week of bed-wetting; apparently, Mattie's routine, so vital to her, had been disrupted.

At the next play therapy session, I told Fiona, 'Mattie's been mentioning her old family a bit lately and saying she misses Jenny. She's had some bad dreams, too, though she won't say what they're about.'

'It's like a house of cards,' Fiona explained. 'I let her down by cancelling the meeting and now other insecurities have begun to bother her, too.'

'What should I do when she mentions her old family?'

'It's natural for her to speak about them. Just listen and answer, if necessary, but don't raise the subject yourself, or prolong the conversation.'

This time, the bangs on the floorboards upstairs were even louder than usual, and there was shouting, too. I'm glad that's not me up there, I smiled to myself, thinking how exhausting it all sounded.

Fiona reappeared, flush-faced, an hour later. Mattie was with her and immediately complained that she was 'starving'.

'It was a really good session,' Fiona said. 'Mattie spent the whole time venting her anger at me – which was good...'

'Excuse me Fiona,' I interrupted, after noticing that Mattie had dropped her apple, out of which she had taken a bite, onto the sitting room rug. 'Please pick it up, Mattie.'

'No,' she shouted at me.

'There has been a lot of defiance lately,' I said, quietly, to Fiona who, I could see, was genuinely surprised, her eyebrows raised above her still rosy cheeks.

But Fiona said nothing to me, simply nodded her head, and gently coaxed Mattie to pick up the apple. She finally relented.

Mattie's defiance, I dared not admit to anyone, had

begun to concern me. How far would it go? Was worse yet to come? I recalled my doctor's words at my pre-adoption medical examination: 'Do they have post-adoptive support for you, for when your child becomes a teenager?' I had lately found myself alternating between the belief that I was the luckiest women alive – and wondering whether I had been tricked by social services into taking a potential monster.

The last thing I wanted to do that afternoon was to cry, but at one point I felt my lower lip tremble and my eyes began to fill with tears. As Fiona left to take her bag of playthings to her car, I hoped she had not noticed.

When she returned to say her goodbyes, Fiona suggested it might be good for the two of us to meet *without* Mattie some time. 'There's been a lot of change in your life, too,' she said calmly, 'a big change, but it's only a change...'

I was touched and relieved by Fiona's sensitivity and awareness of how things were going for me. I knew I was suffering at times but only now did I realise the point I had reached. Perhaps I had simply wanted to maintain the façade of competence that I had presented to Allie and Toby, fearful that any weakness on my part might jeopardise the adoption. But Fiona worked in a separate section of the health authority, she was caring and I felt safe and comfortable with her.

So I agreed that a meeting might be beneficial. At the same time, I was terrified that I might burst into tears in the middle of it.

The irony of it, I thought, the next week as I waited for Fiona to appear for *our* appointment, was that whilst I had been wondering whether *Mattie* had benefited from her play therapy sessions, now – it seemed – some play therapy was necessary for *Mummy*, too. 'Do you want to play with the babies or with the farm animals?' I imagined Fiona asking me. I then heard her knock at the door.

As we sat down at the kitchen table with our cups of tea, Fiona said, 'I thought it would be good to meet and discuss any particular issues you may have…Your life is very much different now.'

'Yes, I suppose it is… I believe I'm doing pretty well, though it can be a bit overwhelming at times… And Mattie *is* lovely,' I told Fiona, 'she's very sweet.' I told her how Mattie would always leave a hand-drawn card on the stairs or by my bedside after she behaved badly.

'Yes, she is a lovely child!'

'I'm surprised that recently, she's begun giving some of her old photos away.' (I didn't tell Fiona that I would not allow her to give away too many, since those photos were all I had of her earlier years.)

'It shows that she trusts you more,' Fiona said. 'She wants to share her old life with those in her new life, that's all… And I want you to know it's natural to want some time to yourself – don't forget, Mattie's only been with you a short time… You're adapting, too.' How relieved I felt to hear her words.

'It's not that I'm missing my job, or the commute, or Canary Wharf,' I said.

'Maybe not, but you're *still* having to adapt…to not having a job, to being home more and to having a new little girl in your life,' she said, in her usual calming tones.

And then, I realised, it was not only Mattie who had been grieving. On some level, I was grieving, too. I was missing the 'me' who no longer seemed to exist.

Later that week, I had a message from my eldest brother, Nick, on my answer-phone when I returned from a cycle ride. 'We're in Brighton and we thought we'd pop over to see you and meet Mattie. We'll be arriving about noon and will bring some lunch.'

On their arrival, Nick and Melanie looked obviously disappointed when I explained that it was one of Mattie's nursery school days.

'How about walking down with me?' I suggested. 'They might let her out for a bit in her lunch-hour.'

Mattie's little face looked bemused when she came into the reception hall to stare up at two strange faces. It soon turned to one of delight when Uncle Nick suggested that he buy her an ice cream.

As we made our way from the nursery school for a walk in the adjacent town gardens, I reminded Mattie about them: 'Pictures of Uncle Nick and Auntie Melanie are in your photo album.' I was pleased to see how well she seemed to get on with my brother and his wife. Nick gave her a piggyback and played with her just like she might have been his own, which I thought very sweet. At the same time, it struck me how strange it must be for Mattie, meeting yet another new uncle and auntie.

Later, I looked at my watch and realised it was time for Mattie to return for her afternoon session. When we arrived back, I was delighted to see that some children had come to the nursery school window and were shouting and waving at Mattie, obviously pleased to see her.

Back home, on the patio, Nick and Melanie and I made a picnic of all the goodies they had brought.

'Are you on an adoption allowance?' Melanie, a health visitor, asked me, as she poured out the wine.

'No, I'm not. Social services said I'm not eligible for any help,' I replied. But my mind was more on the state of the garden, which had been my pride and joy in my childless days. I wondered what Nick and Melanie must think of the overgrown lawn and weed-infested beds.

The next week, at the end of another play therapy session, Fiona asked, 'Has Mattie seemed more controlling lately?'

'No, I don't believe so,' I said, thinking how much more serious Fiona looked than on her previous visits. 'At least, no more than usual,' I added.

'I feel she's becoming so,' Fiona warned. A feeling of apprehension welled up inside me. 'It was evident in today's session. You'll need to ensure you're very firm with her. Make sure you stick to the boundaries…It's nothing to be concerned about,' she quickly added, no doubt due to the expression on my face. 'It's entirely natural as a child bonds more with their new parents. You've become very, very important to her and she's frightened she might lose you.'

It seemed like one thing after another.

Fiona went on, 'I asked Mattie what sorts of things were important to her and she said "cuddles". Remember to give her lots and lots of cuddles.'

'I do cuddle her a lot,' I said, on the defensive. At the same time I knew that, after only a few weeks, it did not always feel entirely natural to me. It did, however, feel natural cuddling her cousin Mei, though. It was the familiarity, I suppose. Occasionally, I felt I was forcing myself to cuddle Mattie – like being with a boyfriend with whom you had fallen out of love.

'She will need constant hugs and cuddles,' Fiona reiterated, as though reading my thoughts. 'You remember that next week will be our last session? I've already spoken to Mattie about it,' Fiona smiled, acknowledging Mattie who had now joined us in the kitchen. 'I've told Mattie I always bring a little cake to the last session and that the three of us will be going through her life history book together.'

'OK,' I replied, feeling somewhat sad that we would be seeing no more of Fiona. I was rather worried, too, as to how Mattie, who had obviously become very fond of her play therapist, would react on saying goodbye.

Fiona arose to leave and Mattie announced: 'You're not

going this way,' blocking Fiona's path. I smiled, thinking it was a game, until I noticed the look on my daughter's determined, little face.

'Really?' Fiona laughed, but she seemed taken aback. Mattie, arms outstretched, refused to budge.

'You can go the back way,' I suggested to Fiona, after several moments of stalemate.

'That might be a good idea,' Fiona said. But Mattie then moved to block that way, too. Finally, after another minute or two, Mattie let Fiona pass.

'Thank you,' Fiona smiled at her. 'Goodbyes are difficult,' she added quietly to me, 'I'll see myself out.'

'I'll come and open the door for you,' I offered, nonetheless, and just as Fiona got into her car, Mattie dashed into the hallway and asked to be picked up. Soon, we were in the doorway waving Fiona off as though nothing had happened.

What is a life history book? It is an account of a child's life in words, pictures, photographs and documents, made by the child with the help of a trusted adult. It can help:

- *organise past events in chronological order*

- *aid ego-development*

- *increase self-esteem*

- *build a sense of trust with the adult*

- *facilitate bonding*

- *help a child accept their past ...*

Why do a life history book? With older children, in particular, who have been in care for a length of time prior to placement, pieces of information can be lost; the life story book can piece them together...It is also a way of communicating events of the past to lessen confusion... Children can be helped to see patterns in their life and to feel more in control of it. The book attempts to give back to the child their past, and allow them to go into the future with that knowledge...

Preparation Course notes

Just before the start of the summer holidays, Fiona arrived to go through the long-awaited life history book with Mattie. I had eagerly awaited this session.

'Has Toby delivered the life history book?' she asked, as soon as she came through the door. She was wearing a look of consternation and carrying a box in which, I assumed, was the cake.

'No,' I replied. 'Should he have?'

'He should have delivered it to my office. It was supposed to be on my desk this morning. I'll give him a ring,' she said, picking up on my obvious agitation. A few minutes later, Fiona came into the kitchen, where Mattie and I were, and said, 'Toby's already left the office and the book, unfortunately, is still on his desk awaiting his review.'

'I don't believe it! It's already two months overdue.'

'I'm sorry about this delay. I'll have to come for another visit when it's ready. It's not good for a child to think they're telling you goodbye only to have you re-appear a few days later.'

Despite the sight of a chocolate cake on the kitchen table, Mattie looked visibly irritated.

'Toby's always late,' she grumbled.

'Let's have a piece of cake together anyway,' Fiona said, 'and perhaps we can just have a short session afterwards.'

But halfway through that session, Mattie suddenly re-appeared in the kitchen. 'It's boring,' she said, 'I don't want to do any more.'

'OK,' I replied, surprised – though secretly pleased, for I had been worried about Mattie missing Fiona's visits.

Fiona then came in hot on Mattie's heels. 'Goodbyes are difficult,' she said. 'Would you like to do some drawing instead, Mattie?'

'OK,' Mattie replied, reluctantly.

Later, Fiona presented me with a sheet of paper on one side of which Mattie had drawn herself and on the other she had drawn me. 'The fact that Mattie has written "Mattie and Mummy" on this picture is very significant,' Fiona told me. 'It reveals how important you are to her now. Mattie was very careful to get all the details, like your hair length, correct. She spent a lot of time on the picture. Make sure you never lose it.'

Fiona left, after making an arrangement to return as soon as possible *with* the life history book. The rest of the chocolate cake, which had turned out to be rather dry, Mattie and I put out for the birds.

'We haven't been back long from shopping,' I apologised, with a smile, when Fiona came later that week. 'Mattie's having her tea… It's interesting how many strangers want to stop and chat since I've had Mattie. It seems we're always running behind.'

Fiona smiled as she accompanied me into the sitting room.

'Look!' Mattie said, appearing in the doorway. She showed Fiona a keyring before returning to the kitchen to finish her tea. I told Fiona how Mattie had admired it dangling from a woman's belt and that the woman gave it to her.

'How sweet of her!' Fiona said.

'She then asked if Mattie was my daughter and she said how much alike we looked.'

'It must have been nice to have received that affirmation,' Fiona replied, 'even though you look nothing like one another.'

I was flabbergasted, for so many people had told me how much alike we were. Could Fiona not see it, too? Her remark took me back to when I had seen that first photo of Mattie. 'She even looks like me!' I'd said to Allie and Toby, expecting some sort of acknowledgement. Instead, they both just looked blankly at me and said nothing, and I remember feeling a little foolish.

Mattie had now finished her tea and joined us in the sitting room.

'Mattie, I suggest you sit between the two of us whilst we go through your life history book,' Fiona said.

Mattie refused, saying she wanted to sit by my side, not in the middle of us.

'That's OK,' said Fiona, 'so long as you can see.'

Before opening the long-awaited life history book, Fiona gave Mattie a goodbye card with a big fluffy white cat on the front. 'Shall I read this out to you?'

'Yes,' Mattie answered, in a low voice.

I noticed how quiet the room had become and I suddenly felt very protective of Mattie who, unusually, wore a very serious expression on her face. She looked so tiny sitting there and I felt a great lump form in my throat as Fiona began to read:

Dear Mattie,

Toby, your social worker, wanted me to see you in case you had any muddles, or big feelings you needed help with when you moved to your new mummy's. We have played and talked about all sorts of things, babies and how mummies look after them; we have made animal families and played about different feelings and we've played with sticky messy stuff and Play-doh.

I've loved seeing you and your mummy really get to know each other, and I know you will be happy together. I have really enjoyed knowing you, Mattie, and knowing you with your mummy, Beth. I hope you and your mummy will have lots of happy times together as you grow up.

Love from Fiona
x

'That was nice wasn't it,' I said to Mattie who, still looking very serious, had taken the card. Fiona then lifted the big pink life history book onto her lap and slowly turned over the first page.

'That's your *old* mummy's name,' Fiona said, pointing to one of the circles in the roughly drawn family tree.

Mattie now moved onto my lap. 'Why has that got nothing in it?' she immediately asked, pointing at the only blank circle on the family tree, the space for her birth father.

It *did* stand out, I thought, that empty circle; it was the first thing I had noticed, too.

'I don't know,' replied Fiona, quickly.

'We'll fill it in together, later,' I told Mattie as I sat there, feeling awkward.

'Yes, that's a good idea,' agreed Fiona.

Mattie was silent as Fiona turned over the page. There was now some information about Mattie's birth date, length and weight at birth, and the fact that she had been bottle fed. It was touching to see how interested Mattie was in all this. She asked Fiona several questions. Then followed a page filled with photos of her half-siblings, one of her birth mother, and something written this time about her birth father, too. Fiona described him as the 'daddy, who made you.'

Mattie listened intently but had no questions. She then said, 'I don't like that photo,' pointing to her birth mother, 'I don't like her hair in it.'

210

It was the photo of her birth mother, with dyed hair, identical to one Mattie had once screwed up.

'I'll put a nicer one in of your old mummy,' I promised Mattie.

I also noted that the colour of Mattie's hair had been entered in the book as black, instead of dark-brown.

Fiona turned the next page to reveal a few photos of Mattie in her foster home. And finally, there was a photo of Mattie and me, her new Mummy, the photo taken by my brother-in-law, Tom, during our first tea. I noted, with irritation, that my name had been misspelled.

Mattie's long-awaited life history book seemed to be little more than a photo album, all duplicates of those she already had in her possession. Where was the information regarding her favourite toys? How had Mattie celebrated birthdays and Christmas? Who were her favourite friends? What special trips had she made?

Later, Mattie lingered with Fiona at her car, chatting.

'Fiona needs to get back for her tea,' I told her.

'Yes, and I need to feed my cat, too,' Fiona laughed.

With a mixture of sadness and relief, I picked Mattie up and we waved goodbye to Fiona for the last time.

Some months later, I asked Mattie, 'What do you remember about Fiona's visits?'

'We could play in any room except the kitchen,' she said. 'Fiona used to be excited and was very nice. I loved the toys we played with. She would say, "Pick out what you want." I played with Play-doh and the Baby Born doll. She left Baby Born's spoon here.'

'Yes, that's right. I remember we later found it in the study.'

Mattie had refused to take it at the time and the spoon lay hidden in a little pot on a bookshelf in my study until one day, while dusting, I found it and put it in Mattie's playroom with her toy cutlery.

'Do you remember anything else?' I said, intrigued by her revelations, given her earlier secrecy about the play therapy sessions.

'I felt upset when she left my house. She was nice. I wish she didn't leave me. I wish the last day when she would finish was when I was six.'

The next day, after nursery school, when I took Mattie's dinner-money tin out of her coat pocket, I felt something else in the pocket. It was the Baby Born spoon.

There were other goodbyes the same week as Fiona's departure: Mattie's last day of nursery school had come around.

'Can we go to the gardens for an ice cream?' Mattie begged, when I collected her that day. '*Oh, please,*' she insisted.

I had no excuses and it was a lovely, hot, sunny afternoon, but I secretly baulked at the thought of again being under the public spotlight. How would Mattie behave? Would it not be obvious to everyone I had only been a mother for a couple of months? And I worried that the social services manager, who had chaired the introductions review meetings, might be there. 'See you in the town gardens,' were his last words back in May.

'OK, then,' I said, finally.

'Hooray!' Mattie exclaimed and we walked in the direction of the gardens. When we entered, we saw established groups of mothers sitting on the grass, nibbling at picnics and chatting whilst their children played. Everyone seemed to know everyone else.

After buying Mattie an ice cream, I suggested we sit on a bench.

'No, let's go and sit with those people,' Mattie insisted. 'I know one of the boys, he goes to my nursery.'

Sit down with a group of strangers? Surely not! But before

I knew it, I was sat on the lawn next to a group of mothers and children, feeling more and more self-conscious as they barely acknowledged our arrival and carried on their earnest conversation. Worse, the boy, whom Mattie had recognised, did not say a word in reply to her greeting.

'He's having "time out", one of the women explained.

'Oh,' I responded, unsure what she meant.

'He's got another 30 minutes,' she added, before turning back to resume her conversation. I stared at the little stone buddha, sitting cross-legged, staring straight ahead.

Feeling more and more like a spare part, I eventually persuaded Mattie that we should have a walk around the gardens. We got up and left, unnoticed.

Mattie announced that she wanted to climb a tree. I squirmed as I watched her, climbing in her new sandals, unsure as to whether tree climbing was something I should allow at her age, and afraid she might fall. Was I being irresponsible, I wondered, anxiously. I looked around and saw that lots of other school children around her age were doing so and their parents seemed unconcerned. After a few minutes, though, I called her down; thankfully, she didn't protest too much.

Later, as we were walking home, we passed the registry office and Mattie asked about some confetti strewn on the ground. I explained that this was a place where people sometimes got married.

'I want you to get married,' she told me. 'And I want a daddy, too,' she added, nonchalantly.

Thank goodness for Mike, I thought, with relief. But again, I had a familiar feeling of isolation. I felt low at the thought of another evening, alone, after Mattie had gone to bed. How different it might have been if Mike were around. I would not have cared if I had not known anyone in the park – and how I would have looked forward to seeing him when we returned home.

e-mail, July 2005

Dear Beth

I am arriving on Continental Flight 104, scheduled to arrive at Gatwick at 10:00 Saturday morning, July 30th...I am very much looking forward to seeing you again, for the first time in your natural habitat. And, of course, meeting little Mattie...

'Who's Mike?' Mattie had asked me one day, not long after she had moved in.

'He's a friend,' I replied. 'Would you like to speak to him when he next rings?'

'Yes,' she said eagerly, and after a few weeks of brief but successful telephone conversations between the two, I asked, tentatively, if she would like Mike to join us on holiday.

'Yes,' she exclaimed excitedly, followed by a long pause... 'What's holiday?' she asked.

Only then did the obvious occur to me: Mattie had never been on holiday and, as a consequence, had no concept as to what a holiday was.

'Holiday is when you go away for a few days. Sometimes by airplane and sometimes by boat and sometimes you go in the car – and you do nice things like go to the beach.'

'And where do we sleep?'

'In a hotel where they have beds and give you breakfast – so you'll have to pack your pyjamas and some spare clothes in a little case.'

'Where's holiday?' she asked.

'Well, this time it's going to be in the same country as we

214

are – England – and near a beach. And, as it's not too far away, we'll be going in the car.'

A few days later, Horsie, a little brown cuddly toy horse with the word 'cowgirl' written on the side of its carrying bag, arrived in the post. Mattie was very excited and asked, 'When's holiday?'

'In just over two weeks' time. You must take care of Horsie; he's come a long way – all the way from a country called America, where Mike lives. And he had to sit all by himself on the plane so he's feeling a bit nervous at arriving in his new home because everything is new and strange to him,' I said, in preparation for Mike, Mattie's next visitor.

Mike often told me he saw himself as my sounding board in the adoption process. He was there to listen and to support me during those months when I talked of nothing other than motherhood and Mattie. (What had happened to that strange and mysterious time in the past when we had discussed books and politics?) He was there to hear me cry and shout, too. He would later recall how stressed and fragile I had been during those early months. 'You were being pulled in so many directions,' he said. 'There was the adoption and that huge adjustment, the continuing stress over your brother's health situation, and you were also dealing with a trans-Atlantic relationship.'

He also told me he often pondered when, and where, we might all live together and, in the end, whether he would even be in the picture at all. In one e-mail, towards the end of June 2005, he said, '*If you think you are cooling on the whole idea of us, and all that entails, I would ask you to please be candid. It was a chance I willingly took. I knew when your life changed, to the degree that it certainly would with the adoption, that things might move in a direction that did not include everyone.*'

And there was the vital goal of Mike's winning over Mattie.

He said he knew that if that should fail, he was certain that our relationship would be over.

When Mike arrived at Gatwick Airport, following a sleepless night flight from Texas, he was forced to wander and wait almost two hours in Terminal South, whilst Mattie and I endlessly searched Terminal North. When we finally met, he said all he wanted to do at that point was to get a beer, find the nearest bench, and spend the rest of his life on it.

After much telephone discussion, Mike and I had decided that 'holiday' would first consist of a few days on Mattie's own territory, to be followed by a week touring the West Country. Whilst Mike's home town in Texas suffered from 100 degrees plus heat, not only was it cold here, it was pouring with rain on the morning he packed the car. Still suffering from jetlag, his clothes sodden, he said it was all he could do to keep his eyes open when we popped in on my parents *en route* to Dorset, so that he could meet them.

For the whole of the day's journey, the rain continued to pour down relentlessly. With Mike at my side suffering silently, and Mattie in the back seat asking every five minutes if we were 'at holiday yet', I became convinced that, far from being the idyllic trip I had been dreaming about, this might well turn into a complete disaster.

'Is this holiday?' Mattie asked when we finally drove up to Frogmore Farm, where we were booked for several nights.

'Yes, it is,' I responded, between clenched teeth. We then dragged our cases out into the downpour.

'I'm sorry about the weather,' the landlady said, as we entered, 'there's normally a lovely view.'

All we could see from our room was a thick blanket of cloud. Soaked, Mike and I sat slumped on the settee.

Mattie, however, loved her little adjoining room. She soon

went exploring, ostensibly to visit the loo, and came back all agog: 'The bathroom's full of frogs,' she shouted.

'What?' I cried, and Mattie dragged me to have a look. She was right. There were hundreds of frogs all over the place: frog flannels, frog-shaped soaps, frogs on the curtains and frogs on the towels; even the toilet-roll cover sported a smiling frog.

Soon, Mike and I were smiling, too, not only about the frogs, but because the clouds had lifted to reveal a most glorious view of the sea.

Mike later recalled it was like a scene out of *The Enchanted April*, that moment when Mrs Wilkins opens the shutters onto all the radiance of April in Italy, with the sun pouring in on her and the sea lying asleep below her, hardly stirring.

As we looked down into the gardens of Frogmore Farm, we spotted the landlady waving up at us, smiling.

It was here in Dorset that Mattie drew what she called her 'photos' – pictures of the cows, the flowers and the beach which, the landlady had informed us, could be reached by a variety of beautiful coastal path walks varying in distance between one and four miles. Mattie accomplished all these walks almost entirely by herself, with the help of an occasional lift onto Mike's shoulders. Her reward was a swim in the sea followed by ham sandwiches and chips, and orange squash with ice ('don't forget the straw') at a nearby beach pub.

On one walk, Mattie unexpectedly asked Mike, 'Will you be my daddy?'

Mike grinned and said, 'Well, I might have to think about it a day or two…but that's the best offer I've had in some time.' He then bent down and tickled Mattie until she was giggling.

'That was a nice thing for her to say,' I whispered to him, later.

'Yes, it was,' he said. 'It's probably best to take it lightly. She may be saying what she thinks *you* want to hear. It *is* encouraging, nonetheless.'

In Dorset, I was pleased that Mattie also had the opportunity to talk and play with other children. One little boy, whom she met whilst we were dining outdoors at the little pub, we later nicknamed Lance 'Boils', after his mother (a Cambridge don as it turned out) discussed in detail her son's skin problems.

Lance was two or three years older than Mattie and quite intellectual for his age. He wore a cap with a long bill and a solar panel on the crown that turned a small propeller. He was quite a sight. But Mattie was intrigued.

'We're very careful to make sure he has a balanced diet,' his protective mother told us.

It was not so much the diet I wondered about but her incongruous partner – a rough and ready biker-looking type, who often seemed irritated by the egghead boy's 'smart alec' remarks.

After three blissful days, and yet another traditional English breakfast, Mike dragged our cases out to the car, this time in beautiful weather, and we all bid a sad farewell to Frogmore Farm, the landlady, and all the little frogs, too.

Driving off that morning, I noticed that the car exhaust sounded loud. As the day wore on, it seemed to be getting louder. In the early afternoon, we roared into the car park at Clovelly. How different this hilltop village was to my childhood memories. At some point during the last thirty years, it had become a world heritage site complete with turnstiles, large, crowded gift shop and hundreds of tourists.

Later, after poring over our maps (Mike was the navigator) we finally saw the turning to Tintagel, and soon after noticed the B&B sign hanging at the head of a narrow lane. We ventured down a tree-lined road and came out at a lovely, two-storey brick farmhouse with large attached greenhouse.

As soon as the roaring car was turned off, an animated-looking couple came out of the farmhouse, dashed towards us and cheerily announced: 'You're the first people to stay here!

It's only stopped being a working farm recently,' they explained, as they led us inside and along a wide hallway to a large, luxurious room with a huge, high bed made up with beautifully-pressed linen sheets. Adjoining the room was a Victorian bathroom where Mattie yet again was agog – not at frog-shaped soaps this time, but at the seemingly hundreds of multihued bottles of bubble-bath, bath salts and scents of every sort.

We were then shown the small children's room just along the hallway and the couple suggested that Mattie might like to stay there. I was a little bothered that Mattie might feel strange on her own, but she cried out gleefully on seeing the pretty bedcover and curtains, the little table and chair, and was adamant about having it as her room.

Later that day, feeling very pleased with ourselves in our new accommodation, we wandered around Tintagel on what turned out to be the day of the town's annual carnival. We made the most of the still warm and sunny weather by eating outdoors – Mike enjoying his first Cornish pasty – and later walked along part of the lovely coastline in the direction of 'King Arthur's Castle'. I had to remonstrate with Mattie for poking her tongue out at a local and for persistently jabbing Mike's backside with King Arthur's plastic sword, which he had kindly bought for her.

Towards the end of our walk it began to rain lightly, and by the time we found shelter in a shop doorway to watch the carnival parade, it was pouring. As the floats rolled past, the sodden participants were all the while smiling and waving to the crowds. Mike laughed and said, 'These are hardy folks. I can't believe they're smiling in the middle of this deluge.'

After a wonderful night's rest, we got up early to bathe and Mattie enjoyed a bath filled to her shoulders with bubbles. Afterwards, we dressed and made our way to the sun-washed dining room where the landlady seated us at a large table.

'This is by far the best traditional English breakfast we've had so far,' Mike told her, with a grin. She beamed with joy. As we finished our breakfast, the landlord joined us and chatted for a while, telling Mike of a trip he and his wife had once made to Houston, courtesy of an American feed company. 'We went to a rodeo and saw a monkey riding a dog,' he laughed.

With some reluctance, we said our goodbyes and were soon on our way to Cornwall. We made a brief stop at Port Isaac, on the landlady's recommendation, and it was *here* that a passing holidaymaker offered to take our photo, the first of us all together. Who would have believed, I thought, looking at it much later, that the three of us had only been together, by that point, for five days? What was obvious in another photo – me in my straw hat holding Mattie – was a look of total happiness on my face.

But it was not all blissful: Mattie's occasional refusal to hold our hand proved irritating – and dangerous, too, as she sauntered on ahead at one point in a narrow street and a car came much closer to her than I would have liked. Though if Mike held *my* hand, Mattie always quickly came up and slipped in between us – partly, she wanted to hold both our hands; partly, she wanted to prevent us from holding each other's. And the kicking that I had at times experienced, was once directed at Mike. But apart from that one incident, Mattie showed little overt jealousy towards Mike during our holiday and she seemed very much to enjoy the extra attention showered upon her.

'Is this holiday?' Mattie asked when we stopped near Veryan on the Cornish Roseland Peninsula.

'Yes, it is,' Mike and I automatically answered – not for the first time.

'It's been two years since I came here with my sister, Caryl,' I told Mike. 'We stayed in an old boathouse that belonged to my friend Lucinda.'

What a difference two years can make. This time, as Caryl foretold, I was revisiting the little hamlet with my new daughter – and with Mike, too, something Caryl had not predicted.

'That's the boathouse Caryl and I stayed in,' I told Mike. 'And this is where my friend Lucinda lives,' I added, as we approached a small cottage. We knocked on the door. 'She must be away,' I said, and we made our way to the footpath that led to the foot ferry to St Mawes.

We were walking back through the hamlet on our return from St Mawes when I looked up to see Lucinda.

'Beth, how lovely to see you! Would you like to come in for a cup of tea and see the cottage?'

'I'd love to,' I responded, hoping for a chance to catch up on one another's news.

But as soon as we entered her cottage and met the man I assumed to be her new partner, I knew it was a mistake. He was obviously uninterested in our visit and read a newspaper throughout. Lucinda was plainly ill at ease. Even Mattie, normally a chatterbox, was silent.

As Lucinda went to make tea in the kitchen, he – without looking up from his papers – called out to her, 'What did you want me to sing for you later, darling?'

'An aria from *Turandot*,' she shouted. She returned with a teapot and a couple of mugs. 'We've just come back from the beach. We went down to read the Sunday papers.'

'And to drink beer,' her partner interjected. 'Are you sure you don't want me to make the tea? You've got enough on today,' he said, going back to his newspaper, apparently unaware that the tea was already made.

'I'm a bit busy at the moment,' Lucinda explained to us. 'There's been a big funeral in one of the villages and I'm preparing food for fifty people tonight.'

'I don't know how you do it,' I said. 'Are you living here full-time now?'

'Yes, but I'm not sure what I want to do for a job,' she sighed and I recalled that when we'd last spoken, a couple of months earlier, she had been working for her partner's fledgling amateur opera company. I remembered her complaining that all he wanted was for her to be his secretary and cook, making dinner for all his friends that loved visiting the cottage.

'We really must be going,' I said a little later, and Lucinda, obviously embarrassed, chastised her amateur opera singer for continuing to read the papers in our presence.

I felt relieved when we were once again in the warm sun. And on our own.

Our accommodation in Cornwall was far removed from the boathouse of two years earlier. It was a very nice B&B, except that instead of the adjoining room we had been promised at the time of booking, a bunk bed, around which you had to navigate in order to reach the loo, had been pushed into the room for Mattie. But Mattie was, as usual, asleep most evenings by 7.30pm.

Traditional English breakfast was served in a large dining room where Mattie regaled an amused Dutch couple with various tales and reminded them constantly of the 'No Smoking' sign on the wall. At least, the husband was amused. His big-boned, expressionless wife, who reminded me of Coppelia with her rouged cheeks and pigtails, appeared to be the jealous type. Amusingly, they did indeed smoke, as we discovered later, upon finding them puffing away outside the breakfast room.

On the trip home, we met Molly, Tom and the girls, who were staying at Frogmore Farm for a few days themselves. The meeting allowed Mattie to enjoy a reunion with her cousins, an afternoon swim, and, of course, her favourite ham sandwiches and chips, and orange squash with ice and a straw, at our favourite Dorset seaside pub.

'We saw Lucinda in Cornwall,' I told Molly, as we sat outside in the sun, watching the children play on the nearby beach. 'She was with her new man.'

'What's he like?' she asked, and I described our meeting.

'Oh dear, it sounds like she's going for the same type. I met a friend of hers recently who said she's committed to him, but unhappy.'

'Committed to unhappiness?' Mike enquired, with a wry smile.

Towards the end of a memorable afternoon on the beach, swimming and chatting, Molly told me, 'Mike's lovely. You're fortunate because there can be so many problems with adopted children when their mother has a new partner.'

'They've been getting on really well,' I commented.

Mattie refused my help in getting out of her wet swimming things. Irritatingly, 'I want Auntie Molly to help me instead,' she insisted, a petulant expression on her face.

We arrived back home the day before Mike was to leave. It was very sad seeing him off at the airport.

Afterwards, Mattie and I were sitting in the garden.

'Mummy, shall I sing a song?' she asked.

After she had finished the rather plaintive tune, I asked, 'Where did you learn that song?'

'I made it up. It's about missing Mike.'

e-mail, 11 August 2005

Subj, Flowers (Mattie's title suggestion)

Dear Mike,

...Mattie and I were both very sad to see you go and the house

223

seemed so quiet back here... Mattie has been in her playroom
making you a gift, which she is currently wrapping. She just
said you are going to be 'really confusing' as to what it is and it's
for you because 'Mike is a special boy'. She wants to phone you
but I just explained you can't call anyone on the plane...I hope
we can all be together one day, I think we sort of fit together.

When, years later, I asked Mattie if she could remember anything about that first holiday, she said, 'I remember I had a bunk bed and there was a place where you could make coffee in the room... There was a parade, particularly I liked the best the music they had and somebody gave me a big, big balloon... I remember the wind was blowing my windmill...'

The first time I felt a real difference in Mattie was after Mike had flown back to America. We had been living together for almost exactly three months by then, and I noticed, as her confidence in her new situation grew, that she began to correct me when I introduced her: 'Mummy, I'm your daughter, not your *new* daughter.' And she would correct me, too, in my use of the possessive pronoun: 'Mummy, it's *our* house, not "my" house.'

At three months, I realised, that although the pieces in our kaleidoscope still rattled, some of them were now starting to settle. I became the devoted mummy watching my daughter at her swimming lessons, the adoring parent who could be heard telling the neighbours that she would be good at everything. I later laughingly apologised to my neighbour, Ann, a retired teacher, saying I must sound like all those dreadful parents praising their children all the time. Ann replied, 'No, not at all! You can't praise her enough!

And although Mattie still brought out her clutch of photos from time to time, to reminisce about her time at Jenny's, she did so less frequently. I decided to put them in my own bedside cabinet for her, leaving in her room the little photo album I had given her during introductions. I was still careful to keep the few special cuddly toys she seemed to enjoy that had been given to her by Jenny, and the one or two from her old mummy and old nanny. I felt like an old battered teddy myself now as I occasionally began to suffer from a virus or a bout of the flu. Mattie, by contrast, was enjoying the rudest of health. 'She's like a flower that's been watered,' announced Ann's partner, Jo, over tea one afternoon. 'That's what happened to me at her age, shortly after I was adopted and moved in with my new mum; I started having growth spurts and filling out.'

'She's lucky to have you,' Ann added, much to my delight. Into a neighbourhood inhabited primarily by widows and widowers, childless couples and single women, this magnetic, affectionate and thoughtful child had brought a breath of fresh air.

At three months into our new relationship, I no longer dreaded the start of the next day. What I did dread a little, however, was the thought of my social worker's first post-holiday home visit. Had word got back to Allie about Mike? Had someone from social services seen me with him? Did they know he had come with us on holiday? And if they did, would this jeopardise the adoption?

'You have no need to worry,' my sister Molly reassured me. 'The only reason they would take Mattie from you now, was if they suspected abuse.'

But I was still a little concerned.

'So how have you found the summer holidays so far?' Allie smiled, as we sat in the kitchen over tea. 'It's difficult to know whether to place children before them or after. On the one hand, it's a good chance to bond; on the other, it could drive one round the bend!'

'It's not been too bad *so far*,' I said. 'I'm lucky that Poppy and Mei are just up the road.'

'And how did your holiday in the West Country go? Did anyone accompany you in the end?' Allie enquired.

'Yes, a friend came along for some of the time,' I replied, and was relieved when Allie did not probe further. As to whether she suspected someone was on the scene, I really couldn't say. 'We managed to meet up with Molly, Tom and the girls on our way home,' I said, moving on to safer territory, 'which brings to mind something I meant to ask you about... Whenever Molly or another female is around, Mattie always wants *them* to do the things for her that I normally do.'

'She's rejecting you a little,' Allie said.

I was taken aback at her use of the dreaded 'R' word. Rather than rejection, it felt to me more like a need for Mattie to show her independence of me – or was that the same thing? Whatever it was, it was proving difficult for me.

'It's not uncommon for an adopted child to show indiscriminate affection towards others,' Allie continued. 'And you're more likely to get it with an older child. But it'll only happen until they've fully bonded.'

'You know, I was feeling rather irritated with Mattie this morning,' I said, changing the subject. I noticed Allie raising her eyebrows. 'She came down from her bedroom holding a piece of paper with thick blobs of green and red paint on it...'

My heart had stopped when I saw her standing there on the pale, stone-coloured stair carpet, her clothes covered in paint. 'Where's your painting apron?' I'd screeched, dreading the mess that awaited me in her playroom.

'It's for Uncle David,' Mattie said, looking upset. 'Because I feel sorry for his bad leg.'

'Following my brother's stroke, one side of his body was left partially paralysed,' I explained to Allie. 'He's walking now, but only with the help of a stick. When I heard Mattie's words, I realised what was important. She's so thoughtful.'

'She's *very* thoughtful,' agreed Allie.

'And when she rings Granddad, she always says, 'How are you, Granddad?' or 'How's your cold, Granddad?'

'You mustn't forget that a lot of *birth* children are not that thoughtful,' Allie smiled. 'And some adopted children,' she went on, 'because of their background, cannot develop empathy. You're lucky to have a child who is so naturally thoughtful and loving…'

The summer holidays continued their relentless march and out of the blue, Mattie asked if little Henry, a nursery school pal, could come and play.

What! A strange child in my house! I didn't know the rules – would I have to make them tea and entertain them the whole time? For days, I fretted about it until the little boy's mother rang the day before, to confirm that she would drop him off. Phew, I thought with relief, at least there would be no forced conversation with his mum.

But when the little red-haired angel turned up at my front door with his mother, he insisted he wanted Mummy to stay with him.

'That's fine,' I said, hoping I sounded genuine.

Did his mum know Mattie was adopted, I wondered, as we sat outside on the patio whilst the children went up to the playroom to fetch some toys. And if she did know, would she think I was behaving just like any other mother?

'Henry was really obnoxious with my parents at the weekend,' little Henry's mother suddenly said.

'Really?'

'Yes, he was quite rude to them.'

I could hardly believe it as I pictured the angelic blue eyes peeping out under a mop of ginger curls. But my main feeling was one of relief: it was not only adopted children who played up to their grandparents.

When Henry's mother mentioned that we shared a mutual

acquaintance, I assumed that gossip had already gone round about the adoption and volunteered, 'Mattie's adopted.' Immediately, I could have bitten my tongue.

'Is she?' she exclaimed, looking genuinely surprised.

Feeling uncomfortable and by way of changing the subject, I added, 'And funnily enough, Mattie stayed with her grandparents, too, this weekend, for the first time. She'd kept on for ages about wanting to spend a night with them during the summer holidays...'

'You can go now,' Mattie had told me in no uncertain terms, when I'd dropped her off at my parents' house.

I wasn't sure whether to ring her or not. I was afraid I might unsettle her, in case she missed me. But, in the end, she rang me herself in the early evening.

'Mummy, I love you very much,' she told me. 'Have you missed me?'

'Yes, I have,' I said (though I was enjoying my rare taste of freedom, too.) Mum then came on the phone and said that she thought it best if Mattie slept in Nana's room as it would be strange for her. She added, quietly, that based on her experience with Poppy, she half expected they might be bringing her home at some point during the night.

That night, *I* was the one who found it difficult to settle! I was surprised at how lonely I felt, and how strange it was, knowing her room upstairs was empty. I felt frightened, for some reason, too, and – unusually – left the landing light on all night.

I rang to speak to Mattie the next morning, but she refused.

'Please say something,' I could hear my mother say in the background, 'or you'll upset your mum.' But Mattie just held the receiver, staying stubbornly quiet until my mother herself came on the phone.

'We'll bring her over earlier than arranged,' my mother said. 'She's been missing you.'

'I wanted to stay longer,' Mattie announced, contrarily, when she saw me.

'She's been good, but quite defiant,' my father told me in an aside. 'She does need two parents – and it's good that you're firm with her; you need to be.'

'She actually threw a hairbrush at your father,' my mother said, when both Mattie and Dad were out of earshot.

'What!'

'Dad wanted to switch to the rugby when Mattie's children's video ended, and she wanted to watch another… But she's gorgeous,' my mother added, 'it'll just be a matter of time… Don't say anything to Mattie about it.'

I felt terrible, especially as it became obvious that my father had been a little upset by Mattie's behaviour. I had assumed that Mattie would exhibit the same model behaviour as when we had visited them for tea, during introductions.

Her night away must have caused her some stress, too, as Mattie, unusually, wet herself on the kitchen chair whilst I prepared her tea.

That evening, I read Mattie a bedtime story then kissed and tickled her.

'In a way, I was surprised that Mattie saw the weekend through,' I told little Henry's mother. 'I read somewhere that adopted children often fear spending a night away from their parents. For years, my niece, Poppy, had problems with sleepovers…'

The conversation stopped dead when the mother suddenly shrieked. I followed her frightened gaze to see Mattie standing on her bedroom windowsill, up in the attic, arms outstretched as though trying to fly.

'Don't worry,' I quickly reassured her, 'the windows are fixed; they only open a few inches.'

'Oh thank goodness,' she said, a look of relief on her face, whilst I felt quite embarrassed – she must be thinking I had a minor delinquent on my hands. *How on earth could Mattie do such a thing!* And where was Henry, I worried, as I rushed up to the playroom thinking she might have led him astray somehow.

I met them on the stairs, carrying a wicker basket and a blanket. 'We're going to play picnics,' Mattie announced.

'Would you like a drink and a banana cake for your picnic?' I asked, as the children and I came back onto the patio.

'Mmm, yummy,' said Mattie as she grabbed a couple for the picnic basket.

'Henry doesn't like banana,' his mother said, 'he'll just have one of the biscuits I brought.'

Oh dear, I thought, even that, I haven't done right. But I had to admit that I was enjoying the visit, and our chat, more than I had expected.

After a while, a knock at the door interrupted our conversation.

I returned with a small package. 'It's a late birthday present,' I said, unwrapping the parcel; I removed a pale turquoise ring and pair of matching earrings.

'They're beautiful,' Henry's mother said.

'Oooh, they're lovely, Mummy,' Mattie exclaimed, coming over to see. 'Are they from Mike?'

'Yes, they are.' I smiled as Mattie disappeared into the house, dragging an obviously reluctant partner behind her, only to reappear minutes later wearing a long white dress and holding Henry's hand. She announced they were to get married.

'She's a lovely child,' Henry's mother laughed. 'Was she with foster parents previously?'

'Yes, she was – for two years. She was very happy there so we plan to visit them next week, before she starts school.'

'Do you remember the way to Jenny's?' I asked Mattie, as I

glanced at her in the rear mirror, noting with satisfaction how cute she looked in her new flowery shorts.

Mattie had wanted (no doubt as a mark of loyalty to her foster mother) to wear her old clothes for this first visit back. But to me, it had felt like an affront and, besides, I wanted her to look especially nice for Jenny. I had eventually persuaded her by saying that Jenny would love to see her new clothes; Mattie put them on reluctantly.

'No, I can't remember,' Mattie replied.

Interesting, I thought, how just three-and-a-half months had erased those familiar landmarks from her child's memory.

But as soon as we turned into the lane – this time bereft of the bluebells that had lined it in May – she immediately cried out in excitement at the familiar sight of the chimney pots, and the cottage which, like magic, grew bigger and bigger as we drove slowly towards it. I parked the car in exactly the same spot as before, the spot where I had turned around to see Jenny wiping away a tear, and I thought how quiet everything was. Just like the last time, I felt a bit tense.

'Hello!' Jenny beamed at us as she opened the front door.

Mattie, I noted with surprise, seemed strangely uncomfortable and, as soon as we stepped inside, she stayed close by my side.

'Mattie, would you like me to go now or shall I stay a little while?' I asked, as Ruby and Sam ran in from the garden, obviously pleased to see her.

'I don't want you to leave,' she said, quietly, making me more than a little pleased.

'What lovely shorts you're wearing, and new sandals, too! Why don't you put your sandals in the back porch,' Jenny suggested, pointing behind her. 'Do you remember? That's where you always put your shoes.'

Although Mattie took off her sandals, she laid them by the *front* door instead.

'She's afraid she's going to have to stay.' Jenny chuckled, quietly. 'Mattie, Jack planted that beautiful fuchsia you brought me as a farewell present. Do you want to come and see where he put it?'

But Mattie still was reluctant to leave my side. 'Why don't you give the presents to Ruby and Sam,' I suggested.

After opening her gift with enthusiasm, Ruby proudly said, 'Look!' and showed me a plastic tube containing fourteen of her milk teeth.

'She had them taken out yesterday,' Jenny explained. 'These children hardly knew what a vegetable or a piece of fruit was when they arrived here.'

I remember Jenny earlier telling me how both children were filthy and full of head lice when they came to her. The state of Ruby's teeth, which she now shook like a child's rattle, had been cited as evidence of neglect when the case for removing the children permanently from their home was presented.

I had met their birth parents during introductions, when they'd been at Jenny's house for a contact session. I was out in the garden, giving Mattie a push on the garden swing, and I remember a woman and a man standing in the background. The birth father smiled over at us, but the mother looked daggers – she, no doubt, saw me for what I was: someone taking away another's child. It made me wonder at the time what my own eventual meeting with Mattie's birth mother might be like. It was something social services encouraged nowadays, to reassure the birth parents as to who was taking over parental responsibility for their child. It also gave the adoptive parents an opportunity to meet the child's mother. I felt uneasy at the thought of such an encounter, but it must be a hundred times worse for the parent, the one *losing* the child. Most likely, Ruby and Sam's birthparents would have sat in the same room where I sat during my prep course, whilst the social workers discussed their case. How on earth must they have felt, pleading for custody of their *own* children? The mother, I remember Jenny saying, was hard and defiant at the meeting, even scornful of her husband when he broke down and wept.

Watching Mattie chatting and playing with the children, I wondered how *she* must have felt, at two years of age, being taken from her mother, then taken to her first set of temporary foster parents and then, a few weeks later, to a second set before, finally, ending up at Jenny's. Would it have been frightening not to have had her brother and sister – or her mother – with her? Or, as it was for Ruby and Sam, would there have been some relief in having regular meals, baths and clean clothes?

Little Ruby had appeared to have been numbed by her life's experience, and in some ways seemed unlike a child. All the times I had seen her previously, she'd expressed little emotion and when she engaged with her little brother, Sam, I noticed her vigilance, how she'd watched him like a hawk – sister and mother merged into one. Now, she and her brother appeared happier and I noticed how much more colour was in their cheeks, and that they had both put on some much-needed weight. 'They're looking so bonny,' I complimented Jenny.

'Sam's talking a lot more, too,' Jenny said. 'Ruby told me she doesn't want to see her parents any more. She wants to be adopted.'

'Is the farming couple still interested?' I asked, when the children were out of earshot.

'I think so, but nothing's been decided yet.'

'You can go now,' Mattie suddenly announced to me, using exactly the same tone and words she used in the recent dismissal at my parents.

'OK, I'll just finish my cup of tea.' I was looking forward to a long hot summer's day of freedom.

'I'm going to have an adoption party,' Mattie then told Jenny who, with a look of surprise, raised her eyebrows at me, quizzically.

'Yes, you are, but not for a little while,' I smiled, making my way to the front door. 'I showed Mattie the adoption forms I filled in,' I explained to Jenny.

'And I'm going to have a cake for my party, too,' Mattie added.

'Oooh that's lovely,' Jenny exclaimed, 'I'm *so* pleased for you.'

I felt strangely alone that day. I had returned home from a bike ride and glanced at the clock; it was only noon. Time to prepare some lunch, I decided, and I would normally have relished the thought of a glass of wine and a meal on my own, but today I felt agitated – agitated at the thought of Mattie being back with Jenny. Would she even want to come back to me if she was having a good time?

After lunch, I tried to read a book, but found I could not concentrate. Had I done the right thing by leaving the time of Mattie's return open? When I asked Jenny at what time I should pick her up, she simply said that she had nothing on all day and would call me. But was that the right decision? What would other mothers, in my position, have done? Some, I am sure, would have stayed the whole time; others would have left their child for no longer than a couple of hours, at most. But Mattie had lived there for two-and-a-half years, I reasoned. I looked at the clock and discovered it was still only two o'clock. If Mattie wanted to stay the whole day, then why not let her? I decided to take out some embroidery. Since my attempt at reading had failed, at least I would be able to think and do something at the same time.

What were they doing now, I wondered, as I attempted a little more of the Hümmel child picture that would go in Mattie's room. Perhaps Mattie would tell Jenny that she was lonely living only with me. Or that sometimes I shouted. But I knew Jenny had sometimes shouted, too… And how would Mattie be after a day at Jenny's? Would it set back our bonding? I again checked the clock and saw that it was now three o'clock. I was annoyed with myself for not enjoying these rare hours of freedom. Even a phone call from Mike had done little to allay my fears. By four o'clock, I even thought about ringing. But if I did so, would Mattie and Jenny feel I was interfering? Then again, if I did not call, would that be interpreted by Mattie as showing a lack of concern? I realised, as I sat there on this lovely late summer's day, that I had rarely felt more miserable.

Shortly after five o'clock, I heard a knock at the door.

It was Jenny and Mattie.

'I'm sorry, but I misplaced your phone number,' Jenny laughed. 'So we brought her back ourselves.'

Mattie, I thought, seemed happy – and certainly did not appear sad to be back. I was pleased, and relieved, too, to see her. I kissed her on the head, wondering how she came to be dressed in clothes I did not recognise. She had a Winnie the Pooh in her arms that Jenny told me had been left behind in the move and was a gift from her old mummy. I was pleased to see the blue ball, too.

'She's had scrambled eggs and six sausage rolls,' Jenny said, evidently having enjoyed spoiling her. She handed me a plastic bag of damp clothes. 'I'm afraid she got messy in the mud and I didn't have time to dry them. The top and skirt she's wearing used to belong to her,' Jenny added, as Mattie beamed up at me in her 'new' attire.

'They're really nice,' I said (the little devil!).

As soon as Mattie and I were together once more, she announced, 'Mummy, Jenny said you have to give me carrots and apple in future.'

What a cheek! I thought, given all the fruit and vegetables I had fed her and here she was telling Jenny what I did and did not give her.

'Ooh, my toys!' Mattie then exclaimed, noticing the pile I had exhumed from the bowels of the basement boiler room. It had seemed a good idea to bring them out for culling the day Mattie had gone back to Jenny's. But still, I stood there with bated breath, whilst she went through them excitedly. 'This is from my old mummy,' she said, grabbing a pink Care Bear.

I was pleased that Mattie had something else that she could identify with her birth mother. She seemed to show little interest in the other toys.

Meanwhile, still feeling a bit left out of Mattie's day, I realised I was experiencing a sense of rejection. I decided to carry on where I had left off with my sewing. But Mattie, tired at the end of her special day and, most likely, now annoyed by my lack of attention towards her, started to play up a bit.

'Come on, bath time,' I announced, thinking how she, no doubt, had been a model child at Jenny's.

Whilst I later sat on the side of the bath and Mattie played in the water, she whispered to me, like a collaborator, that she had *not* had a bath every night at Jenny's after all.

'Really?' Drat! To think of all those bath-time sessions I had carried out each evening during introductions, the dozen or more times I had bathed her, all the while feeling like an interloper, in Jenny's home. But I did appreciate Mattie sharing this news with me.

Just as I felt something change within Mattie after Mike's visit, so, too, I felt something had been laid to rest with the visit to Jenny's.

It was about this time, too, that Mattie began to 'write' for me little 'letters' and 'invitations' she liked to read aloud, expressing her love in wiggly lines:

'Dear Mummy, Welcome.

'I love you so much. Especially I love Tibbles.

'I like tuna and I love all your cooking.

'I love staying with you.

'I want to stay with you for the rest of the days.

Mattie'

Things took an unexpected downturn a few days later. The first pieces of evidence were the empty bubble-bath and shampoo bottles in Mattie's bathroom, the contents of which had disappeared down the drain. Similar things had been happening recently, and coupled with my ongoing feeling of exhaustion and the unaccustomed stress of living with my new daughter, I was upset and confused. Mattie, on the surface, seemed even more settled and happy following her visit to Jenny's, so why was she now exhibiting such behaviour?

I had just dropped Mattie off to play with her cousins, and I knew Molly and Tom loved having her but I remembered Tom's recent offhand comment about her being a handful.

'I hope Mattie doesn't play up here,' I said to my sister, 'she's been doing some childish things lately.'

'No, she's lovely,' Molly smiled. 'But you know, taking on a child can be difficult.'

And only then, as their two dogs – strays they had also 'adopted' during their years in Hong Kong – came up to greet me, did I realise what a difficult time they might be having with three-year-old Mei, who had been with them longer but who was still testing them. I recalled Molly once saying, with a certain amount of relief, 'We've just learned Mei is on the

237

normal side of ADHD.' For she had been sure at times that Mei might have been suffering from the syndrome.

That evening, when Mattie returned from Tom and Molly's, I decided to deny her a bedtime story and then told her we needed to have a talk about her behaviour. I detailed what I lately had found unacceptable and in the process of doing so, I'm afraid, out of frustration, raised my voice a bit.

Later, as I lay in bed, concerned by the enormity of what I had taken on with this child, I decided to go over the folder that contained all the information I had been given by social services. Had I overlooked something, I wondered, as I rummaged intently through countless reports and forms. Nothing untoward caught my attention, no hint of anything sinister, but just as I replaced the documents in the folder, I caught sight of a red book at the bottom. I had completely forgotten the Red Book, which Jenny had handed to me on the day Mattie moved in. Perhaps there was something in here? It looked innocuous enough as I glanced through the pages, thinking how strange it felt to be handling a book Mattie's birth mother might once have handled herself. Then, I saw the written comments of her health visitor concerning Mattie's challenging behaviour after contact with her birth mother and birth auntie. I saw words like 'attention-seeking', 'naughty chair', 'uncompliant' and 'difficult at nursery'. Only now, as I saw those words sprinkled throughout the pages, did it finally sink in.

Yes, Mattie was lucky to have been removed from her dysfunctional family at an early age. Yes, Mattie had enjoyed a stable two years in the foster home where Jenny and Jack had proved to be loving and caring surrogate parents. Yes, she was a loving, confident and self-assured child. But only now, as I looked at those scribbled words, did I fully realise that it was inevitable that Mattie was going to be affected by some of the issues affecting other adopted children. There was the separation from her half-siblings; the two short-term periods of fostering; the long foster stay at Jenny's interrupted by visits to the old family – to say nothing of the mother's frequent failure to turn up for contact and the parade of new mummies and daddies who, during the two years of her stay, had walked out through the little white gate at Jenny's house to disappear with her foster friends. There were all the goodbyes that had been said. And, no doubt, the thought of 'big school' was now on Mattie's mind, too.

The phone rang. It was Molly. We picked up our conversation where it had stopped earlier that afternoon.

'Adopting a child is sometimes frightening,' Molly said, adding that Mei's behaviour had sometimes left her anxious, too.

Suddenly, I felt a sense of relief. It *was* sometimes frightening, but it was normal to feel that way, too.

'She's a lovely child,' Molly went on, 'and you're still in the middle of bonding – she's only been with you *three* months. It might take a year before you're both there... You're accustomed to controlling your life, but it can't be like that with a child. But, no matter how bad it becomes, never threaten her with going back.'

'I could never do that.'

'The good thing is,' Molly continued, 'Mattie seems very in touch with her feelings. Always tell her you love her, no matter how angry you feel. And always be sure to make up before you leave her at bedtime. Make up, no matter how hard it is,' she advised. 'Each time you make up, it will bring you closer.'

I put down the phone and lay there, feeling relieved, but a little saddened, too. If only Mattie and I had made up before I left her that evening.

I decided to go up, as I always did, to check that she was OK. I hoped that perhaps she might still be awake so I could cuddle her and tell her I loved her. But only the sound of her steady breathing met me at the top of the stairs. Disappointed, I returned to my room where, only with difficulty, did I manage to fall asleep.

I awoke in the middle of the night to see Mattie standing by my bedside.

'I want a cuggle,' she said.

'I love you, Mattie,' I said, as she climbed into my bed.

'I love you, too, Mummy,' she said, snuggling up to me.

'I came up to see you earlier. I wanted to tell you I was sorry I raised my voice but you were asleep.'

'Do you always come up to see me?' she asked.

'Yes, I do, just to check that you're all right.'

'Jenny never did that,' she said, falling asleep.

Over the next few days, Mattie began to open my post, even though I had told her not to. I threatened to deny her some treat if she tore it open again.

'But I love opening the post,' she moaned. At that point, I decided to examine Mattie's room. Under the bed, I came across a number of containers filled with food items, and in her bathroom I discovered that all the toothpaste had been squirted out of its tube.

Later, when I gave Mattie her goodnight kiss, I said, 'I love you,' although I was not completely sure I meant it at the time.

'Even when I'm naughty?'

'Yes, even when you're naughty. I don't like your behaviour then, but I still love you.'

I left her room without giving her the usual number of 'cuggles' and hugs.

Later, lying in bed, I felt lonely and worried. I had eschewed re-reading *The Primal Wound* since Mattie moved in: the last thing I had wanted to do was spend my precious free time reading about adoption. But it might have some helpful insights now.

As I leafed through the book, I discovered there was a

separate, albeit small, section on adopting an older child that I could not remember having read. Most of it was a reiteration of things I had already been told by social workers, but it was a relief to see it spelled out on the page in front of me: the occasional regressing to a younger age; the need for security and boundaries; trying to be in control as a foil against future loss; thriving on routine and consistency...

As I put off the bedroom light, I was very aware of not having made up properly with Mattie before saying goodnight.

Again, Mattie came down in the early morning hours for a cuddle. 'I love you as much as the whole sky,' she told me.

'Like the shiny sun in a big blue sky?' I asked.

'No, like a big blue sky,' she insisted.

The next day, I made an agreement with Mattie that henceforward, I would give her all of the junk mail to open.

The Saturday before Mattie's first day at big school, I had awoken earlier than usual and immediately felt overwhelmed by a feeling of entrapment. It had been a while since I felt like this, and I was surprised.

Later, as I made breakfast, I wondered how I would feel if Mattie were not in my life. What would it be like if I were the one living on the other side of the road and every morning I saw the woman opposite – me – coming out of her front door with Mattie? I know I would have felt lonely at the sight of them, and envious, too. Even so, I still felt suffocated by being tied to the house. I decided to ring Molly. When there was no answer, I assumed she had gone out for a walk with the dogs. How nice that sounded: to go for a walk on the Downs.

'Are you all right, Mummy?' Mattie asked, as I was deep in thought.

'Yes, I am,' I mumbled, quickly seizing from her a little container of tomato sauce in which she was about to mix some pecan nuts Mike had brought over. Then, the obvious occurred to me. 'How about going for a walk with me to see the horses in the stables and pick some blackberries?'

I expected her to groan and say 'no'.

'Oooh, yes,' she said, to my amazement.

Why on earth, had I not thought of it before – especially after all the walking she had accomplished with me and Mike in Dorset. Whilst she hurried to put on her 'Barbie' trainers, I packed some little snacks and her water bottle.

After we had walked a fair distance, I looked back over the town to see the church spire and the castle below, realising this had been a good chance for me to blow a few cobwebs away. And Mattie was lovely company, too, I thought, as she asked me to pose for photos made with her cow-parsley pretend camera. And when an older, bearded walker went by – no doubt reminding her of her foster father, Jack – Mattie gave me a mischievous look and said she wanted *him* to be her daddy.

'Shall I go up and ask him?' I said, and we both burst out laughing.

'I can't wait to tell you my plan,' said Big-Ears.

'Is it a bee-oooo-ti-ful one?'

'Yes, I've come to say that we ought to have a holiday – and we ought to go to the seaside – at once, this very day, because it's such lovely weather. We can paddle—'

'What's paddle,' said Noddy, looking excited. 'And where's the seaside? And what is it?'

242

'Oh, Noddy, – I keep forgetting how little you know,' said Big Ears. 'The seaside is a lovely place. It's got heaps of yellow sand and a lot of blue water, and you dig in the sand and paddle in the water. And you go right into it, too – up to your neck, if you like.'

'I don't like it,' said Noddy, looking rather scared. 'I don't even go up to my neck in the bath.'

'Oh, don't be silly, Noddy,' said Big-Ears. 'You'll love it all. Everyone likes holidays.'

Noddy at the Seaside, *Enid Blyton*

'Mummy, that was like me,' Mattie giggled, months later, as I read her a story from an old Enid Blyton *Noddy...* book that we had found in a charity shop.

'Yes, you didn't know what a holiday was either, did you,' I smiled. 'Or the sea – you thought it was a big pond.'

'I knew it wasn't, I just liked to call it that.'

'And whenever we left the beach at the end of the day, you used to say: 'Will it still be there tomorrow?'

Mattie looked up at me and laughed.

I always find a particular pleasure in looking back through the photos of those summer days that Mattie spent with her cousin, Mei. There they are dressed up in their fairy dresses or splashing about in the paddling pool, or eating lunch out on the patio under the big sun umbrella.

And I remember those times when I would take a glass of wine to the bottom of the garden and sit under the pergola where, hidden by the scarlet of the American honeysuckle and the deep red-purple of the Falstaff rose bushes, I would listen to the faint sound of their chatter and laughter carried down to me on the breeze.

There are photos, too, of those long, hot days we spent at the seaside. The timeless feel of a day, the noise and laughter of children on the beach, the plaintive cry of the gulls. And I remember cooking sausages on the barbecue, which we ate with potato salad. And that sometimes I would simply lie there under the sun umbrella, watching Mattie and Mei paddle at the water's edge or play with the pebbles. And how they loved to wrap up in their beach towels and have me rock them, in turn, like babies and sing lullabies whilst they pretended to sleep.

Missing from those photos but etched in my mind, is the memory of a woman lying close by on her own. How different my life has become, I remember thinking. I looked over and thought how alone she seemed, and I recalled all those times I had lain on that same beach, alone but seemingly contented. I wondered whether anyone had ever looked over at me and thought how I looked lonely, too.

'Where does the sea end?' Noddy said.

'Don't bother about where it ends,' said Big-Ears. 'It begins here…'

Noddy at the Seaside, *Enid Blyton*

On the morning of Mattie's first day at big school, I was feeling tense. I looked out of the study window to see Tibbles chasing away Ginger Tom, and I thought back to my own first day at our new junior school in England. How upset we had been – my brother, David, and sister, Molly, and my mother, too – in the office of the headmistress, an elderly spinster and JP, whose grey hair was tightly combed into a taut, compact bun. And how relieved we became at her suggestion that we come back the next day instead.

I was surprised to hear the sound of Mattie's sweet melodic singing as she entered the room.

'It's been a while since I've heard you sing, Mattie. That was lovely,' I smiled, turning round.

'I sing when I'm feeling sad,' she replied.

'Are you feeling sad about big school?' I asked, as she climbed onto my lap. 'Or maybe a little nervous?'

'What does nervous mean?'

'It means worried.'

'I'm excited *and* nervous,' she replied.

I took Mattie's photo on the doorstep that afternoon, just before we set out for school. She stood there, smiling, in her new school uniform, holding an apple in her hand.

'I'm proud of you,' I told her, as we walked, hand in hand, down the street. I thought how adorable she looked. What was most pleasing, however, and I could see it from her walk, was *how* proud she felt of herself, too.

Mattie clung to me for a few minutes in her classroom before she would let me go. Then there was the same little 'handing over' ceremony, or transfer of security, that we had performed each day at nursery – or in any similar situation where I had to leave her in the hands of a trusted adult. When one of the teachers came over, Mattie simply gave me a kiss on my arm and then turned around. And although I waited for her to turn back, she never did, and never would. This was her way of dealing with our partings.

Later that day it struck me, as I went to pick Mattie up, that up until only six months before, I had been commuting to Canary Wharf every day and now, at the age of 48, I was on the twice daily school 'run', or rather 'walk'. Not only did I wonder how she had got on, I was also interested to see what the other mums looked liked, and especially how old they might be. My own mother was only 27 when she picked me up from primary school, but I assumed the average age would be higher now, given that I lived in a town where many mums were in their forties, women like me who had had a career before children.

As soon as I arrived at the school, I noticed numerous what I assumed to be grandparents waiting there – the unpaid granddads and grannies who did the afternoon school run and looked after the children until their parents came home from work. There were some older mums, too, and even some dads, who had turned up with pushchairs to pick up their children.

Looking at all those strange faces for the first time, I felt like a fish out of water, but soon, I was looking at my own little fish peering out of the glass door of the classroom, as though she were looking out from an aquarium, mouthing 'Mu-mmy, Mu-mmy'.

Mattie rushed out and jumped up into my arms, exclaiming with pleasure how much she had enjoyed her afternoon. I was both relieved and pleased because she would be full-time from the next day.

'Shall we go to the library on our way home?'

Mattie chose some books and a Disney cartoon DVD and then, as we were about to leave, I noticed an *Anne of Green Gables* DVD on the shelf. 'I love this one, Mattie. Shall we watch it together?'

Mattie and I lay on the settee, both distressed to see Anne treated so unkindly by the first family who took her in.

'Mummy, why is she so horrible to her?' Mattie asked when Anne at one point began to cry.

'I don't know,' I told her, 'but *soon* she's going to live with someone really nice.'

'Anne can live with me,' Mattie offered.

Even though Anne was thirteen when she was adopted by Matthew and Marilla, I saw some interesting parallels with my own situation: Marilla's initial insensitivities – in wondering whether she wanted to take the child on – recalled my own scrutiny of Mattie's Form 'E' and checking for hyperactivity or any behavioural issues. And I knew exactly how Marilla felt when she voiced her fears to Matthew as to whether Anne would want someone as *old* as her to look after her. Early on, and in Jenny's presence, Mattie had asked me how old I was.

'Forty-eight,' I told her.

'Oh, you're very old!' she replied.

Jenny had chuckled and though I laughed outwardly, inside I was shocked.

How relieved I had been that afternoon at school to see the older mums and grandparents.

Watching the DVD, I felt a little ashamed of myself, too, when Marilla assumed that Anne had stolen her missing brooch. I reflected on my own totally unfounded suspicions in the early days when something had gone astray.

'You don't know what a social persecution it is to be adopted,' Anne had said at one point in the film. There is, no doubt, still a stigma in society about being adopted.

I smiled to hear Anne exclaim excitedly that it was the first time she had tasted ice cream. I thought of Mattie's firsts: her first taste of peanut butter, of tuna fish, and pasta with pesto sauce. With me, she experienced her first dip in the sea, her first holiday, her first trip on a train, her first visit to London, her first ballet, her first trip to the theatre. And soon, there would be her first bonfire night, her first Halloween, her first time on an airplane. There were her first musicals on DVD, too – Mattie loved *The Sound of Music* and *My Fair Lady*. 'I'm a good girl I am,' she would often mimic. And we would sing 'Get me to the church on time' as we dashed to Sunday School.

'But there are so many firsts with an older child!' I remarked to Allie during one of her visits. She had just told me how few prospective adopters wanted older children. I expected 'older' to mean, perhaps, eight or nine. I was amazed to hear that 'older' meant 'over two' in adoption circles. 'Most people don't want to miss out on the walking and talking and all that,' Allie explained, 'even though with an older child, the outcome is more certain – you know far more what you're getting!'

Mattie's second day at 'big' school was also the day of my second Looked After Children or LAC review. After seeing that Mattie was settled in at school, I rushed back to put the kettle on. This time there was less tea and coffee to make, for only the chairperson, Allie, Toby and the school nurse were present

'There have been a couple of blips,' I reported to them, 'where Mattie was particularly defiant – but I feel, on the whole, I managed them well. There seems to be a bit of a pattern: I begin to feel she's become even more settled, and then there's a blip. But I do feel that our bonding has grown stronger.'

'You might find there's always that pattern,' the chairperson responded.

There was general agreement that Mattie appeared to be doing well and it was unanimously agreed that Allie's and Toby's home visits should be reduced to once a month each.

'Could you make it alternate months?' I asked.

'No, I'm afraid we *each* have to make a monthly visit,' Allie said, 'but it should work out to be only one every other week.'

The chairperson moved on to the next item on agenda – that of contact.

Toby stated that they had come to an agreement on direct contact. 'There will be no meetings between Mattie and the birth mother,' Toby said. 'We don't believe it would be beneficial. We think the grandmother is the only stable adult in the family, therefore she will be the only one to have direct contact with Mattie.'

'I'm happy with that,' I replied, feeling relieved.

'And we're also suggesting a maximum of three visits per year with the siblings.'

I said that I was happy with that, too.

'I think the contact arrangements are fair,' I said (although secretly, I still thought direct contact with the gran was probably an overkill because I felt Mattie needed to move on).

'Is there a subject anyone wishes to raise?' the chairperson asked.

'Yes. The record of the first LAC meeting stated that I was against *all* direct contact. I've never been against contact – so long as it's in the interests of Mattie.'

'That's right,' Allie agreed, 'I've never known Beth to say she's against contact.'

'Would you make sure that's corrected,' the chairperson told Toby, who made a note of it. 'Now, we need to put a date for the next meeting – March 2006 – but I believe it's unlikely to be needed, as Mattie should be legally adopted by then.'

'It might still take another six months,' Toby protested.

'It's a straightforward case,' Allie said, looking at him, 'I would have thought it'll be completed by Christmas. Beth's already sent off the amended adoption forms to the solicitor.'

Whilst the bonding process begins the moment one meets one's new son or daughter, the legal process of adoption does not really begin until that child has been living in your home for a minimum of thirteen weeks.

'Some of our parents wait longer than that,' Allie had once told me. 'Sometimes, they feel they need a longer time to be absolutely sure they've made the right decision.'

Almost from the time Mattie moved in, I could only see a downside in waiting. There was the stress of the continual intrusion into our lives by social services; Mike and I were unable to make serious plans for a life for the three of us, and I simply could not envisage my life without Mattie now.

So in mid-August I had decided to initiate the process.

'You'll need to ring the children's court in Brighton to

obtain the requisite forms,' Allie had told me at the time; and following a rather surreal experience of searching under 'Brighton', 'Children', 'Law Courts' and 'County Court' for that magical telephone number, I finally found it.

'I'll send you the adoption forms straightaway,' an officious voice on the other end of the line finally told me. 'Have you filled them in before?'

'No, I haven't.'

'They're quite complicated,' she said, doubtfully, 'and you have to fill them out three times, by hand. If there's any difference – however small – we'll have to send them back for you to amend. You'll probably need some help from your social worker... Do you know if there's a freeing order or a care order in place?'

'No, I don't. I think there might be a care order in place.'

'And do you know if the adoption is being contested?'

'I'm not sure.'

'It's much more straightforward if there's a freeing order in place,' she said. 'You'll need to check with your social worker to see if there is one...but with regard to the forms you can always ring me, too, if you need help in filling them in.'

'Thank you,' I replied, feeling suddenly overwhelmed.

As I pored over the adoption forms a few days later, I became more and more confused. The boxes on the first few pages were obvious, but then I came to a page in which I had to input the birth mother's address – what on earth was that? And the name of the child's father: was that the person who appeared on her birth certificate, i.e. her stepfather, or did they mean her birth father? And who, or what, was the child's 'Guardian'? And what should I put in the box as to whether the child's parents had consented to the making of an adoption order? And if they had refused, I wondered, glancing down the page at the next box, on what grounds had they done so?

After rummaging through the plethora of forms and documents I had been given by social services over the months, I entered what I thought to be appropriate. I then discovered I needed the *original* care order. I again went through my box of documents to find I only had a copy. The original birth certificate of the mother was needed, too. I rang Allie, who told me I had to deal with Toby in regard to the application – and Toby, she reminded me, was away on his summer holidays. She suggested I ring his office for the documents.

'Has a freeing order been applied for?'

'I don't believe so.' Allie said. 'Again, you'll have to wait for Toby to return, or perhaps check with his office.'

'The mother's birth certificate is locked away in a safe,' I was told, when I rang Toby's office. 'I'll need approval to send it,' the clerk added, and I felt my stress levels rise. 'But it shouldn't be a problem and I'll ensure it goes by first-class post.'

As soon as the care order and birth certificate arrived, I attached them to the three forms and put them in an envelope, along with a cheque for £140 to cover legal costs (this, Allie told me, I would later be reimbursed) and popped it, blithely, into the postbox.

A week later, I found a badly torn envelope in my post, a large brown one from the County Court, and I was immediately at the end of my tether with Mattie; she had been opening my post again.

Out of the torn envelope dropped my cheque for £140 and a letter torn in half which, when put together, advised me that the adoption forms were unacceptable because the three forms were incorrect, were not identical and, furthermore, I had filled in two sections that should have been completed by Toby.

In great frustration, I immediately rang Allie for guidance.

'Toby will be back from holiday on Monday. In his absence

I'll ring the court myself to go over the errors with them and as soon as he's back, we'll get the other portion completed for you.' The second time around, with everything hopefully corrected, I checked and re-checked the forms. The last thing required was to reattach the cheque for £140. I retrieved the original torn envelope from the court, but there was no cheque inside. I was at a loss as to where it might be. I hunted high and low in the sitting room and kitchen in case it might have fallen out. I was certain I had left the cheque in the brown envelope on the dining table. I looked in the envelope one more time but it contained only the original incorrect forms and the torn parts of the court's accompanying letter. There was definitely no cheque. The whole thing was a complete mystery.

As Mattie and her cousin, Mei, played happily in the garden, I extended my search to each room in the house, including Mattie's bedroom and playroom, but could not find the cheque anywhere. At my wit's end, I finally decided the court must have forgotten to return it and that in my stressed condition I had only imagined its inclusion. I rang them up and was assured that it *had* been sent back to me. I eventually decided to go outside and check the rubbish bin.

'What are you doing, Mummy?' Mattie asked.

'I'm looking for something that came in the post,' I muttered, rummaging through the bags of rubbish. I soon came across the contents of Mattie's wastepaper bin that I had emptied the previous day. Gingerly, I went through the bits of paper now stained by teabags and covered with vegetable peelings. At last, there it was! Or at least part of it. I held half of a cheque, in my own writing, to the value of £140, all scribbled over in felt-tipped pen. I then went up to Mattie's playroom where, after another search, I found the other half of the cheque in her desk.

I went back down to the garden and told Mattie off.

Exasperated, I considered the corrected adoption forms now all ready to dispatch just as soon as I wrote another cheque. Wavering, I decided not to rush after all to catch the post. Perhaps it would be better to wait a while longer.

Later that afternoon, Allie rang to see if I would be agreeable to attending the next preparation course and speak briefly to prospective adoptive parents about my experiences. 'We hope it might encourage people to think about adopting older children, too. It was your comment about how there are so many firsts with an older child that made me think you'd be ideal to talk to them…'

I told her I would happy to do it, and then laughed as I came off the phone. *If only she knew!*

The next morning, I sucked in my breath and put the corrected forms, along with a new cheque, in the post.

It was quiet in the room, save for the sound of the solicitor's pen scratching on his notepad, the occasional query he tossed in my direction and the faint sound of the busy street and the buses transporting passengers up and down from the railway station. Like a compliant child, I sat there, answering his questions obediently and – in my exhausted state – rather dispassionately, too.

I was sitting in front of a man who, with his large, round features and balding pate, was finally putting in motion the legal portion of the adoption process.

I saw the previous four years flash before me in an instant. I recalled June questioning my motivation; Sylvia questioning my desire to be a mother biologically and my significant relationships; Elaine showing me the catalogue of available children; Allie attending the second Approval Panel with me; Toby bringing along the video; Jenny entering my hallway with baby Charlotte; and the first moment I met Mattie.

If I had known what it would be like, would I have gone through it all? Would I recommend it to anyone else?

'Have social services appointed a Guardian?' the solicitor asked, interrupting my thoughts.

'I'm not sure.'

'Will there be any contact with the birth family?'

I told him of the latest agreement.

How would it have been if Mike had not been in my life, I wondered. I had been a single adopter in one sense but in another, I had not.

'I know you and you *would* recommend it,' Mike later told me. 'Because you're happy.'

'Is the birth mother contesting?' the solicitor asked me.

'I'm not sure,' I replied.

I glanced down at my watch, hoping he would not be too long; Mattie would be coming out of school soon.

I'm sure I would have felt lonelier without Mike. With him, there was a whole future to anticipate for the three of us, not just two... Yes, I now decided with a smile. *Yes*, I know I would go through it all again...because of Mattie.

'Are you on an adoption allowance?' the solicitor asked.

'No,' I replied, once more like an automaton. I saw him note down my answer.

'What *is* an adoption allowance, by the way? No one's ever told me.'

He raised his eyebrows at my question, and for the first time his lips formed a wry smile. 'What you don't ask for, you don't get,' he said. 'What have you been living on these last few months?'

'My personal savings,' I replied, and his eyebrows rose again.

'And what was the foster mother receiving before Mattie came to live with you?'

'A foster allowance.'

'Exactly.' It was his belief, he told me, that as I had had to give up work to adopt Mattie, and would eventually be earning far less on a locally-employed salary, I should be given some sort of an allowance, at least for the interim period until Mattie was legally mine.

'I must say I always thought it strange that I have no parental rights until the adoption order goes through and yet I have the financial responsibility.'

'Quite. But the allowance is something you will have to raise yourself with your social worker.'

'I did ask about finance just before Mattie moved in, but I felt embarrassed about it.'

'No one likes to talk about money in a case like this,' he replied, 'but you have to.'

'She *is* a lovely child,' I said, on the defensive.

'That's *why* you need to raise the subject,' he said, looking directly at me.

What relief I felt as I made my way to the station – relief that, finally, someone in a position of authority was taking my view on finances. I felt a bit hoodwinked by social services. All those years I had been paying off my mortgage and putting money aside for my year of unemployment and now, it appeared, I was entitled to an allowance.

Finance must have been on my daughter's mind, too, for she brought it up on our way to school one day, not long after my meeting with the solicitor.

Astonished at what I had just heard, I stopped dead in my tracks. 'Mattie,' I told her. 'I don't get money for you.'

'But you *did* buy me.'

'No, I didn't buy you,' I said firmly. 'I chose you.'

'But you did sort of buy me,' she persisted.

'No. *I* chose you and *you* chose me.'

'I didn't choose you,' she said, after a moment.

'Oh yes, you did. You could have told Jenny that you didn't

like me or that you didn't feel you could live with me,' I fibbed, wanting Mattie to feel that she had had some control over her own fate.

Mattie paused for a long moment and then, looking pleased with herself, announced, 'Mummy, I chose you and Toby helped me to.'

'That's right,' I smiled.

'I'm so sorry about Mattie's picture,' the teacher said, when I dropped Mattie off at school.

'What picture?'

'Oh, perhaps you haven't seen it. There was a class photo in the local newspaper at the weekend. The form we asked you to fill in said you didn't want any photos of Mattie publicised outside the school. I'm afraid, it somehow got lost.'

'Oh no!'

'Don't worry! It hardly looks anything like her. I don't think anyone would recognise her. And we'll make sure it doesn't happen again.'

My mind went into overdrive. Perhaps her birth family had been scouting the local paper and would be lurking outside the school. I went straight to buy a paper and there she was. I had to admit it was a little blurred, so it was possible no one would recognise her.

The next morning, one of my neighbours stopped to chat as she took in the milk from her doorstep. 'I loved the photo of Mattie!'

'Oh did you see it?' I said, with a feeling of dismay.

'Yes, I recognised her immediately,' she laughed, 'you couldn't mistake her.'

Despite all my worries about the school's photo error, thankfully nothing happened and Mattie and I moved on. I was pleased how remarkably seamless had been her transition to 'big' school. She would later tell me, 'When I miss you when I'm at school, I think of you in my head.' But the blip I was warned to expect whenever there was a major change in her life didn't happen.

Then, ten days after Mattie's first day at school, she came into my bed early in the morning and began to cry.

'Are my brother and sister going to a new mummy?' she sobbed.

'Yes, they are; they'll be moving in with their new foster mummy before Christmas and you'll be seeing them soon after,' I assured her.

'No I won't.'

'Yes, you will. If I say you will, then you will.'

'What about Ruby and Sam? They might never have a mummy, so maybe they could live with us?' Mattie said, still crying.

'Ruby and Sam are soon going to have a new mummy and daddy and go and live on a farm.'

'I want to ring Jenny.'

'OK, let's give her a ring.'

Ringing Jenny occasionally, I had come to realise, was beneficial in that it allowed Mattie to feel more grounded. I believe it helped in the transition from her old home to her new one.

'I'll go and find her number and you can tell her all about 'big' school. But first, I raced up to Mattie's bathroom to check the shampoo and bubble-bath containers. They were full.

Later that morning, the postman brought a letter from the solicitor. It stated that although it was thought the birth mother would not contest, she refused to sign a form of consent so an application to dispense with her consent must be made.

And in regard to contact, once an adoption order had been granted, the solicitor explained, I would be the person who

257

had sole legal responsibility for making decisions as to what was in Mattie's best interests. If she became unduly excited or stressed prior to, or exhibited disturbing behaviour after, contact then it would be appropriate for me to reconsider the contact arrangements.

And finally, he warned me of the likelihood that Mattie's new surname and address might become known to her half-siblings during contact, and that they might well pass the information on to other members of the birth family. He outlined the steps I could take in the event of a member of the birth family causing disruption by calling at my home or telephoning. He also reminded me that as the mother was reclusive it was unlikely she would do so. Even so, this information caused me much anxiety for several days thereafter.

A few weeks later, I had taken Mattie and her cousin Mei on an outing to the beach when I noticed a woman watching me as the children played together happily. The water was too cold in October for them to go into the sea but the sun shone and they were enjoying rolling down the little hills of pebbles that formed part of the breakwater.

'I want sausages!' Mei called out to me.

'There's no barbecue today,' I laughed, as I sat watching them. 'But you can have an ice-cream in the park later.'

I noticed the woman still passing glances in my direction and that she was with a little boy and girl, and a man whom I presumed was her husband. I simply assumed she was looking because the two girls did not look English.

She then approached me and asked, 'Is that Mattie?'

'Yes, it is,' I replied, a bit taken aback.

'I *wondered* what had happened to her. I know her family well. My son, Billy, used to go to the same nursery. Someone told me she was being adopted.'

I looked at Mattie, who showed no interest at all in little Billy, but I began to feel uneasy and so after a brief word or two more, I called out to the girls and suggested we might go for ice creams.

'Are you looking after Mattie?' the woman asked me.

'Yes I am,' I replied, cautiously.

'So, are you her mother?'

'Yes.'

'Do you live here?'

'No, but we come here a lot.' I could have bitten my tongue as soon as the words came out.

'Do you know what happened to Mattie's sister? My daughter used to be her best friend.'

'No, I don't,' I lied. 'I do know that she's with her brother though.'

'They should have made sure the family stayed together. I think it's a shame they split them up.'

Well, perhaps you should have taken the three of them on yourself, I thought, ungraciously. 'It's not always that simple with families.'

'And it's a pity that Mattie didn't have a farewell party at her nursery.'

'But she did!' (I *knew* because I had specifically remembered Toby talking about it.)

'No, she didn't. Billy would have definitely gone to it – he was Mattie's best friend and she would have definitely wanted Billy there.'

I have never had my home burgled, but the feeling I experienced then was similar to what I expect one feels when such a thing happens. I felt as though someone had just gone through my belongings.

Not long after, when I had taken Mattie to see Jenny during the October half-term, I mentioned my meeting with Billy's mother.

259

'Mattie *did* have a leaving party,' Jenny confirmed, 'but I don't remember her ever mentioning a boy called Billy in all the years she went to nursery. He certainly wasn't one of her close friends.'

Allie and Elaine were in my home to discuss finance when I mentioned that the solicitor had said that I might have to obtain an injunction if any member of the birth family tried to contact me.

'That would be a very unusual situation,' Elaine said. 'I've never known it to happen.'

'I've never known it either,' said Allie.

'The solicitor said he had had experience of this on a few occasions,' I repeated. 'And someone approached us at the beach recently. She said she knew Mattie's birth family and kept asking me questions about them.' I still felt somewhat uneasy about that encounter.

Neither Elaine nor Allie said anything for a moment. Then Elaine said, 'There's very little chance of your having any problems from the birth family – especially as the mother is reclusive… Now as far as the finance issue is concerned, *yours* is an unusual situation,' she continued.

'Yes, I want to apologise,' said Allie. 'When I came in, I regarded you as an independent woman who didn't need additional financial help. I thought you might even be offended if I brought it up. I'm sorry about my error and hope it hasn't affected our relationship.'

'No, of course not,' I assured her.

'If we gave you financial assistance we would be discriminating against couples,' Elaine stated.

'But with a couple,' I responded, 'I assume one of them would give up work, at least whilst the child settles in, but there would still be a regular salary coming in from their partner. In my case, there's none.'

'Yours is an unusual situation,' Elaine repeated. 'I only know of one or two single adopters and they're on income support. In your case, because of your savings, you would be ineligible.'

'But most of my savings are tied up in shares. Perhaps I should sell them – my cash savings are getting low already.'

'No, you shouldn't have to do that, and you shouldn't be living off your savings,' Elaine said. But you should have asked us about it, if it was an issue.'

'I had the impression from Sylvia that if I raised the subject of finance, it wouldn't go in my favour with regard to my adopting a child.'

'What!' they both exclaimed, in unison.

'Sylvia – and June, too – always said that if I couldn't show I had the means to take time off work for at least six months, I probably wouldn't be allowed to adopt. It seemed a bit like blackmail.'

'That's absolutely *not* what we want people to think,' Elaine replied.

'I read on the BAAF [British Association of Adoption and Fostering] website last night that it's the duty of social services to raise the subject of finances with the applicant, not the other way round.'

'Yes, that's right,' Elaine admitted. 'That's one of the things we're doing now. We're about to hire someone who'll go through the financial side of things with new adopters.'

'So, presumably that person will advise people about things like tax credits? I happened to be listening to the Radio 4 *Money Box* programme the other day, and it appears I'm eligible for working tax credits. I thought that was something you only qualified for when you were working. If I hadn't heard that programme I would have no idea I was eligible… The BAAF website also states that when an adoptive parent is self-employed, which is effectively what I was, the local authority should be urged to give them the equivalent of a maternity allowance…'

'We'll go back and discuss it with our bosses,' Elaine said. 'I'll get back to you as soon as I can. I'm sure we can come to an agreement on this.'

'Thank you,' I replied, relieved that the meeting was over and that it had apparently gone well.

'Anything else we can help with?' Elaine asked.

'Actually I need to rush off now,' I apologised. 'I have my parenting course today.'

'How's it going?' Allie smiled.

'I'm enjoying it! I've surprised myself. And listening to some of them, I realise how easy I have it in comparison – Mattie's an *angel*,' I laughed. I then told them how I had had a recent revelation. 'They had a session on the need for boundaries and they said that all children needed boundaries. But all the while *you* talked about boundaries, I thought they were just for adopted children.'

'Oh, no,' Allie replied with a smile, '*all* children need boundaries.'

It was Molly's suggestion that I sign up to a series of twelve parenting classes held at a local church. Mattie and her cousins often attended Sunday school there. Molly thought that it might be useful – she had completed a similar course with Mei – and at the least, it would give me a chance to meet some new people. I assumed that, with my City background, I would have little in common with the other participants. But I *had* lost touch with most of my friends and acquaintances, hardly any of whom had been in contact since Mattie's arrival, and I still felt rather frazzled from my experiences as a new mother. So I thought it would be worth giving it a go.

By the morning of that first class in late September, I was quite looking forward to the event and even put on some make-up before making my way down the hill towards the small church.

The course leader was a very nice, petite blonde I guessed to be in her mid-fifties, and she began by focusing briefly on her own experiences. '…I suffered from depression for a while after each of my children was born,' she said. But it was the word 'claustrophobic', and the phrase 'not able to think a thought through', that made me prick up my ears.

This sounded like it might be better than I expected.

She then asked us to introduce ourselves, one by one, to the group and say a word or two about our circumstances.

Oh no, I thought, immediately feeling stressed: what will they think when they learn I don't have a birth child, but I've only adopted?

'Let's start with you, Heide,' she smiled at the woman sitting by her side. I recognised her as the parent of a child in my daughter's class; now word about Mattie being adopted was going to fly around the school like wildfire.

'I'm married and I have three children,' the well-built, handsome-featured Austrian announced proudly, as an infant suckled at her breast.

Why did she say that she was married? I panicked, thinking of my own single parent status.

'I always wanted five children but I did not meet my husband until I was 35 and I only have managed to have three,' she went on. 'That's why I'm here – I'm worried about the middle child. They say that the middle child always suffers from being sandwiched in between. That's why I wanted four so there would not be a middle child.'

Wait a minute, doesn't that mean there would then be two middle children?

'I'm worried about putting them in daycare,' Heide continued. 'I want to carry on with my career, but I heard on the radio recently that children who have daycare *do* suffer.'

'Thank you Heide.' The course leader beamed and motioned for the next woman to start.

'I'm married, too,' she said.

Oh, no! Everyone's now mentioning their marital status, I thought, heart sinking.

'I have a two-year-old and a baby, but the two-year-old is very jealous of the baby. My husband works on night shifts, which means I'm often taking care of them both on my own… '

Her situation sounded worse than mine.

'I'm married with just the one baby,' the next participant announced. 'But I hardly see my husband who works long hours up in the City. I've just gone back to my job as a graphic designer part-time, which I'm enjoying…'

How interesting – the last two women sounded more like single mums.

'I'm married with a baby,' another said, 'but I have my husband's teenage sons from his previous marriage every weekend, too. They can be quite difficult to manage…'

That sounded horrible!

'…And I can't understand why, although I'm not working at the moment, I never seem to be able to get on top of everything…'

That resonated with me, too. Apart from the kitchen floor, which I still resolutely swept, I never felt anything in the house was under control.

A shaggy-haired, brunette mother of three then introduced herself; she was married, too, and had what sounded like a monster older son. Or was the mother the monster? She said she once managed to get him to sit and chill out, or take time out, or whatever it was called, for nearly two hours. This led me to recall the little brat who had sat in the town gardens, that last day of Mattie's nursery.

Finally, the spotlight was turned on me. Mentioning nothing about my marital status, I said, 'I had a long career in the City before I adopted my daughter, Mattie, four months ago. She's almost five now…' I mentioned that I was spending a few hours a day writing, lest they think I lounged around all day painting my nails. 'My difficulties come partly from having to adapt from being a career woman to a mother. In my job, I was accustomed to being in control and having logical and sequential thought processes. Now, I have a child at the centre of my life. In addition, I'm still dealing with the ongoing adoptive process... '

To my surprise, a barrage of questions immediately came my way. *But these are all married women who have had their own birth children, so why would they be interested in me?*

I soon realised, it was not just children we shared. All of us were lacking in confidence and, to a greater or lesser extent, felt frazzled, isolated and claustrophobic. Having children was a great equaliser: six months before, we would have had little in common; now, I was one of them.

At the end of one session several weeks later, a woman I did not recognise introduced herself to me. 'Hello! I'm Mattie's Sunday school teacher. Would you like to come and see where she does her lessons?'

'Yes I would,' I smiled back. On my way out, I poked my head into the room, the walls of which were covered all over with children's drawings and the word 'Welcome'.

'That's interesting,' I said, turning to her. 'Do you say "Welcome" to them? Mattie's been writing little invitations and letters to me and they all start with, "Dear Mummy, Welcome."'

'Yes,' she laughed, 'we always say welcome to them, at the start of each lesson.'

Dear Mummy, Welcome

Would you like it if I said I love you so much. I could bless you. I love you so much. I could keep you for a whole day for ever and ever.

Mattie

265

'Toby will be visiting after school today,' I said, lightly, to Mattie one morning as she dressed for school. It had been quite a while since he had been in touch and she no doubt had put him to the back of her mind.

'I don't want to see him.'

'He still has to see you now and then, just to be sure you're all right.'

But Mattie did not look very happy about it, and for the remainder of the time before we left for school she became particularly – and unusually – aggressive towards me. I felt exhausted when I dropped her off, but thought no more about it until I picked her up later that day.

'Could I have a word with you?' her teacher, an attractive, motherly type, asked. 'Is there anything wrong with Mattie? She hasn't been herself at all today; in fact, she wasn't very nice to me, which is *very* unlike her.'

Mattie adored her teacher and I could hardly believe my ears. 'She wasn't very nice to me either this morning,' I said. 'I think it must be to do with the fact that I mentioned her social worker is due to visit this afternoon.'

'I'm so sorry,' she replied. 'I didn't know they were still visiting. Do they have to?'

'Yes, unfortunately, up until the time she becomes legally mine. I think a child reaches the point where they get fed up and the visits affect them adversely – *next time*, I won't tell her in advance.'

'That might be a good idea,' she smiled.

On our way home, Mattie said, 'Will Toby already be there when I get home?'

'He'll be arriving just after you get in but will only stay a short while.'

'I'm not going to talk to him.'

I said nothing.

'Will he be inside the house?' she asked, as we were almost home.

'Yes, he'll be inside when we talk to him.'

'Then I'll be outside.'

And true to her word, she refused to say a word to Toby when he arrived. She instead went upstairs and would not come down.

'*We* can still have a talk,' Toby told me. 'I wanted to say something about the legal process.'

After a few minutes, Mattie shouted down that she was hungry and I took her up a tangerine. Later, she came downstairs and sat in the sitting room. She put on a DVD, despite my request not to do so.

'I don't want to push her,' I said to Toby. 'Allie told me there comes a point when children want to move on, and that it can disturb them when they continue to see their social worker.'

'Oh, really?' Toby said.

I was surprised at his response, expecting him to agree, but he sat there and said nothing more on the subject.

'So are you bonding?' he asked, a little later.

'Yes, we are,' I smiled. 'It's getting better and better. My sister said she'll become like my right arm in the end.'

Toby did not respond to that comment either; I began to wonder if I was being a little naïve.

Mattie did at least say goodbye and give Toby a nice smile when he left. Thank goodness, that's over, I thought.

Perhaps not surprisingly, the bed-wetting restarted that night, after a long dry period.

Two days later, Mike arrived for his second visit, bringing a little cowgirl outfit for Mattie.

Since our August holiday he had stopped sending me e-mails, saying he felt I no longer needed them and besides, he was calling me at least twice a day now. I always looked forward to his phone calls.

I met him at the airport and we drove to our favourite country pub for lunch. Later, we both went to Mattie's school to pick her up. Mike could not wait to see Mattie again, although she had lately become unusually reluctant to speak to him on the phone. After his initial surprise, Mike hadn't made a big deal about it, though I thought it very odd.

Given how well the summer holiday had gone, I was sure Mattie would be delighted to see Mike. I could not have been more wrong! When we arrived at her classroom, she completely ignored him. I quietly told Mike that it was probably Toby's recent visit that had done it.

'It's fine,' he replied, but I could see his feelings were hurt.

The following afternoon, I had to attend a brief parents' meeting at the school and left Mike to sit with Mattie for an hour, never dreaming it might be a problem.

'Mattie is a most delightful child!' the teacher beamed, and then asked about her background. I filled her in a little and she mentioned that they would soon be talking about babyhood in class and was it OK if Mattie joined in? I replied in the affirmative – I didn't want her to be treated differently to anyone else and she did have a baby photo she could bring in. It was the earliest photo I had of Mattie, taken at her SureStart nursery when she would have been about nine months old.

'Oh good!' said her teacher. She then showed me some of Mattie's artwork and said they had been painting self-portraits recently. 'Mattie said we didn't have the right colour for her skin and she was absolutely right – we only have a pale pink! I'll make sure we add some colours to our palette.'

After the school meeting I met Mike and Mattie coming

down the hill, chatting and laughing together. I would never have believed it then, but Mattie apparently had panicked when I had left. Mike said she had become almost hysterical, shouting that I had left her and gone to America.

I felt I had made it completely clear to Mattie that after the meeting Mike would bring her down to the school, after which we would go out for an early birthday dinner for her.

At least everything seemed all right now, and the three of us happily went to Pizza Express, where Mattie sat right next to the pizza maker and, of course, enjoyed her frequent trips to the loo.

But although Mattie was on the whole receptive towards Mike during his visit, she now often showed jealousy whenever he openly displayed affection towards me. And the kicking that had occurred on that one occasion in August now happened to him once or twice more. Mattie's growing attachment to me had apparently made her more vulnerable; on some level it would appear that she realised she had more to lose.

Even before Mike's latest visit, Mattie in fact had become particularly possessive of me, and expressed disapproval if I showed any affection towards her cousin Mei – or even poor Tibbles, whom she would slyly kick off the bed when she thought I was not looking.

During Mike's visit, I received several letters from the solicitor. He wrote that Mattie's birth mother had not responded to the statement made for dispensing with her agreement to the adoption and therefore, at the next directions meeting in December, he hoped to arrange a date for a hearing to dispense with consent, most likely to take place early in the New Year. At that hearing, a date would be fixed for the making of the adoption order.

'Is everything OK?' Mike asked, after I finished reading the letters.

'Yes, everything seems fine. It looks like the adoption order will be made in January.'

Despite occasional difficulties with Mattie objecting to Mike's presence, we would look back and agree that that week in October, during which we enjoyed beautiful weather, had been one of our loveliest weeks. After walking Mattie to school each day, Mike and I would have a walk on the Downs and then go to a favourite pub for a long lunch in front of an open fire. In the afternoon, we would pick Mattie up from school and treat her to a hot chocolate in a café or perhaps her favourite tipple, a glass of orange squash with ice and a straw.

After Mike returned to Texas, he called and told me he had never seen me looking happier than during that October.

On the eve of Mattie's birthday, I walked into the kitchen to ice the chocolate cake that I had left on the cooling rack. 'Mattie,' I shrieked 'what have you done to the cake!' A big piece had been taken out of it.

'I wanted some. I love it!' she cried out.

'But it's your birthday cake! That hole is so big, I can't even cover it up with icing.' I groaned, realising I would have to make another layer and sandwich the two together, putting the partially eaten one underneath to hide the big chunk taken out. I was feeling nervous enough, as it was, at the prospect of hosting a party of five-year-olds the next day at the children's farm. It was ridiculous: after years in the diplomatic service and a long career in the City, I was feeling anxious about a children's party! And now, I had to make another cake.

Mattie rushed into my bedroom very early the morning of her birthday. We both then raced downstairs together to open her presents, which included a Baby Annabel doll that laughed and cried realistically. I was pleased that she seemed particularly delighted with it, for I had so wanted to give her a very special doll. Although she had brought several from Jenny's, none of them was particularly pretty and I felt that if there was one gift a Mum should give her daughter, at least once, it was a doll.

I often wondered how Mattie had celebrated her earlier birthdays, but she had either forgotten or did not wish to tell me. The only tangible memento appeared to be a photo of a caterpillar chocolate cake, which she had screwed up the first time we went through her photos together.

The postman arrived and added to her excitement – mine too – by delivering more cards and presents. Around 10.30am, still in my dressing gown, I iced the now perfect-looking cake and our neighbours, Jo and Ann, arrived with another present. They stayed for an hour or more, delighted to share in Mattie's big day, and were particularly fascinated when Mattie showed them what Baby Annabel was capable of. Then, without warning and much to Jo and Ann's amusement, she turned the doll off, announcing that she now found her 'annoying' and instead dressed up in the fairy costume Mike had bought for the occasion.

Later, with the refurbished cake safely packed into a basket, Mattie and I stood in the porch, sheltering from a steady downpour, awaiting Molly who was to give us a lift to the children's farm.

When Molly arrived, she told me that cousin Poppy was sick, so instead of her staying to help me as planned she would drop Mei off with us and then return home to nurse the invalid. *Oh, no…*

A short while later, I was waiting nervously for the rest of the children to arrive, certain they must have got the date wrong, whilst I studied the hands of the clock creeping slowly past one o'clock. Then they all seemed to arrive at once, with much noise and laughter, all in various fancy dress costumes.

'Can I take your number, in case I need to call you,' I quickly announced to the mothers before they had a chance to tell me they wanted to stay.

'But I've never left him on his own before,' one of them lamented. Her little lad nonetheless looked delighted to be able to run off, unhindered.

I could hardly believe how quickly the three hours went by, and soon the mothers were returning to pick up their little Katies and Joels.

'How did Henry enjoy it?' a familiar face asked me as I was packing away some things. Henry's mother had been particularly bothered about leaving him on his own, he being the youngest child there.

'Oh, he's had a wonderful time,' I smiled, and then saw her aghast expression. I looked over to see little Henry crying and running away at top speed from one of the boys dressed in an especially grotesque Dracula suit. She must think I'm irresponsible, I thought guiltily, as she rushed off to save her threatened son.

For the most part, though, I felt rather euphoric at how well our first birthday celebration together had gone. It was a poignant time for me, as well. I realised that Mattie was losing some of her babyishness and, with some sadness, I thought about how quickly the time had been passing.

I was relieved there was little in Mattie's behaviour over the following days to indicate that her birthday had been difficult for her. Special mention about birthdays, and the trauma often associated with them for the adopted child, had been made in *A Primal Wound*.

Mattie did unexpectedly bring up the names of two birth cousins during that period, names I had never heard before; she said that they had been her favourite cousins. She told me about them one morning, when she came into my bed for her usual morning cuddle.

Mattie also said she wanted to see her brother and sister, and she especially wanted Ruby and Sam to come and live with us. She wanted Anne of Green Gables to be all right, too. And, in her usual Mattie way, she said something very special, that I will never forget:

'I haven't given you a "thank you" card, Mummy.'

'You don't need to give *me* one; you've already said thank you for your birthday present.'

'Thank you for *you*, Mummy.'

'That's a sweet thing to say, Mattie.'

'Will you give me a big cuggle, Mummy?'

I drew her to me and hugged her even tighter.

'Fanks,' she said.

It was now five months since Mattie had moved in and I began to sense a positive change in her, a sense that she was more settled. I believed that we had probably reached another milestone in our relationship.

I often thought back to Molly telling me that Mattie would become more and more like my right arm. I could look back and see that even one month before, there was still an occasional blank look when I picked her up from somewhere as if, for a moment, she did not know who I was. And the times when she would run to someone else for a tissue to wipe her runny nose were occurring less often. More and more, Mattie wanted my cuddles and to hear my giggles, too – she always knew how to make me laugh. And how nice it was that her natural confidence and enthusiasm had not diminished at all! I remember laughing delightedly on the way to school one morning when she cried out with excitement at the thought of a part in the school play. And now, when she grazed her knee she *would* cry, which I found more natural than her need to always fight off the tears and force herself to be brave.

By now, I had stopped nearly all of my planning and some

of the *nicest* days were those with nothing scheduled. I would get up and do some baking with Mattie's help and after lunch we might go for a walk with her doll's pram to a park. When the evening drew in, we would have tea and watch some TV together. We had, I realised, fitted ourselves into each other's routines like two cats. Mattie still had to be the first to go up the stairs to put in the bubble-bath and still had to be the one to pull out the bath plug – these things I would not dare do.

Our early mornings had a routine, too, but sometimes with a slight variation. She would at times let me have a lie-in whilst she went down to watch 'tots' TV and help herself to some fruit and rice cakes. I would follow down later, having perhaps snatched another half-hour of sleep – if other mothers did not let their children watch morning TV, who cared?

Mattie, doubtless, was still sorting things out in her head, and although I never knew for sure what went on in it, I did have some help from an unexpected quarter: her cuddly toys. Which toys she took to bed with her or played with in her pram, would tell me a little of what was going on.

One morning, she brought the pink Care Bear that her old mummy had given her, into my bed.

'I'm glad that you have your Care Bear,' I said, 'because you can think about your old mummy when you see it.'

'I can't think of *her* because I'm also thinking of you,' she said.

'You can think of *both* of us, Mattie. Me and your old mummy at the same time.'

When my biological clock had been ticking away, and when I was faced with the adoption deferment, time seemed to have been against me. And time seemed to have been against Mattie, too, as she waited impatiently for a new mummy. *Now*, time was the bonder. Time had become our friend.

On a cold, sunny November afternoon, I dropped off my daughter at a classmate's birthday party. It was the first party invitation she had received and we were both excited about it.

That morning, after dressing, Mattie had asked what shoes she would be wearing.

'Why, your school shoes,' I replied (they were actually rather pretty ones).

'I always wore party shoes when I was at Jenny's,' she grumbled. I could see she was not very happy about it and after I had left her at the birthday boy's house, I slunk off making a mental note to buy her party pumps for the next occasion.

I now had a whole two hours for walking on the Downs, but just as I was about to ascend the muddy trail that led to the old farmyard, I bumped into a couple I knew, going the other way.

One of them beamed. 'We've seen Mattie coming out of the house on one or two occasions and she looks lovely – you can tell even from a distance. We're delighted for you! How's it going?'

'It's going really well, thanks,' I smiled. 'I'm lucky to have her. She's settled in quickly and seems so happy and stable.'

'That's down to the foster mother,' the woman said.

'Yes, it is.' Suddenly, though, I was fed up at hearing this particular refrain.

'Does she have a life history book?' the woman asked.

'Yes, she does,' I replied, and she went on, good-naturedly, extolling the benefits of a life history book.

I became a little agitated. 'Actually, that reminds me, I haven't gone through it with her for a while. I keep it in a cupboard.' I thought she looked at me slightly oddly and added, quickly, 'I don't like the thought of her alone in her room with questions in her mind. I really should get it out again.'

'Yes, you should,' she smiled.

I knew she was well-meaning but as I continued on my way, I thought of how many views people had on something they had little or no firsthand knowledge of, and how often they felt the need to share them.

I said as much to Allie, at our next session. 'All these programmes on TV about adoption don't help,' Allie said. 'Everyone thinks they're an expert.'

I did indeed get the life history book out of the cupboard a few days later, to go through it with Mattie, but after putting it down to answer a phone call I completely forgot about it.

'Mummy, we haven't looked at this for a long time,' Mattie said, catching sight of it on the chair in my study.

'Yes, I know, let's have a look at it now.'

I sat down with her and I thought it interesting how this time she didn't mention the blank circle in the family tree. Interesting, too, that she had (or said she had) forgotten her auntie's name and that she did not want to talk about her old cousins when I asked after their ages. But she was always drawn, I noticed, to the photos taken during her foster placement with Jenny, and those of her half-siblings and of her birth mother.

'Have you found you're always hearing people's views about adoption since you've had Poppy and Mei?' I asked Molly, when I next saw her.

'Come to think of it, I have,' she said, 'and especially from mothers taking the side of the birth mother. It especially happened when I adopted Mei,' Molly went on. 'There was a lot of bad press then about the Internet baby business and people often asked if I'd got Mei on the black market, and how much I paid for her.'

'I think it's because people tend to look on an adopted child as community property,' I said. 'Everyone feels they have a right to her, and a right to their view. I don't believe I'd have heard half the things said to me if Mattie were my birth child…'

'Is your daughter of your own blood?' the woman on the park bench beside me had asked. I was watching Mattie clambering up the slide; several children were queued up behind her.

'No, she's adopted,' I replied, thinking what a presumptuous question it was coming from a total stranger.

'I know your sister slightly, and I *thought* I'd seen her playing with your sister's children,' the woman explained.

I assumed that Molly must have told her I had adopted – or perhaps, like so many, she just wondered about Mattie's darker skin.

'I tried to adopt, too, once,' she said, quietly.

'Oh, really?' I said, slightly taken aback.

'Yes, but there was a problem with him from the beginning. We were just unable to bond.'

'How old was he?' I asked.

'Only eighteen months. He was a beautiful child, but it was very difficult. In the end we asked social services to take him back.'

Take him back? A disruption? Had I heard correctly?

'It wasn't just a case of them coming and taking him away, however,' she added. 'He'd already been with us several months so the social worker said they must do it gradually, to limit disturbance to him.'

I thought how awful that must have been, for both her and the child. I didn't know quite what to say.

'Just before they took him away, we finally had begun to bond,' she continued. 'I was so happy. And around the same time I found I was pregnant… My husband and I by then had decided we wanted to keep him, but my social worker refused. She said I'd only change my mind again and they took him away.' She was quiet for a few moments. 'It would have worked out just fine, I know… I often wonder how he is.'

'Do you know what happened to him in the end?'

'Yes, I heard he went to another family and that it worked out really well there… I do hope though, that one day he'll want to come back and see us.'

At the end of the month, I had my last session of the Parenting Course. Everyone agreed that the course had been a big confidence booster – I even went so far as to make an appointment at a trendy new hairdressing salon in Brighton.

The course leader, as she was finishing, said she would like to take ten minutes to explain to everyone why she was a Christian. As she spoke, I looked around and saw that everyone's head was bent down. Indeed, you could have heard a pin drop, I thought with amusement, recalling all those times when it had been difficult to get a word in edgeways.

'You're very brave to have adopted, all alone,' the course leader told me after the session. 'We've all been saying that.'

An attractive blonde-haired woman in her forties now joined us and said to me, 'I found it so interesting, listening to you.'

'I never thought women who had had their own children would be interested,' I replied.

'*I* find it fascinating. I think you're very brave, too.'

One important thing I took away with me from the parenting course was that whilst *some* issues were specific to adoptees, most affected *all* children. I would always try to remember this.

When I arrived home from the hairdressers, I shrieked when I got a good look at myself in the mirror. Not only had I been nearly scalped, but what remained of my hair was almost black. What had happened to all those subtle tints I thought had been mixed in? What would Mattie think? I remembered the photo of her birth mother in the life history book – the one in which her mother's hair had had an obvious dousing of peroxide. 'I don't like that one. I don't like the colour of her hair,' Mattie had said.

'Why is your hair a different colour?' Mattie asked, without her usual sunny smile, when I picked her up from school.

'I've had it coloured. Don't you like it?' *Please say yes!*

'No.'

I felt terrible, and wondered if her teacher thought me heartless: poor little thing, she's just getting used to her new mummy and then she goes and changes her looks. 'Keep change to the minimum' was one of the rules of adoption.

But what worried me more was that I had a housewarming party to attend that evening. It was my first time to dress up in ages, my first opportunity to get out of the house and I had very much looked forward to this event – now, what would everyone think when they saw my hair?

'I like your hair,' the host commented, sweetly, upon my arrival. 'How's Mattie?'

'She's doing really well,' I replied, as he handed me a glass of wine. 'What a beautiful apartment you have! I recognise some of the paintings from your old flat.'

The doorbell rang and he left me to greet another group of guests. Sue, an acquaintance of mine now approached and smiled, 'Was it how you imagined?'

'No, it wasn't – but I don't think anyone could adequately prepare themselves for the experience,' I said. (*Her* hair was very dark, I noted, and obviously coloured – so why did it work for her?)

'How has it changed you?' was her next question. I was stumped for a response at first.

'I think I'm probably more flexible,' I then replied, 'which isn't a bad thing.'

I realised, for the first time since adopting Mattie, I was

able to stand at a distance from all I had gone through and get a little perspective.

I reminded Sue how, years earlier, she had asked for a tour of my newly renovated house. That day, I had noticed a mark on the wall outside the attic rooms (now occupied of course by Mattie) and I had felt rather annoyed as I tried to rub it away. 'Houses are made for living in,' she had quipped, a comment that irritated me at the time.

'How right you were!' I now laughed with her. Six months after Mattie had moved in, I realised it no longer mattered if there were some felt-tip pen marks on the kitchen table; even the marks on the carpet outside her room, which had annoyed me when she made them, no longer bothered me. And Sue chuckled to hear me recount how sweeping the kitchen floor was the last remaining vestige of control I might experience.

'Where's her bedroom?' she asked.

'She has a bedroom, playroom and bathroom in the attic,' I smiled.

'Well, you've certainly got enough room in your house.' She chuckled and I recalled how guilty I had felt at times on moving into my new house when the odd comment was thrown in my direction about it being far too big for one. Why should I have ever given a toss?

'But what about you?' I asked, thinking that given all Sue's questions she might have an interest in adoption, too. 'Did you ever want children?'

'Oh, no, I never wanted them,' she said, abruptly, and the shutters came down.

'Do you get any money for adopting?' Cicely asked, out of Mattie's earshot.

Cicely was my vinegary neighbour, whose handsome old face resembled a gnarled oak tree; she would have made a perfect Dame Slap.

'No I don't – it's not like fostering,' I said, handing her a glass of wine.

'They get quite a lot for fostering, don't they.'

'Yes. I believe, they do.'

'Far better value in my view,' Cicely opined.

'I feel adoption is better for Mattie and it's better for me, too,' I told her.

'Quite,' she said. 'Are you behaving yourself?' she asked Mattie, who had now approached.

'Yes,' Mattie nodded.

I had threatened Mattie, before Cicely came round, that she would be unable to watch a DVD if she misbehaved. She was now the model child, playing with a dolls' house given to her by another elderly neighbour.

'You've undergone an astonishing transformation since having her,' Cicely announced, looking at me.

I was amazed. Cicely rarely gave out compliments and secretly, I felt rather pleased. I took a sip of my wine whilst I waited for more of the same.

'I can hardly believe you're the same person who had a job in the City and went to the theatre and opera all the time and *now* you're completely child-focused.'

I listened, a bit bewildered now, wondering whether this was going to turn out to be a compliment, after all.

'I suppose, though, it's expensive going to the opera and ballet,' she said.

'Yes, it is.'

But it was more than the cost of a ticket. I felt I had been keeping my head barely above water the previous few months, dealing with all the changes in my life. I had had to bond with my new daughter, discover the dishes that she liked, revamp my list at the supermarket and remember to get Calpol from the chemist. I was often suffering, too, from some bug Mattie brought home from school. And, all the while we were

281

adjusting to one another, I was also dealing, on a weekly if not daily basis, with social worker visits and the solicitor, and trying to maintain a trans-Atlantic relationship. For the moment, I felt I had enough on my plate.

I mentioned to Cicely that I had lost touch with a lot of people since Mattie moved in.

'It's *because* you've changed that your single friends are no longer in touch,' Cicely said, knowingly. 'You've changed your focus. You're no longer interested in local gossip or want to do the things singles like to do.'

So there I had it, in one.

'It's like when I was a girl,' she went on, 'the first one to get married was ostracised because they weren't like the rest of the gang any more.'

'I hadn't thought of it that way.'

'When are you going back to work?'

'I'm taking at least a year off.'

'Oh really? Don't you miss it?'

'I don't, actually. And anyway I'm quite busy,' I added as I re-filled our glasses, 'I've started to write a book.' That will show her, I thought – completely child-focused indeed! 'There's been a lot of interest in the adoption, from all sorts of people.'

'I think it's immensely interesting,' she replied. 'But I find it especially interesting that you've had a man in tow as well. Most women would find it *enough* to adopt a child; they wouldn't want a man around.'

'Really? I've only spoken to one other woman who adopted as a single parent and, come to think of it, she *did* sound content just being on her own with her daughter.'

'Are you staying here for Christmas?'

'We're actually going to Texas. I'll be cooking an early Christmas dinner for the family before we go, so that Mattie will have a sort of family Christmas here, too.'

282

'And are you thinking of settling over there?'

'I don't know yet. We want Mattie to settle in first – that's the main thing.'

'I think you're far better off over here. Your sister's such a splendid woman; make sure you don't move too far away from her.'

After Cicely had gone, and I was making Mattie's lunch, I wondered whether I was still the same *me*. Was I different? It *was* true that I was no longer interested in the latest play, film, book, art exhibition or restaurant. And I had long thrown away the list of countries I still wanted to visit. Rather than planning an exotic trip, now I was taking Mattie on the bus to see *Jungle Book* at the Brighton theatre. And our holiday with Mike in the West Country – the glorious walks, making sand pies on the beach and eating ham sandwiches and chips in the nearby pub – had given me far more pleasure than walking around some exotic street market.

Where I *was* the same *me*, was in feeling a sense of guilt at going away from my family for Christmas. Until recently, Mike had planned to come over here, but I later decided that four weeks away from the entire adoptive process would do me much good. I also felt it would be good for Mattie to have a break, too, a break from 'big' school and the long string of social workers.

'I'm going to southern India for Christmas this year,' Allie told me, on her last visit before the holidays.

'How lovely!'

'What are you doing with Mattie?'

'We're going to Texas.'

'Oh, that's a long way,' she laughed.

I had checked with Allie and Toby about the possibility of my taking Mattie abroad for a short holiday whilst she was still not legally my daughter. Both had been positive about the idea and Toby had arranged Mattie's passport; since it had to be under her birth surname, he had also given me a supporting letter to show immigration, if necessary.

'Do you have friends there?' Allie asked me.

'Yes I do, and Mattie's very excited about it, too.'

'I come from a big family and I've always spent Christmas with them,' Allie said. 'So it feels a bit strange making the break this year.'

'That's exactly how I feel!'

'Big families can be both a boon and a bane,' she laughed. 'Have you found that the dynamics have altered since Mattie moved into your family?' she added, taking me by surprise. 'The introduction of a new child often can change family relationships and roles.'

'I suppose *my* role has changed. I was first and foremost the eldest daughter and sister. Now I'm also Mattie's mother. That probably took some adjustment for all of us. I was in my former role for nearly 40 years,' I laughed. 'My mother made an interesting comment recently. She said she'd never thought about it before but it must be *more* difficult for a family adopting an older child. She said she's found it more difficult herself. When Molly adopted her children, they were babies, just like any other babies. But Mum said it's different knowing how to deal with an older child. She said it would have been useful to have had something to read.'

'I *did* give you something for them to read,' Allie smiled.

'I know, and I remember thinking, why on earth should I be giving this to my parents? I never dreamed an adoption would have much effect on anyone else in the family. Now, of course, it's obvious that it did... Actually in some ways, my mother reminds me of Jenny.'

'They probably both have what would now be called an "old-fashioned" way of bringing children up,' suggested Allie.

'Yes, they both know the comforting things that can only come with experience – such as my Mum's recent suggestion of a hot water bottle when Mattie complained of a stomach ache. Why hadn't I thought of that, I wondered, after ringing her.'

'And what about your relationship with your nieces?' Allie asked.

I remembered Molly telling me how Mei had become more aggressive after Mattie's arrival – and how surprised and guilty I had felt on hearing those words.

'Yes, it's been a big change for Mei, too,' I said.

'She was probably the baby of the family and now she's got competition,' Allie smiled.

'Yes, though Mattie can be a little devil, too. Their relationship is indeed uncanny. Mattie even copies the way Mei speaks.'

'Really?' Allie laughed.

'Yes. Because of a hearing problem Mei says some words in a different way and Mattie mimics her perfectly...But she's also helped with Mei's speaking and social skills. Mattie, being a little older, is higher in the pecking order and sometimes plays the little mother – though sometimes she acts like a three-year-old with Mei. It's given me a brief glimpse into her toddler years that I missed.'

'What about Poppy?' Allie asked.

'I don't see so much of Poppy now. That's partly to do with the fact that Mattie and Mei play a lot together. But Poppy also likes to be with friends her own age. She's grown up a lot in the last year.'

I felt sad that Poppy and I had grown apart, although it had already begun when Mei arrived on the scene.

I mentioned Molly's recent comment about how demonstrative and in tune with her feelings Mattie was, and that because of that, she had had a positive impact on the entire family. Although my family *was* very close, we were not particularly effusive. Mattie, it seemed, had brought us out of ourselves. Often my father would look at her, seemingly mesmerised, and I thought back to the old black and white photo of him carrying me in the garden many years ago; he wore the same look in the photo that I now saw when he looked at Mattie.

I was excited by the prospect of Mattie and I spending our *first* Christmas together visiting Mike in Texas. Not only did we both very much look forward to seeing him again, but we would be a family again. *And* I would have a breather from my single mother/housewife life and the usual madness of a modern-day Christmas.

But, on the other hand, I still felt guilty. 'I'll be cooking an early Christmas dinner for the family before we go,' I told Mattie's teacher on the last day of term – 'so that she will have a sort of Christmas here, too.'

'Do take care of yourselves, won't you,' she smiled, laying her hand on my arm; and for a moment, I felt a little disconcerted.

On the morning of our departure, I was feeling strangely nervous about taking Mattie out of the country and on such a long flight, and was therefore relieved when my brother-in-law, Tom, offered to drive us to Gatwick.

But it was with a feeling of excitement and liberation that I entered Gatwick Airport with Mattie, and I was rather amused to note that with her backpack from Auntie Molly stuffed with crayons, a book about Muffin the Mule and, of course, Horsie, she carried a whiff of the seasoned traveller about her.

Our ten-hour day flight was surprisingly enjoyable, despite the fact that it was punctuated with numerous requests to visit the loo, which totally fascinated Mattie. She had been presented with a children's gift bag (colouring book, crayons, cuddly toy) as soon as we boarded and she was entranced by the inflight Disney cartoons – a godsend. Mattie also made friends with a little American girl in the row behind.

Mike greeted us at Dallas-Fort Worth airport with two bouquets of flowers – a large bunch of yellow roses for me and a small lavender-coloured bouquet for Mattie.

Our first stop that afternoon, which would fast become a ritual, was lunch at Pappadeaux Seafood Kitchen where Mattie gorged on chicken fingers and french fries. That night, Mattie went to sleep early but due to jetlag, she woke us up at four in the morning. She came in, wide awake and giggling, and although we attempted to coax her back to bed, she refused. Eventually, Mike got up, made her some toast and jam and turned on children's TV for her, allowing us an hour or so more of precious sleep. The following evening, following an afternoon nap for Mattie, Mike escorted us to Bass Hall for a concert featuring the Blind Boys of Alabama whose Christmas CD, coincidentally, I had bought just before I met Mike in Puerto Vallarta. I would never have dreamed then that only a few days later I would be meeting someone who would one day take not only me, but my new daughter, to hear them sing live. Their rendition of 'Joy to the World' would thereafter always bring tears to my eyes when I thought back to the three of us celebrating our first Christmas together.

Mattie experienced another 'first' the next day with her first trip to a zoo. I was excited for her, remembering how much as a child I had enjoyed our family trips to Bristol Zoo and to Longleat Safari Park. My excitement soon changed to bemusement, for apart from showing some curiosity about a white Siberian tiger, her primary concern seemed to be the bottle of Coca Cola which she managed to coax out of Mike as a 'treat' and her fascination with each and every button on the several interactive screens she encountered.

Mattie's interest *was* stimulated by our visit to the Fort Worth stockyards and her first rodeo. Later, at the Cowgirl Hall of Fame she rode a mechanical bucking bronco and instead of riding timidly as the other children had done before her, she rocked about in the saddle and yanked vigorously on the reins, all the time shouting 'Yee hah' much to the amusement of the other visitors. The next day, Mike bought Mattie her first pair of cowboy boots.

Christmas Eve afternoon was a rare chance for Mike and I to spend a few hours alone, and it was a treat.

When Mike had first mentioned the possibility of leaving Mattie with a babysitter for us to do some shopping, I was concerned at the thought of leaving her with a stranger. But when Mike brought round the daughter of a couple he knew to meet Mattie and me beforehand, I felt much better. And Mattie was quite excited about having an older girl and her younger sister look after her for the afternoon. Besides, she knew that the primary reason was so the two of us could buy Christmas presents for her. Mattie did cling to me for a moment when I made to go that afternoon, and I thought it might not be possible after all. But, almost immediately, she let me go again and when I left she was playing happily with the girls.

After a relaxing, quiet child-free lunch at a south-western-style restaurant, during which Mike called a couple of times to check that Mattie was OK, we did our Christmas shopping.

On Christmas Day, it was a joy for us, bleary-eyed, to watch Mattie tear open her gifts and stocking, laid under the tree that she and Mike had decorated on the first day of our visit. Needless to say, we took lots of photos.

After seeing what Santa had brought and phoning the family back home, we all dressed up and went out for Christmas dinner. We dined at the Hotel Ashton, an elegant, traditional hotel downtown, and enjoyed a special four-course

Christmas menu along with an enticing assortment of desserts – how Mattie's eyes popped out at the sight of those chocolate-coated strawberries! There she is in our scrapbook, standing by the large Christmas tree in the lobby, wearing the pretty cardigan that Mike bought her for her birthday, and her brand new boots. What you could not guess from the photo, but something that always made me smile, was Mike's irritation at Mattie's numerous requests to go to the loo – for the most part simply to play with the golden-coloured taps and other paraphernalia of a high-class WC. 'She hardly did anything,' he would say upon his return to the table, Mattie at his side, beaming.

A few days later, we all set out on the eight-hour drive to Marfa, in far west Texas. We traversed miles of flat countryside containing cotton fields and oil pump jacks, all the while accompanied by Mattie's relentless chatter. 'How can anyone talk non-stop for eight hours?' Mike shook his head with an exhausted smile. The landscape gradually changed to open grassland with cacti, pronghorn antelope and the odd roadrunner, all set against the backdrop of the Davis Mountains. Considering the length of the journey, Mattie was a real trooper.

It was during our visit to the Donald Judd Museum in Marfa that it occurred to me how far I had come. I remembered reading one evening, on the commute back from London, of this collection of former air hangars once used to house German prisoners-of-war, which Judd had converted into a venue to display his sculptures, and I had dreamed of visiting it one day. Here we were now, the three of us together in the middle of nowhere, walking around the large installations in this vast open landscape

Shortly after Mattie's and my return from Texas, I bumped into Gillian and Donald at the swimming pool. We found it hard to believe that it must have been three years since our last meeting. Gillian asked lots of questions about the adoption and after Donald swam off, I reminded her of her comment about having adopted *him*. She laughed and said, 'Wash my mouth out with soap!'

The following week, Mattie and I drove over the Downs to have tea with them. I was touched to hear Gillian sing lullabies to Mattie, and Donald play nursery rhymes for her on the piano. 'She's so pert!' Gillian kept exclaiming. And when Gillian asked what American words Mattie had learned at Christmas, to everyone's amusement Mattie replied, in perfect imitation of Mike's southern drawl, 'Quit it.'

At eight months, I felt like Mattie and I had reached another milestone. I *thought* we had finally 'got there'. But hadn't I thought the same at five months? I pondered. I decided, however, that the eight months' point *really* was important because the cuddly toys told me so: Mattie was now nurturing them all. The row of assorted stuffed animals on her pillow at night – a mixture of those from both her new and old families, and of course from Jenny – was the undoubted proof of it. Previously, she had switched them around each night, although Horsie, I noted, was always on the pillow. He now was joined each night by Pink Bear, a Christmas gift from Mike.

About this time, Mattie told me of a dream she had in which she had hugged all of her mummies, new and old, and all of her families, new and old...all at the same time.

As I lay in a hot bath in early January, listening to the radio, I heard John Lennon speaking on the Wenner tapes. 'What's the point of it all, if you are alone at night,' he said. And as I listened, I realised how lovely it had been for the three of us to be together again, this time feeling much more like a little family. Mattie occasionally showed some jealousy but it was minor, in reality. It occurred to me that I was no longer always looking ahead, wondering what came next and where we would one day live. In some ways, looking ahead had been a form of escapism for me during the times when I had felt particularly challenged and stressed by the adoptive process.

Going away for the four weeks had allowed me to rest and recharge my batteries. I had come back feeling quite relaxed...*until* I saw the letters from social services and my solicitor that awaited me in the large pile of Christmas post.

Neither of the two letters from social services made any sense. One proposed a date for a meeting with the foster mother of Mattie's half-siblings, and the second a meeting with the birth grandmother. What was going on? The meetings with the foster mother and the grandmother were not supposed to occur until February – *after* the adoption order had been granted. Things became clearer when I opened a third letter, this one from my solicitor.

He wrote that he had had a lengthy conversation with Mattie's Guardian (the Guardian's role is to do a 'health-check' on the care proceedings, acting as a sort of social worker on behalf of the Courts) and that she had told him that she would *after all* need to meet Mattie. Because of the need for this additional meeting, she therefore had not filed her report with the court in December, as previously agreed. As a result, the court meeting to dispense with consent of the birth mother had been delayed.

I could not believe it. I read on, a gnawing sense of anxiety in my stomach. Another issue causing the Guardian concern was that of the proposed future contact between Mattie and her half-siblings and with her maternal grandmother. So, before the Guardian would file her report, I must first meet with the foster carer of the half-siblings and with the maternal grandmother.

Frustrated, I began to open the pile of Christmas cards that had also arrived in my absence. What had my friends thought when they received my Christmas card announcement, along

291

with the photo of Mattie? 'I'm delighted,' my former best friend at school had written and I couldn't help but think of our different paths – she had met her Mr Right at sixteen.

Then came a nice surprise when I opened two cards from local friends, Lucinda and Mary, both of whom I had often seen in the past. Each suggested meeting up, and after eight long months of motherhood I was ready to do lunch.

Listening to a Radio 4 news programme the morning I was to meet Lucinda, I heard about a new designation of woman, the SADFAB (single and desperate for a baby). I felt awful – was that how *I* had been perceived? I heard the sound of the cat-flap and looked up to see Tibbles come in from the garden. I put some food in his bowl, checked the clock and realised that if I did not get moving I would be late for lunch.

'Hi, Beth,' Lucinda called out on seeing me enter the pub. 'What's yours?'

'I'll have a half of Guinness, thanks,' I replied, settling myself down on a wooden window bench.

'So how are things?' Lucinda asked.

'Very well. Mattie's thriving, I think.'

'That's great. And how's your relationship going?'

'It seems to be going well, too,' I said, taking a sip of my drink.

'You all looked good together,' Lucinda said.

I recalled the man rudely slouching over the newspapers in Cornwall. 'What about *your* relationship?'

'It's all over,' she announced. 'You *did* hear about my miscarriage?'

'No! When was it?'

'Last summer, actually, just a few days before I saw you at the cottage.'

'Oh no! How awful for you.'

'I'm OK now. I hadn't been particularly happy when I found out I was pregnant and assumed at my age there might be problems. But as the weeks went by, I grew used to the idea and began making plans. Christopher was absolutely delighted, too. Our relationship wasn't really going anywhere but he wanted the child. It happened right at 12 weeks and although I rushed to the doctor I knew that was it…'

It had been a terrible time for Lucinda, made worse because her partner seemed to blame her, rather than give support through such a hellish time.

'I'm so sorry,' I said.

'Oh, I'm getting over it now… Christopher was adopted, too, by the way.'

'Good heavens!' I exclaimed, thinking how little interest he had shown in Mattie.

Lucinda told me that as she was 45 now, she felt her last chance had gone. I thought back to what Mike had said, when we left her cottage that hot, sunny day, that he sensed a sadness about her.

'What are your plans now?' I asked.

'I'm thinking of adopting.'

'Really? That's wonderful!'

'But it took a long time for you didn't it?'

'Yes, it was nearly four years before Mattie arrived. But I did postpone it for a year; even so, you'd have to allow about two.'

'But I also want to get a job. I don't want to go back to teaching. I'm looking into working in London. And Christopher wants to get back together. I just hope I'm strong enough to resist him.'

'When I look back on my life, I can see a pattern in some of the relationships I've had,' I told her.

'The same goes for me.' Lucinda smiled, wryly. 'How are you managing financially? I suppose that's important in adoption.'

'Well, I don't have a huge amount put away but you do need enough to prove you can take at least six months off – though I would say a year off would be better.'

'That would be no problem with me, and I have the cottage, of course. But I *would* worry about being in Cornwall away from all my friends…'

How amazing, I thought, as I walked home later – someone else who might adopt. I felt quite excited at the prospect. I glanced over at the other side of the street, at the café where, only a couple of days earlier, I had had a meeting with the permanent foster mother of Mattie's half-siblings. I was pleased to learn from her that the children, a few years older than Mattie, were apparently fine – albeit distressed over the Christmas period, when their mother had failed to turn up for their first contact meeting. I had enquired after the children's birth grandmother, too, and the foster mother replied, 'She seems nice; she said she couldn't have handpicked a better mummy for the children.'

I continued on my way home, wondering what Mattie's birth gran would think of *me*.

I had forgotten the traffic that could mount up on the Hastings road and I was late. With an increasing sense of agitation, I glanced at my watch as I tried to remember which exit I should take at the roundabout. I looked in the windscreen mirror and passed my hands through my hair. Gosh, it looks awful – I really should have gone to the hairdresser. But I *had* put some makeup on. Then I smiled as I remembered that time, almost a year ago – the day I first met Mattie – when I had laughingly applied some lip-gloss. On that occasion, I had worn jeans, which I thought more appropriate for visiting a farm (although Mattie later complained about them, saying, 'Why didn't you wear a dress?'). This time, I decided to wear some smart casual clothes – fitting, I thought, to meet one's daughter's birth grandmother.

What if she's already there? I looked at my watch again, and with a sense of relief saw that I was only five minutes late.

When I found Toby and Alice (my contact liaison officer), I discovered Mattie's grandmother was late, too. This did not augur well – perhaps she hadn't cared enough to turn up.

'You *did* send the letter?' Alice asked Toby.

'Yes I did,' Toby replied. 'I sent copies both to her and to Beth confirming the meeting.'

'Actually I didn't get a letter from you,' I told him. 'I got a letter from Alice mentioning the date and time of the meeting as though I already knew about it. But I received nothing from you.'

'They definitely went out,' Toby insisted. 'I'll give her a call anyway; she might have forgotten all about it.'

What? Forgotten about meeting the new mother of her grandchild?

After calling her on his mobile, Toby announced, 'She's on her way. She'll be here in just a few minutes.'

'I'm so sorry,' the short, greying and slightly overweight woman apologised as she entered the meeting room. 'I never got your letter, Toby.'

'I didn't get one either,' I said, in order to make her feel better.

'I wouldn't have missed this for the world,' she said, sitting down. 'We haven't introduced ourselves yet,' she added, uncomfortably, but not in an unfriendly way, as she leaned over the table towards me. 'Hello, I'm Rose.'

'We leave introductions to the participants themselves,' Toby explained.

'I'm sorry I'm late,' she said. 'I haven't been well and I was lying on the bed when Toby rang. I didn't even have time to do my hair… You look like her,' she suddenly announced to me. I was surprised to hear her say that, and pleased, too.

'I think Mattie has a bit of you in her, too,' I replied,

genuinely. 'You both seem to have the same energy.' She looked pleased at my pronouncement, although I could not imagine how she must have *really* felt, looking over the table at me.

'I want to say, first and foremost, I'm sorry I wasn't able to care for Mattie myself – I'm not well enough.'

I realised, then, the feelings of guilt she must be living with.

'And it would have been impossible having Mattie's mother living nearby,' Toby added. 'I'm afraid it wouldn't have worked.'

'But I'm delighted about the contact,' she said. 'I'd been told I wouldn't be having any.'

Oh really? I thought. But I said nothing.

'Here's a recent photo of Mattie,' I said to her.

'Is this for me to keep?'

'Yes, of course you can keep it.'

'Oh, she looks so happy! And such a lovely purple top – is purple still her favourite colour? She always used to say that she wanted to live in a purple house one day and have a white cat. Such an imagination.'

'Actually she always points out a purple house when I take her to Brighton,' I said. 'It even has a purple door. She always says she loves it.' Suddenly, though, I felt anxious that by mentioning Brighton, I might have given a clue as to Mattie's whereabouts. 'I've got quite a lot of information from Jenny, her foster mother, but she only had Mattie from the age of two,' I went on quickly. 'Is there anything you can tell me about her – perhaps the first time she walked or talked?'

'I'm not sure about the dates exactly, but I think she was walking by about eleven months and I believe she started to talk when she was a little over a year old. She was a very happy baby, though. Laura always said that she bonded more with Mattie than with her other two children. And Mattie loved

296

her dummy. She loved the water, too. She was quite fearless; she used to frighten me.'

'Actually, she's just started swimming lessons,' I smiled, 'and she's really good.'

'Oh, that's lovely!'

'How is her mother?' I asked.

'She's not well,' she responded and then, with Toby's assistance, she began to talk about some of Mattie's birth mother's more recent difficulties.

'Would you mind sending me a photo of her?' I asked Rose. 'There's one in the life history book, it was after she had her hair bleached, which Mattie says she didn't like. I'd rather she had a nicer photo of her.'

'Yes I will. Of course.'

'And I was wondering how tall her mum is – there's a different height given in the life history book than in another document. One of them makes her quite short. I'd like to get it correct for Mattie.'

'Oh no, she isn't short…I'd say she's about the same height as you.'

'Did you ever meet Mattie's birth father?'

'Yes, we met him a few times. He was a smiley, gentle man. He had a lovely personality.' She told me his first name; it was all she knew. I made a mental note to add the info to Mattie's life history book.

At the end of the meeting, Mattie's birth grandmother hugged me and thanked me for having Mattie. 'I couldn't have handpicked anyone better myself,' she told me.

After she left, I asked Alice, 'Did I make a mistake mentioning Brighton? Will that give her an idea as to the area where Mattie lives?'

'No, that was fine,' she replied.

'This meeting must have been very difficult for her,' I said. 'And it was very nice of her to say how Mattie looked like me.'

'Yes, I thought that was very generous of her,' Alice agreed.

On the way home, I felt relieved that the meeting had gone so well. Two down, one to go, I thought: one more obstacle to overcome before Mattie became legally mine.

I soon received a call from Jill, Mattie's Guardian, who confirmed to me her need to meet Mattie face-to-face.

'Yes, I know,' I replied tersely. 'My solicitor wrote to me.' I'm sure my voice sounded rather cool.

'It's really just to check for myself that she's happy,' Jill explained. 'I also want to know that she's happy with the contact arrangements.'

I felt my hackles rise. I had already met Jill last December, when she had told me there was *no* need for her to meet Mattie. Haven't you read all the reports? I felt like saying. How many of you need to see her before you decide she's OK? But I said nothing.

'I'm aware our meeting has to be handled sensitively. Perhaps, I could go with you to pick her up from school one day. It might feel more natural than if I just arrived at her home.'

'I don't think that's best,' I said quickly, thinking of the occasion when she had dead-eyed Mike back in October. 'School is Mattie's patch – and knowing her, I think she would prefer meeting you here.' And school is *my* patch, too, I thought, annoyed by yet another intrusion on our privacy.

'Then it's probably best to warn her in advance.'

'That's what I did just before Toby's last visit,' I responded tartly, 'and she ended up being aggressive to me *and* her teacher. I'll play it by ear on the day.'

'She *should* remember me; I saw her a lot at Jenny's and at some of her contact sessions with her birth family.'

'Mattie, there's someone coming to see you as soon as we get

298

back home,' I announced, as we met after school on the appointed day.

'Who?' she asked, looking intrigued.

'It's Jill. She used to visit you when you were at Jenny's. Do you remember her?'

'No.'

'She's just coming to have a few words with you and see that you're well. Is that OK?' I asked, tentatively.

'Yes.'

How relieved I was later when I opened the front door to Jill and saw from Mattie's expression that she was pleased to see her.

'Do you remember me?' Jill asked.

'Yes,' Mattie responded, excitedly.

'Would you like a cup of tea, Jill?' I asked.

'Yes, I would,' she answered, with a look of surprise, as though expecting a frostier reception.

I was relieved at how relaxed Mattie appeared. *I* was the one on tenterhooks as I waited in the kitchen for the kettle to boil. Would Mattie mention Mike in some connection since we had just been over to see him? My eyes caught sight of the scrapbook I was making of our trip to Texas and after checking that there were no photos of Mike in it I quickly put a tea towel over it.

'Thank you,' Jill said, taking the cup of tea from me as she chatted with Mattie.

I felt uncomfortable being there, fearful that Mattie would let the cat out of the bag about Mike, so I excused myself and left the room.

'I've just been on holiday,' I heard Mattie say as I ascended the stairs. I could hardly believe my ears and stopped in my tracks.

'Have you? How exciting! Where did you go?'

'To America.'

'To *America*! Do you have any photos?'

'No, but we're making a scrapbook,' I heard Mattie say proudly.

'Can I have a look at it?'

'Mummy,' Mattie called out. 'Can you get the scrapbook.'

Shall I say I can't find it? That was my immediate thought before I realised how ridiculous that would sound. 'Yes, of course,' I said, between clenched teeth.

'This is *lovely*,' Jill told her as Mattie took great delight in going through every page, each of which Jill studied in depth. I grew increasingly agitated.

'Didn't you get tired?' Jill asked Mattie, when she saw that she had been to see the Blind Boys of Alabama concert, visited a number of museums and made a trip to far west Texas.

'No, never!' Mattie exclaimed, shaking her head.

'And was this your Christmas dinner?' Jill asked, when she came to the photos of our Christmas meal at the Ashton, in Fort Worth.

'I did cook a Christmas dinner here for my family before we went,' I informed Jill.

'Do you have friends in America?' she asked me.

'Yes, I do,' I told her, feeling distinctly uncomfortable. During the rest of the time they spent on the scrapbook I left the room a few times pretending to busy myself, dreading what Mattie might say next.

'That belongs to Mike's daughter,' Mattie said, pointing to one of the photos in which she was holding a guitar. I sat there and held my breath for a few moments, waiting for the inevitable enquiry. Nothing was said, and much to my relief, Jill closed the scrapbook and began to talk to Mattie and me about the day we would appear in court for the adoption.

'Do you think you'll feel able to talk to the Judge?' Jill asked Mattie. 'They'll probably want to ask you a few questions.'

'Maybe just a little bit,' Mattie said, and Jill drew a picture of a table with the Judge sitting behind it.

'Who will be going from your family?' Jill asked me.

'My parents, my sister Molly, my brother Nick and his wife, and my other sister, Caryl, and her partner...'

'Gosh, Mattie, you'll have a lot of people there,' Jill said.

Mattie told Jill she was going to have a party afterwards. And a cake, too.

The next day, Jill rang to thank me for making her visit possible, and told me how much she had enjoyed seeing Mattie again. She also assured me that her report for the court would clearly state that she believed the adoption to be in Mattie's best interests. I was delighted.

'You mentioned at our meeting that I could see a copy of your report,' I reminded Jill.

'You can, so long as the court agrees to it. You'll need to mention it to your solicitor.'

During Mattie's half-term, a few days later, I had one of her school friends round for tea. I was now an old hand at this, although I did notice an occasional bemused look when I presented them with an apron; I thought every little girl wore an apron at tea-time!

Mattie also spent a couple of days with my parents, and this time it went seamlessly. 'She's been excellent,' my father told me, after I anxiously asked about Mattie's behaviour.

'I noticed how much more settled and calmer she seemed after her Christmas holiday,' my mother said. 'And she's very much like her new Mum – it's like seeing a little you.'

The Guardian's report was enclosed with a letter from my solicitor in early February.

In his letter, he confirmed that I was to be paid a lump sum from the local authority covering the time Mattie moved in with me until her legal adoption. He also stated that the Judge was absolutely satisfied that Mattie's placement with me was the best way of promoting her interests and safeguarding her welfare during the remainder of her minority and beyond. He wrote that the birth mother was unreasonably withholding her consent to the adoption, which consent was therefore dispensed with, on the grounds that a reasonable parent would recognise the advantages of the present situation and that it was the next best thing for Mattie to be within my family unit if the mother was unable herself to meet Mattie's needs.

He also gave the date of Mattie's adoption in March, with a reminder that we should not forget our camera.

I was rather amused when I read in Jill's Guardian report, 'how relaxed the two of them appeared.' I remembered how I twitched the whole time she went through those photos of Texas. 'There is no doubt a strong bond and attachment has built up between them,' I read on, with pleasure, and Jill further commented on the spontaneous affection between Mattie and me, and that there was no sign of anxiety from Mattie who was unequivocal that this was her 'forever family'. Jill also noted that she had seen Mattie's 'Enthusiasm Award' given to her at school and that she was still the bubbly, assertive girl whose excellent command of language helped her to negotiate her relationships and manage and understand her world.

The birth relatives will be expecting to receive a letter from you at the agreed time and may well be watching the post. Allow plenty of time for it to be processed... Your letter does not need to be lengthy but a warm, friendly letter will be a great help in reassuring birth parents and will make it much easier for them to respond to you...

Social services handout

There was a late burst of snow in early March. Mattie was out in the garden as soon as we got up, wearing her little pink jacket with the 'B' on the pocket, her pink hat and scarf. She was in her element stomping around in the thick snow. Like a bright pink sugared almond on the top of an iced cake. I noticed an elderly neighbour watching her as well, from her bedroom window.

I thought how Mattie's Barbie jacket was becoming too small for her, and I was reminded of how her little face had stared up at me that first day; she looked so tiny. When Mattie came in from the snow, I asked, 'Do you remember how you felt when you first saw me?'

'I thought Toby brought me a big flower,' she replied, with a smile. She told me she had been watching out of the window for my arrival. She had then walked, all alone, out of the door and through the little white gate to meet her new Mummy.

'I was happy,' Mattie said, 'but also this much nervous,' she added, making a small circle with her forefinger and thumb. 'What does nervous mean?' she then asked me.

'Nervous means a little worried,' I told her.

'Yes', she said, 'I was a bit worried. 'I didn't want to move. I wanted to stay longer at Jenny's… I didn't know what it was like with you. Now, I'm happy I'm here. I'm happy, happy, happy. I love you for the rest of time… I love you as big as the sky.'

Mattie then picked up a pencil and drew a picture of a big smiley face with alligator-like teeth, and told me, 'This is how I looked when I saw you.'

Later that morning, Mattie asked whether, after her adoption day, she would be seeing any of her old family.

'Yes, of course,' I answered, tentatively. 'You'll be seeing your brother and sister soon and you'll be seeing your old nanny later in the year… Is there anyone else you'd like to see?' I asked, filled with apprehension.

'No,' she replied, 'but can I write a letter?'

'Of course, you can. Who would you like to write to?

'My brother and sister and to my old nanny and my old mummy.'

Mattie herself had now decided what *she* wanted in the way of written contact and it was a load off my mind. And, strangely enough, March was the very month I had told the letterbox coordinator it would be done.

'Shall we do it now?'

'Yes,' she replied, gleefully.

Mattie first made a card for her old mummy, on which she stuck cotton wool to represent snow. On the front she wrote 'Mummy' and inside: 'I love you and miss you.' Mattie had first dictated the words to me and then copied them from a sheet where I had written them out.

Although it was strange to see her write those words to someone else, I sensed a peace within her after she had done so. On some level, this gave me a feeling of peace, too.

Mattie then drew a card for her nanny, and then one for her brother and sister. She wrote that she loved them all.

Now for my letter to Mattie's birth family.

According to the social services handout, the letter should start with 'Dear', and we were told to use first names. I related a little of how Mattie was getting on at school, how she had been to America at Christmas and the fact that she had grown quite a bit. And I included some lovely photos of Mattie, ensuring – again according to the handout – that they be clear but not contain any identifying features, such as school uniform. I read out the letter to Mattie, and she wrote her name at the end of it.

The next morning, when I looked out onto the garden and the Downs beyond, I would never have guessed that we had had snow. Not one flake was left, not even of the snowman that Mattie had made. The elderly neighbour later told me how much she had enjoyed watching Mattie play in the snow that day.

'Toby's hurt that Mattie refuses to talk to him,' Allie told me at our final meeting before the adoption. 'He said he enjoyed a close relationship with the entire family and now Mattie doesn't want to know him.'

'I think he had a close relationship with the rest of her family,' I replied, 'but I never thought he really knew Mattie. And didn't you tell me there comes a time when a child sees the social worker as an intrusion into their life – at the point where they're becoming more and more attached to their new family and home?'

'That's right.'

'Well, Toby doesn't seem to see that. I can't *make* her talk to him. I'll do my best when he next calls though. We've just been out to buy the decorations for her adoption cake, so that might make her feel less threatened by him.'

'That's a good idea – it'll make it all seem more real for her,' Allie said.

'I bought her a new dress, too.'

How magical that moment had been, watching Mattie try on her dress in the Monsoon changing room. She knew immediately the one she wanted; it looked as though it was made just for her.

'Don't forget to take your camera,' Allie called out, as she made her way to her car and I waved her off from the doorstep.

'I won't talk to him,' Mattie told me a few days later, when I broached the subject of Toby's final visit.

'Oh, come on. He doesn't want to visit you *either*. His boss makes him do it.' I saw her begin to relent. 'This will be his last *ever* visit.'

'When's my adoption party?' she asked.

'It's just over four weeks away now... I tell you what, if you talk to him nicely, I'll make you sausage and chips for tea.'

'Oh, OK then,' she grumbled.

Toby was at the top of the hill when I spotted him, pacing up and down. He had just got out of his car and I noted that it was a blue one now, not the grey one I had seen parked at the farm cottage, almost a year ago.

Mattie and I waved to him and he waved back.

'Hello,' he smiled, as we approached him.

I looked quickly at Mattie, and was relieved to see her smiling up at him.

'When I saw you in the distance,' he said, 'I thought back to that first meeting, when you and Mattie were walking towards each other over the grass. Do you remember? It was like a scene out of *The Sound of Music*.'

'Yes, I do,' I smiled. 'I'll remember it forever.'

Mike flew over for Mattie's adoption day laden with several fine bottles of Californian sparkling wine. We felt it important that he be present to help celebrate Mattie's special day, but thought it might be unwise if he accompanied us to court since we had thus far hidden his existence from the numerous social workers. He instead opted to stay behind and put the finishing touches to the eats for the family celebration that would follow.

On the big day, both of us kissed Mike goodbye at the door and Mattie and I, laughing with excitement, dashed to Molly's car and clambered in.

'You look like two princesses,' Molly told us.

If we don't get a move on, I thought, looking at my watch, we'll be late.

Once there, we had difficulty working out which building we were supposed to enter. No parking space was available so Molly dropped Mattie and me off at one of the court buildings in the howling wind. There, we were told to go to the building next door. Mattie began to play up a bit as we entered the family court building and I had to chastise her. I prayed no one was watching! We ascended the stairs only to find a whole row of Mattie's new family in the waiting room. Apparently, extra seats had had to be brought in for them!

In the middle of our greeting one another, a middle-aged lady popped her head out of a doorway.

'Are you waiting for your certificate?' she asked, looking in my direction.

'Yes, we are,' I replied.

'Then would you like to come in?'

'Can I bring my daughter and her cousin with me?'

'Yes, of course, that'll be fine,' she smiled. 'I'll give you all a little tour of our offices, if you like.'

Mattie and Mei soon became the centre of attraction amongst the court administration staff. Then, what must have been ten minutes later, she came over, a concerned look on her face.

'That's strange, I can't find the certificate.'

'Do you mean Mattie's adoption certificate?'

'Yes.'

'But won't she be given it after the Hearing is over?'

'Haven't you had your *Hearing* yet?'

'No, we haven't!' I looked up at the clock and saw it was only a couple of minutes to ten. 'It's due to take place at ten!' I said, panicking a little.

'I'm so sorry,' the lady said, 'You'd better go quickly.'

Just as we made our way out of the office, we met my solicitor.

'There you are,' he said, sternly and flush faced. 'I was beginning to think you weren't going to turn up.'

'This woman asked us to go into her office,' I explained to Toby, Allie and Jill, all standing in the waiting room, opposite my family.

'I was becoming very worried,' Toby laughed, a look of relief on his face. 'You've brought your camera haven't you?'

Jill said that she didn't always come to the hearings, but she particularly wanted to attend this one.

'This is Allie,' I told my mother, when she came up to have a word.

'Hello,' Mum smiled.

'And this is Toby, Mum.'

'Hello Toby,' Mum announced, 'I've heard a *lot* about you.'

'Oh good, I'm glad about that,' Toby grinned.

Shall I take the photos inside the courtroom for you,' Jill kindly offered. I gave her the new digital camera that Mike had bought for the occasion.

Within minutes, we were all seated in the courtroom. Mattie and I, my parents, Molly and Mei were all in the front row; everyone else – my brother Nick and his wife, my sister Caryl and her partner, my solicitor and all the social workers – sat in the second.

There was first some gentle questioning of Mattie by the Judge. It took me back to Toby's first visit with Mattie in her new home, and how she had done a brilliant PR job.

'Do you have a new dress for the occasion?' the Judge asked her. Mattie was wearing the beautiful one, in Indian colours, that she had taken great delight in choosing at Monsoon.

'Yes, and I have new shoes, too,' Mattie said, as she swung her legs up onto the table to show the Judge.

'*And* new tights,' Mum smiled.

'And who chose the dress?' the Judge asked.

'I did,' Mattie said, proudly.

'And I notice you're wearing a pretty silver bracelet. Who gave you that?'

'They did,' Mattie said, pointing to Nick and Melanie.

'Who are *they?*' the Judge laughed.

'My auntie and uncle.'

'And are you ready to have Mattie in your family,' the Judge asked my parents, with a wry smile.

'Oh yes, we are,' Mum laughed.

The Judge then passed the adoption certificate around, we all signed, and it was done.

I looked at Mei, sitting on her mum's lap, and thought she might be feeling left out of it all with the attention all on Mattie, so I put my hand out and gave her a little squeeze.

'I have something for you, now,' the Judge told Mattie and she escorted her to her desk and gave her a big balloon. More photos were taken as Mattie and I posed with the Judge and the balloon.

As we all came out of the courtroom, my solicitor approached me and said, 'I just need to address the change you want made to Mattie's middle name. The Judge will need to approve it, but I'm sure there's no problem.'

'It's just a slight change – and she'll now have the same middle name as both her birth mother and me. I thought that would be nice, and Mattie is happy about it.'

I felt a lump in my throat when I said my goodbyes to Toby and Jill.

'Do you feel sad?' I asked Jill. 'You knew the birth family well; it must be strange to see Mattie with a new family.'

'No, I only feel very happy. Happy that she's safe now.'

'I know you'll be happy with your *forever* mummy,' Toby said to Mattie, with a sad smile. He handed her a farewell card and told her he had written inside: 'Wishes do come true'.

'How did it go?' Mike asked eagerly when we all trooped triumphantly into the house.

'Wonderfully,' I said, with a tearful smile, and then surprised myself by having a little cry.

The table was laden with chicken drumsticks basted with

fajita spices, numerous salsas with tortilla chips, cheese and onion tartlets, variously topped crostini and, of course, Mattie's adoption cake, a chocolate one topped with bright pink icing. Mike opened the bottles of Californian sparkling wine and toasts were made all round, welcoming Mattie into the family. It was truly a time for rejoicing.

A little later, Jo and Ann from next door popped in to join us, more wine was opened and Mike began to regale them with his repertoire of anti-Bush stories.

A few days later, a letter arrived from the solicitor stating that the adoption order had been granted and that the formal court order would arrive in ten days. I could expect a new birth certificate showing me as Mattie's mother in about ten weeks.'What do you remember about your adoption day,' I asked Mattie, several months later.

'I remember I had a cake and I got a balloon,' she said. 'And someone else got adopted that day, too.'

'That was the court reporter, Mattie, but she didn't get adopted, she got engaged to be married,' I said. I recalled how the Judge had smiled at us all gathered there, and explained that the court reporter had been proposed to that very morning and it therefore was a particularly happy day for everyone.

One thing I will never forget, is meeting Mattie at school the day following her adoption. We were walking home together and Mattie announced, 'I told all the children at school about my adoption day.'

'Did you? That's nice.'

She was silent for a moment and then asked, 'Are *all* children adopted?'

'No,' I answered, astonished. 'Being adopted is something that is very special.'

Never, until that moment, would I have guessed that

Mattie did not realise that she was *different* from the rest of her class.

I thought back to Jenny's first visit to my home, and how she had chuckled when she told me about Mattie playing at 'social workers' with her dolls, and how Mattie pretended they were all foster children waiting for their new mummies and daddies...

'So, do you feel a great load's been lifted off your shoulders, now that it's finally over?' Allie asked me, at our final meeting, a week after Adoption Day.

'No, I don't actually,' I smiled. 'I know you *said* that would happen, but it doesn't feel that way at all. It feels more like an anti-climax.'

'Well,' she said, 'at least you'll have all of us out of your hair now. But I *will* say it's always with a certain amount of sadness that I pay my last visit. You get to know so much about the applicant – and their family – but once an adoption order's granted, you hardly ever see them again. It feels very strange.'

'Thank you for making the most perfect match for us,' I told her, later, at the door. And for the last time, I waved Allie off. And that was that, I thought. It *was* finally over.

But I felt strange. If anything, I felt even more weighed down *after* Mattie's adoption day. I certainly didn't expect to feel this way. On adoption day, Mattie became mine in the eyes of the law, but I was expecting something more. I also was surprised to find myself strangely saddened by saying goodbye to Allie. All those months when I thought how glad I would be *not* to hear that knock at the door announcing yet another home visit or LAC review. And Mike had gone back to the States, too. I felt strangely alone.

I slowly began to realise that just because a major event in my life was over, the months and months of stress that led up to it were not going to disappear overnight.

311

It was a difficult time for both Mattie and me. Each morning, it seemed, there was a little tantrum or tears, and for the first time Mattie even tried to bite me a time or two. I recalled having listened smugly to the other parents on the parenting course talk about their children biting, and now *mine* was doing the same.

A few days later, Mattie and I passed by a building where she asked about the pictures of different hairstyles pasted on the windows.

'That's a school where you learn how to be a hairdresser,' I told her.

'Is that where you learned to be a mummy?' she asked me. And sure enough, a few days later, she accused me of not being a good mother. How I rued my comment to Molly, back in February, that Mattie and I had finally got there.

Mattie was now adopted, she had a new life and a new family – but on some level, surely, the loss of her old family, and Jenny, at times tugged at her. And even though Mattie was not sorry to say goodbye to Toby, Jill and Allie, they were *still* goodbyes. And she had had to say goodbye to Mike once again, too.

With Mothering Sunday on the horizon, I hoped things might improve and I looked forward to celebrating this day, for the first time, with Mattie. She had already been out shopping for my gift with my mother.

On the day itself, Mattie brought home a card she had made me whilst attending Sunday school with Mei. It had the words 'MY MUM' and a picture of the sun on the front, and 'Thank You' written inside. But I was ill that Sunday and Mattie seemed particularly reluctant to leave Auntie Molly and Mei when they dropped her off after Sunday school. I admit, it hurt my feelings a bit. She was also especially fussy about the meal – her favourite, roast chicken – I had prepared. This was out of character for her. And when Mattie wished me a Happy *New* Mother's Day, it felt strangely hollow.

Around this time, Mattie had also asked about her birth mother and I tried to explain, in a way that a five-year-old might understand, that her mother was not well enough to look after her – just as Poppy and Mei's mums had not been well enough to look after them.

Mattie replied 'I still love her.' I took this to mean, 'I still love her despite all that.'

'Of course you do, Mattie. And I know she still loves you, too.'

During the Easter holidays, I rang Jenny and arranged for Mattie to spend the day there, and she also spent a weekend with my parents during the same period. Both visits Mattie thoroughly enjoyed, and just as suddenly as the blip began, it finished, she nurtured her teddies and dolls even more than usual, and was especially affectionate towards me. Everything was back to normal.

And Mattie didn't appear to suffer any setback when an envelope from social services arrived containing a card from her birth grandmother, which I immediately read to her. It held a little card for me, too. In my card, the grandmother said she was sure that Mattie and I would both benefit greatly from what we could give each other. She added that she had made the enclosed beaded bracelet for Mattie and hoped I would not mind her having it. She said she had made one for her before, and that Mattie had refused to take it off.

So that had been the bracelet that Mattie had worn to her new nursery, I realised. I remembered the nursery school teacher telling me, on handing me a handful of tiny beads, how upset Mattie had been when it broke.

Mattie seemed pleased with the card and immediately asked me to help her put the bracelet on.

Enclosed was also a pretty picture of Mattie's birth mother that I had requested from the grandmother. Surprisingly, Mattie just looked blankly at it and then set it aside. I would later place the photograph in her life history book. I was sorry that there was no word from her birth mother. I wondered if she had even received the card with the cotton wool snow that Mattie had made for her.

Mattie said nothing about the lack of something from her mother and I decided it was best, at this point, to say nothing as well.

Things have a way of coming around full circle, I reflected, as my youngest sister, Caryl, Mattie and I sat under the pergola on a beautiful, late May day.

'Mmmm that was delicious,' Caryl said as she finished the pudding. 'I didn't like to tell you but that was the first time I've eaten treacle tart since school. There was a horrible dinner lady who used to force it down me,' she laughed. She went back to reading the first few pages of my manuscript whilst Mattie sat contentedly on her lap, looking through some photos. I gave a sigh of contentment myself as I sat back in my chair, beneath the blue and white blossom of the wisteria.

'I love that quote you've included,' Caryl said, a little while later, as she lay down the pages. 'The one from Kierkegaard.'

'Yes, I like it too. 'Life must be lived forwards, but it can only be understood backwards',' I quoted aloud.

'It *does* seem like fate brought you and Mattie together. You're so like each other. And she's very attached to you.'

'Mum and Molly both said it would probably take a year for us to "get there", and it's a year now… So what about you? Are you still thinking of having a little one?'

'Yes I think so,' she replied, hesitantly, 'though it would be difficult financially.'

'I remember someone from social services, a long time ago, telling me that one can *always*, somehow, have their own child on a wish and a prayer,' I replied, big sister-like. 'Just make sure you don't leave it too long.'

Things had come around full circle for Mike and me, too, I thought, whilst Caryl and Mattie began to sing 'I saw a mouse under the chair'. I had not long returned from a holiday in Puerto Vallarta. What a luxury a week together had been. Mattie had stayed with my parents and everyone had got along well. Mike and I both, at times, had missed her, but it was nice to concentrate on our relationship, too. Mike had always said he wanted to take me back to Puerto Vallarta; he felt there was something unfinished about our brief encounter there two-and-a-half years earlier.

'The photos are lovely,' Caryl said.

'I love that one of Mattie,' I told her, pointing to one I had taken of Mattie on the day of my return from Puerto Vallarta. She is wearing an embroidered, white cotton dress that Mike bought her in Mexico and she is lying on the sun-lounger, laughing up at her mum, in exactly the same pose as the one I took the day she moved in and smiled up at her new mummy. I later compared the two photos, to see if I could detect any difference in Mattie's expression. There was no difference at all. She was wearing exactly the same joyful expression in both photos. But how much our lives had changed in the space of that year!

When Dad had brought Mattie home the morning I returned from Mexico, I'd had a shock when she walked into the hallway. The little face that looked up at me intently was nothing like the one that had been in my mind the whole of my week away. The face that looked up at me in the hallway was the same earnest, expectant little face that had looked up at me the first time I met her. It was the face of my tiny tot.

Epilogue

The childless niggle had begun in my mid-thirties. An old friend of mine from Berlin was visiting at the time, and as he lent a dispassionate ear to my fears of a childless future, I remember him saying, dismissively, 'There are other things in life you might choose to do. For instance, you might write a book.'

Who, on earth, wants to write a book, I had felt like shouting. I want a child!

How strangely things turn out sometimes. I now have that child, but I have also written a book.

My purpose in writing this account was to give Mattie a more comprehensive life history book. Some years have passed now since she moved into my home, and she is still the same loving, affectionate little girl who walked towards me, hands in her pockets, on that first day. Her 'signature' touch to most of her paintings and drawings is a heart.

As expected, there have been blips in our time together – usually small – but they have become fewer and farther between. And afterwards, our bond has felt even stronger.

Two years after Mattie moved in, little Mei and the rest of her family – my sister, Molly, Tom and Poppy – went to live abroad. It was a significant loss for both of us, but especially for Mattie who lost not only a family she had connected with from the first day of meeting, but Mei, her best friend, too. To this day, Mattie still feels her absence. Luckily, they do not live too far away. Mei visited recently, and as I took both girls pond-dipping and later watched them playing with their dolls – both dolls were, of course, 'adopted' – I was reminded of that first summer when Mattie and Mei 'read' and sang together on the patio, and swam in the 'big pond'.

Mattie periodically visits her foster parents, Jenny and Jack, at the little farm cottage with the chimney pots. Jenny recently suffered a life-threatening illness, but against all odds she seems to have recovered.

As predicted, Mattie has experienced some moments of grieving as she has struggled to make sense of the loss of her birth family, and for a time she even expressed a wish not to have any more contact with them. But lately, she has resumed seeing her sister at regular intervals and both girls seem to enjoy the meetings.

My neighbours, Jo and Ann, have filled the gap in the support network created by my sister's moving away – funny to think that they never even occupied one of those little boxes in the social worker's diagram, years ago. They have both become much devoted to Mattie. Jo, who herself was adopted as a four-year-old, has been particularly helpful to Mattie and the two of them have an occasional chat about their common experiences over tea.

At Jo's suggestion, I recently decided to read to Mattie some extracts from the 'life letter' that Toby had given to me just before her adoption day. Mattie seemed to benefit from this, and she appeared delighted when I also handed her a copy of some poems written by her birth mother. As Mattie sat there on the arm of my chair in the study, and read one of the poems out loud, it was as though, for a moment, time stood still. I do admire my little girl.

My youngest sister, Caryl, doesn't remember the words of 'advice' that I uttered under the pergola on that warm May day, but she is now a proud mum, too.

And Mike? I smile when I look through those early e-mails and recall our 'one-year plan'. It took Mattie much longer than a year to truly settle in and bond with me, and I know it was best for Mattie that we didn't make any significant changes too early.

During our most recent get-together in Oaxaca – Mike had always wanted the three of us to one day go there together – their relationship seems to have become complete. And this year, for the first time, Mattie sent Mike a Father's Day card. He was very touched. Dare I say it…? Within the next year, we hope to all be on the same continent.

One of the sweetest – and certainly the most unexpected – things anyone ever said to me about the adoption, was on a day Mattie and I were out shopping in a nearby town. I asked Mattie to choose where to have lunch and she chose a tiny Bangladeshi restaurant that we had never noticed before.

During our meal, the Bangladeshi waiter asked if I was Mattie's mother. I replied that I was and he then enquired as to her father. With Mattie's permission, I replied that her birth father was from Bangladesh, her mother was British and that I had adopted her. The waiter then began to tell us a little about his country. I said that I hoped to take Mattie there one day.

He looked at Mattie, then at me, and smiling sweetly, said, 'You were made for each other.'

Also available from Honno

STRANGE DAYS INDEED
edited by Lindsay Ashford and Rebecca Tope

ISBN: 9781870206839 £7.99

Motherhood is a strange country – you can't tell what it's going to be like until you get there and you have no idea how long the journey is going to be. A collection of true stories of motherhood from fears about birth to the challenges posed by grown-up children.

LOSING TIMO
by Linda Baxter

ISBN: 1870206665 £7.99

In the early hours of June 18th 1999, Timo Baxter and a friend were walking home. On Hungerford Bridge they were accosted by muggers, beaten unconscious and thrown into the Thames. Timo's friend survives the attack, Timo does not. Counterpointing prose of great emotional restraint with blazingly candid poetry, Timo's mother draws an achingly honest picture of slow-burning grief at the senseless death of her only child.

WALKING TO GREENHAM
by Ann Pettitt

ISBN: 1870206762 £8.99

A young mother bringing up her children on a smallholding in rural Wales, Ann Pettitt began a movement that changed the face of modern history. With three other women determined to challenge government policy and the postwar status quo she set out on a march to stop nuclear warheads being launched from British soil. This is her story: where she came from, how the Peace Camp at Greenham Common came to be and of taking the message to the heart of the Kremlin.

ABOUT HONNO

Honno Welsh Women's Press was set up in 1986 by a group of women who felt strongly that women in Wales needed wider opportunities to see their writing in print and to become involved in the publishing process. Our aim is to develop the writing talents of women in Wales, give them new and exciting opportunities to see their work published and often to give them their first 'break' as a writer.

Honno is registered as a community co-operative. Any profit that Honno makes is invested in the publishing programme. Women from Wales and around the world have expressed their support for Honno. Each supporter has a vote at the Annual General Meeting.

To receive further information about forthcoming publications, or become a supporter, please write to Honno at the address below, or visit our website:

www.honno.co.uk

Honno
Unit 14, Creative Units
Aberystwyth Arts Centre
Penglais Campus
Aberystwyth
Ceredigion
SY23 3GL

All Honno titles can be ordered online at
www.honno.co.uk
or by sending a cheque to Honno.
Free p&p to all UK addresses.